THE OLD WOMAN OF THE MOUNTAIN.

First Published by
Sampson Low in 1880

This facsimile edition has been carefully scanned
and reprinted in the traditional manner by
THE LOST LIBRARY
5 High Street,
Glastonbury UK BA6 9DP

The LOST LIBRARY is a publishing house based in
Glastonbury, UK, dedicated to the reproduction
of important rare esoteric and scholarly texts for
the discerning reader.

Cataloguing Information
British Goblins
Wirt Sikes

ISBN 978 1 906621 12 4

Printed by Replika Press Pvt Ltd,
Haryana, India

**THE LOST
LIBRARY**

British Goblins:

Welsh folk-lore, fairy mythology, legends and traditions.

BY

WIRT SIKES,

UNITED STATES CONSUL FOR WALES.

·WITH ILLUSTRATIONS BY T. H. THOMAS.

In olde dayes of the Kyng Arthour . . .
Al was this lond fulfilled of fayrie.

CHAUCER.

PUBLISHED BY

THE LOST LIBRARY

GLASTONBURY, ENGLAND

TO

HIS ROYAL HIGHNESS,

ALBERT EDWARD, PRINCE OF WALES,

THIS ACCOUNT OF

THE FAIRY MYTHOLOGY AND FOLK-LORE
OF HIS PRINCIPALITY

IS BY PERMISSION DEDICATED.

PREFACE.

———◆———

In a certain sense Wales may be spoken of as the cradle of fairy legend. It is not now disputed that from the Welsh were borrowed many of the first subjects of composition in the literature of all the cultivated peoples of Europe.

In the ground it covers, while this volume deals especially with Wales, and still more especially with South Wales—where there appear to have been human dwellers long before North Wales was peopled—it also includes the border counties, notably Monmouthshire, which, though severed from Wales by Act of Parliament, is really very Welsh in all that relates to the past. In Monmouthshire is the decayed cathedral city of Caerleon, where, according to tradition, Arthur was crowned king in 508, and where he set up his most dazzling court, as told in the 'Morte d'Arthur.'

The Arthur of British history and tradition stands to Welshmen in much the same light that Alfred the Great stands to Englishmen. Around this historic or semi-historic Arthur has gathered a throng of shining legends of fabulous sort, with which English readers are more or less familiar. An even grander figure is the Arthur who existed in Welsh mythology before the birth of the warrior-king. The mythic Arthur, it is presumed, began his shadowy life in pre-historic ages, and grew progressively in mythologic story, absorbing at a certain period the personality of the real Arthur, and becoming the type of romantic chivalry. A similar state of things is indicated with regard to the enchanter Merlin ; there was a mythic Merlin before the real Merlin was born at Carmarthen.

With the rich mass of legendary lore to which these figures belong, the present volume is not intended to deal ; nor do its pages treat, save in the most casual and passing manner, of the lineage and original significance of the lowly goblins which are its theme. The questions here involved, and the task of adequately treating them, belong to the comparative mythologist and the critical historian, rather than to the mere literary workman.

UNITED STATES CONSULATE, CARDIFF,
August, 1879.

CONTENTS.

———◆———

BOOK I.

THE REALM OF FAERIE.

CHAPTER I.

CHAPTER II.

CHAPTER III.

CHAPTER IV.

CHAPTER V.

CHAPTER VI.

CHAPTER VII.

CHAPTER VIII.

CHAPTER IX.

CHAPTER X.

CHAPTER XI.

BOOK II.

THE SPIRIT-WORLD.

CHAPTER I.

CHAPTER II.

CHAPTER III.

CHAPTER IX.

BOOK III.

QUAINT OLD CUSTOMS.

CHAPTER I.

CHAPTER II.

CHAPTER III.

CHAPTER IV.

CHAPTER V.

CHAPTER VI.

CHAPTER VII.

BOOK IV.

BELLS, WELLS, STONES, AND DRAGONS.

CHAPTER I.

CHAPTER II.

CHAPTER III.

CHAPTER IV.

CHAPTER V.

BRITISH GOBLINS.

⋙◆⋘

BOOK I.

THE REALM OF FAERIE.

At eve, the primrose path along,
The milkmaid shortens with a song
    Her solitary way;
She sees the fairies with their queen
Trip hand-in-hand the circled green,
And hears them raise, at times unseen,
    The ear-enchanting lay.

REV. JOHN LOGAN : Ode to Spring, 1780.

CHAPTER I.

Fairy Tales and the Ancient Mythology—The Compensations of
Science—Existing Belief in Fairies in Wales—The Faith of Culture
—The Credulity of Ignorance—The Old-Time Welsh Fairyland—
The Fairy King—The Legend of St. Collen and Gwyn ap Nudd
—The Green Meadows of the Sea—Fairies at Market—The Land
of Mystery.

I.

WITH regard to other divisions of the field of folk-lore, the views of scholars differ, but in the realm of faerie these differences are reconciled; it is agreed that fairy tales are relics of the ancient mythology; and the philosophers stroll hand in hand harmoniously. This is as it should be, in a realm about which cluster such delightful memories of the most poetic period of life—childhood, before scepticism has crept in as ignorance slinks out. The knowledge which introduced scepticism is infinitely more

A

valuable than the faith it displaced; but, in spite
of that, there be few among us who have not felt
evanescent regrets for the displacement by the *foi
scientifique* of the old faith in fairies. There was
something so peculiarly fascinating in that old belief,
that 'once upon a time' the world was less practical
in its facts than now, less commonplace and hum-
drum, less subject to the inexorable laws of gravi-
tation, optics, and the like. What dramas it has
yielded! What poems, what dreams, what delights!

But since the knowledge of our maturer years
destroys all that, it is with a degree of satisfaction
we can turn to the consolations of the fairy mythology. The beloved tales of old are 'not true'—
but at least they are not mere idle nonsense, and
they have a good and sufficient reason for being in
the world; we may continue to respect them. The
wit who observed that the final cause of fairy
legends is 'to afford sport for people who ruthlessly
track them to their origin,'[1] expressed a grave truth
in jocular form. Since one can no longer rest in
peace with one's ignorance, it is a comfort to the
lover of fairy legends to find that he need not sweep
them into the grate as so much rubbish; on the
contrary they become even more enchanting in the
crucible of science than they were in their old
character.

II.

Among the vulgar in Wales, the belief in fairies
is less nearly extinct than casual observers would be
likely to suppose. Even educated people who dwell
in Wales, and have dwelt there all their lives, cannot always be classed as other than casual observers
in this field. There are some such residents who
have paid special attention to the subject, and have

[1] 'Saturday Review,' October 20, 1877.

formed an opinion as to the extent of prevalence of popular credulity herein ; but most Welsh people of the educated class, I find, have no opinion, beyond a vague surprise that the question should be raised at all. So lately as the year 1858, a learned writer in the ' Archæologia Cambrensis ' declared that ' the traveller may now pass from one end of the Principality to the other, without his being shocked or amused, as the case may be, by any of the fairy legends or popular tales which used to pass current from father to son.' But in the same periodical, eighteen years later, I find Mr. John Walter Lukis (President of the Cardiff Naturalists' Society), asserting with regard to the cromlechs, tumuli, and ancient camps in Glamorganshire : ' There are always fairy tales and ghost stories connected with them ; some, though *fully believed in* by the inhabitants of those localities, are often of the most absurd character ; in fact, the more ridiculous they are, the more they are believed in.'[1] My own observation leads me to support the testimony of the last-named witness. Educated Europeans generally conceive that this sort of belief is extinct in their own land, or, at least their own immediate section of that land. They accredit such degree of belief as may remain, in this enlightened age, to some remote part—to the south, if they dwell in the north ; to the north, if they dwell in the south. But especially they accredit it to a previous age : in Wales, to last century, or the middle ages, or the days of King Arthur. The rector of Merthyr, being an elderly man, accredits it to his youth. ' I am old enough to remember,' he wrote me under date of January 30th, 1877, 'that these tales were thoroughly believed in among country folk forty or fifty years

[1] ' Archæologia Cambrensis,' 4th Se., vi., 174.

ago.' People of superior culture have held this kind of faith concerning fairy-lore, it seems to me, in every age, except the more remote. Chaucer held it, almost five centuries ago, and wrote :[1]

> In olde dayes of the Kyng Arthour, . . .
> Al was this lond fulfilled of fayrie ; . . .
> I speke of many hundrid yer ago ;
> But now can no man see non elves mo.

Dryden held it, two hundred years later, and said of the fairies :

> I speak of ancient times, for now the swain
> Returning late may pass the woods in vain,
> And never hope to see the nightly train.

In all later days, other authors have written the same sort of thing ; it is not thus now, say they, but it was recently thus. The truth, probably, is that if you will but sink down to the level of common life, of ignorant life, especially in rural neighbourhoods, there you will find the same old beliefs prevailing, in about the same degree to which they have ever prevailed, within the past five hundred years. To sink to this level successfully, one must become a living unit in that life, as I have done in Wales and elsewhere, from time to time. Then one will hear the truth from, or at least the true sentiments of, the class he seeks to know. The practice of every generation in thus relegating fairy belief to a date just previous to its own does not apply, however, to superstitious beliefs in general ; for, concerning many such beliefs, their greater or less prevalence at certain dates (as in the history of witchcraft) is matter of well-ascertained fact. I confine the argument, for the present, strictly to the domain of faerie. In this domain, the prevalent belief in Wales may be said to rest with the ignorant, to

---

[1] 'Wyf of Bathes Tale,' ' Canterbury Tales.'

be strongest in rural and mining districts, to be childlike and poetic, and to relate to anywhere except the spot where the speaker dwells—as to the next parish, to the next county, to the distant mountains, or to the shadow-land of Gwerddonau Llion, the green meadows of the sea.

III.

In Arthur's day and before that, the people of South Wales regarded North Wales as pre-eminently the land of faerie. In the popular imagination, that distant country was the chosen abode of giants, monsters, magicians, and all the creatures of enchantment. Out of it came the fairies, on their visits to the sunny land of the south. The chief philosopher of that enchanted region was a giant who sat on a mountain peak and watched the stars. It had a wizard monarch called Gwydion, who possessed the power of changing himself into the strangest possible forms. The peasant who dwelt on the shores of Dyfed (Demetia) saw in the distance, beyond the blue waves of the ocean, shadowy mountain summits piercing the clouds, and guarding this mystic region in solemn majesty. Thence rolled down upon him the storm-clouds from the home of the tempest; thence streamed up the winter sky the flaming banners of the Northern lights; thence rose through the illimitable darkness on high, the star-strewn pathway of the fairy king. These details are current in the Mabinogion, those brilliant stories of Welsh enchantment, so gracefully done into English by Lady Charlotte Guest,[1] and it is believed that all the Mabinogion in which these details were found were written in Dyfed. This

[1] 'The Mabinogion, from the Welsh of the Llyfr Coch o Hergest. Translated, with notes, by Lady Charlotte Guest. (New Edition London, 1877.)

was the region on the west, now covered by Pembroke, Carmarthen, and Cardigan shires.

More recently than the time above indicated, special traditions have located fairy-land in the Vale of Neath, in Glamorganshire. Especially does a certain steep and rugged crag there, called Craig y Ddinas, bear a distinctly awful reputation as a stronghold of the fairy tribe.[1] Its caves and crevices have been their favourite haunt for many centuries, and upon this rock was held the court of the last fairies who have ever appeared in Wales. Needless to say there are men still living who remember the visits of the fairies to Craig y Ddinas, although they aver the little folk are no longer seen there. It is a common remark that the Methodists drove them away; indeed, there are numberless stories which show the fairies to have been animated, when they were still numerous in Wales, by a cordial antipathy for all dissenting preachers. In this antipathy, it may be here observed, teetotallers were included.

IV.

The sovereign of the fairies, and their especial guardian and protector, was one Gwyn ap Nudd. He was also ruler over the goblin tribe in general. His name often occurs in ancient Welsh poetry. An old bard of the fourteenth century, who, led away by the fairies, rode into a turf bog on a mountain one dark night, called it the 'fish-pond of Gwyn ap Nudd, a palace for goblins and their tribe.' The association of this legendary character with the goblin fame of the Vale of Neath will appear, when it is mentioned that Nudd in Welsh is pronounced simply Neath, and not otherwise. As for the fairy queen,

---

[1] There are two hills in Glamorganshire called by this name, and others elsewhere in Wales.

she does not seem to have any existence among Cambrian goblins. It is nevertheless thought by Cambrian etymologists, that Morgana is derived from Mor Gwyn, the white maid ; and the Welsh proper name Morgan can hardly fail to be mentioned in this connection, though it is not necessarily significant.

The legend of St. Collen, in which Gwyn ap Nudd figures, represents him as king of Annwn (hell, or the shadow land) as well as of the fairies.[1]   Collen was passing a period of mortification as a hermit, in a cell under a rock on a mountain. There he one day overheard two men talking about Gwyn ap Nudd, and giving him this twofold kingly character. Collen cried out to the men to go away and hold their tongues, instead of talking about devils. For this Collen was rebuked, as the king of fairyland had an objection to such language. The saint was summoned to meet the king on the hill-top at noon, and after repeated refusals, he finally went there ; but he carried a flask of holy water with him.   ' And when he came there he saw the fairest castle he had ever beheld, and around it the best appointed troops, and numbers of minstrels and every kind of music of voice and string, and steeds with youths upon them, the comeliest in the world, and maidens of elegant aspect, sprightly, light of foot, of graceful apparel, and in the bloom of youth ; and every magnificence becoming the court of a puissant sovereign. And he beheld a courteous man on the top of the castle who bade him enter, saying that the king was waiting for him to come to meat. And Collen went into the castle, and when he came there the king was sitting in a golden chair. And he welcomed Collen honourably, and desired him to eat, assuring him that besides what he saw, he should have the

[1] ' Greal ' (8vo. London, 1805), p. 337.

most luxurious of every dainty and delicacy that the
mind could desire, and should be supplied with
every drink and liquor that the heart could wish;
and that there should be in readiness for him every
luxury of courtesy and service, of banquet and of
honourable entertainment, of rank and of presents,
and every respect and welcome due to a man of his
wisdom. "I will not eat the leaves of the trees,"
said Collen. "Didst thou ever see men of better
equipment than these of red and blue?" asked the
king. "Their equipment is good enough," said
Collen, "for such equipment as it is." "What kind
of equipment is that?" said the king. Then said
Collen, "The red on the one part signifies burning, and the blue on the other signifies coldness."
And with that Collen drew out his flask and threw
the holy water on their heads, whereupon they
vanished from his sight, so that there was neither
castle nor troops, nor men, nor maidens, nor music,
nor song, nor steeds, nor youths, nor banquet, nor
the appearance of anything whatever but the green
hillocks.'

V.

A third form of Welsh popular belief as to the
whereabouts of fairy-land corresponds with the
Avalon of the Arthurian legends. The green
meadows of the sea, called in the triads Gwerddonau
Llion, are the

> Green fairy islands, reposing,
> In sunlight and beauty on ocean's calm breast.[1]

Many extraordinary superstitions survive with regard to these islands. They were supposed to be
the abode of the souls of certain Druids, who, not
holy enough to enter the heaven of the Christians,
were still not wicked enough to be condemned to

[1] Parry's 'Welsh Melodies.'

the tortures of annwn, and so were accorded a place in this romantic sort of purgatorial paradise. In the fifth century a voyage was made, by the British king Gavran, in search of these enchanted islands; with his family he sailed away into the unknown waters, and was never heard of more. This voyage is commemorated in the triads as one of the Three Losses by Disappearance, the two others being Merlin's and Madog's. Merlin sailed away in a ship of glass; Madog sailed in search of America; and neither returned, but both disappeared for ever. In Pembrokeshire and southern Carmarthenshire are to be found traces of this belief. There are sailors on that romantic coast who still talk of the green meadows of enchantment lying in the Irish channel to the west of Pembrokeshire. Sometimes they are visible to the eyes of mortals for a brief space, when suddenly they vanish. There are traditions of sailors who, in the early part of the present century, actually went ashore on the fairy islands—not knowing that they were such, until they returned to their boats, when they were filled with awe at seeing the islands disappear from their sight, neither sinking in the sea, nor floating away upon the waters, but simply vanishing suddenly. The fairies inhabiting these islands are said to have regularly attended the markets at Milford Haven and Laugharne. They made their purchases without speaking, laid down their money and departed, always leaving the exact sum required, which they seemed to know, without asking the price of anything. Sometimes they were invisible, but they were often seen, by sharp-eyed persons. There was always one special butcher at Milford Haven upon whom the fairies bestowed their patronage, instead of distributing their favours indiscriminately. The

Milford Haven folk could see the green fairy islands distinctly, lying out a short distance from land ; and the general belief was that they were densely peopled with fairies. It was also said that the latter went to and fro between the islands and the shore through a subterranean gallery under the bottom of the sea.

FAIRIES MARKETING AT LAUGHARNE.

That isolated cape which forms the county of Pembroke was looked upon as a land of mystery by the rest of Wales long after it had been settled by the Flemings in 1113. A secret veil was supposed to cover this sea-girt promontory; the inhabitants talked in an unintelligible jargon that was neither English, nor French, nor Welsh ; and out of its misty darkness came fables of wondrous sort, and accounts of miracles marvellous beyond belief. Mythology and Christianity spoke together from this strange country, and one could not tell at which to be most amazed, the pagan or the priest.

CHAPTER II.

Classification of Welsh Fairies—General Designation—Habits of the Tylwyth Teg—Ellyllon, or Elves—Shakspeare's Use of Welsh Folk-Lore—Rowli Pugh and the Ellyll—Household Story Roots—The Ellylldan—The Pooka—Puck Valley, Breconshire—Where Shakspeare got his Puck—Pwca 'r Trwyn—Usual Form of the Pooka Story—Coblynau, or Mine Fairies—The Knockers—Miners' Superstitions—Basilisks and Fire Fiends—a Fairy Coalmine—The Dwarfs of Cae Caled—Counterparts of the Coblynau—The Bwbach, or Household Fairy—Legend of the Bwbach and the Preacher—Bogies and Hobgoblins—Carrying Mortals through the Air—Counterparts and Originals.

I.

FAIRIES being creatures of the imagination, it is not possible to classify them by fixed and immutable rules. In the exact sciences, there are laws which never vary, or if they vary, their very eccentricity is governed by precise rules. Even in the largest sense, comparative mythology must demean itself modestly in order to be tolerated in the severe company of the sciences. In presenting his subjects, therefore, the writer in this field can only govern himself by the purpose of orderly arrangement. To secure the maximum of system, for the sake of the student who employs the work for reference and comparison, with the minimum of dullness, for the sake of the general reader, is perhaps the limit of a reasonable ambition. Keightley[1] divides into four classes the Scandinavian elements of popular belief as to fairies, viz.: 1. The Elves; 2. The Dwarfs, or Trolls; 3. The Nisses; and 4. The Necks,

[1] 'Fairy Mythology' (Bohn's Ed.), 78.

Mermen, and Mermaids. How entirely arbitrary this division is, the student of Scandinavian folk-lore at once perceives. Yet it is perhaps as satisfactory as another. The fairies of Wales may be divided into five classes, if analogy be not too sharply insisted on. Thus we have, 1. The Ellyllon, or elves; 2. The Coblynau, or mine fairies; 3. The Bwbachod, or household fairies; 4. The Gwragedd Annwn, or fairies of the lakes and streams; and 5. The Gwyllion, or mountain fairies.

The modern Welsh name for fairies is y Tylwyth Teg, the fair folk or family. This is sometimes lengthened into y Tylwyth Teg yn y Coed, the fair family in the wood, or Tylwyth Teg y Mwn, the fair folk of the mine. They are seen dancing in moonlight nights on the velvety grass, clad in airy and flowing robes of blue, green, white, or scarlet—details as to colour not usually met, I think, in accounts of fairies. They are spoken of as bestowing blessings on those mortals whom they select to be thus favoured; and again are called Bendith y Mamau, or their mother's blessing, that is to say, good little children whom it is a pleasure to know. To name the fairies by a harsh epithet is to invoke their anger; to speak of them in flattering phrase is to propitiate their good offices. The student of fairy mythology perceives in this propitiatory mode of speech a fact of wide significance. It can be traced in numberless lands, and back to the beginning of human history, among the cloud-hung peaks of Central Asia. The Greeks spoke of the furies as the Eumenides, or gracious ones; Highlanders mentioned by Sir Walter Scott uncover to the gibbet and call it 'the kind gallows;' the Dayak will not name the small-pox, but calls it 'the chief;' the Laplander calls the bear 'the old man with the fur coat;' in Ammam the tiger is called 'grandfather;' and it is thought that the maxim, 'Speak only good of the dead,' came originally from the notion of propitiating the ghost of the departed,[1] who, in laying off this mortal garb, had become endowed with new powers of harming his late acquaintance.

II.

The Ellyllon are the pigmy elves who haunt the groves and valleys, and correspond pretty closely with the English elves. The English name was probably derived from the Welsh *el*, a spirit, *elf*, an element; there is a whole brood of words of this class in the Welsh language, expressing every variety of flowing, gliding, spirituality, devilry, angelhood, and goblinism. Ellyllon (the plural of ellyll), is also doubtless allied with the Hebrew Elilim, having with it an identity both of origin and meaning.[2] The poet Davydd ab Gwilym, in a humorous account of his troubles in a mist, in the year 1340, says:

> Yr ydoedd ym mhob gobant
> Ellyllon mingeimion gant.
>
> There was in every hollow
> A hundred wrymouthed elves.

The hollows, or little dingles, are still the places where the peasant, belated on his homeward way from fair or market, looks for the ellyllon, but fails to find them. Their food is specified in Welsh folk-lore as fairy butter and fairy victuals, ymenyn tylwyth teg and bwyd ellyllon; the latter the toadstool, or poisonous mushroom, and the former a butter-resembling substance found at great depths in the crevices of limestone rocks, in sinking for

---

[1] John Fiske, ' Myths and Myth-makers,' 223.
[2] Pughe's ' Welsh Dictionary.' (Denbigh, 1866.)

lead ore. Their gloves, menyg ellyllon, are the bells of the digitalis, or fox-glove, the leaves of which are well known to be a strong sedative. Their queen—for though there is no fairy-queen in the large sense that Gwyn ap Nudd is the fairy-king, there is a queen of the elves—is none other than the Shakspearean fairy spoken of by Mercutio, who comes

> In shape no bigger than an agate-stone
> On the forefinger of an alderman.[1]

Shakspeare's use of Welsh folk-lore, it should be noted, was extensive and peculiarly faithful. Keightley in his 'Fairy Mythology' rates the bard soundly for his inaccurate use of English fairy superstitions ; but the reproach will not apply as regards Wales. From his Welsh informant Shakspeare got Mab, which is simply the Cymric for a little child, and the root of numberless words signifying babyish, childish, love for children (mabgar), kitten (mabgath), prattling (mabiaith), and the like, most notable of all which in this connection is mabinogi, the singular of Mabinogion, the romantic tales of enchantment told to the young in by-gone ages.

III.

In the Huntsman's Rest Inn at Peterstone-super-Ely, near Cardiff, sat a group of humble folk one afternoon, when I chanced to stop there to rest myself by the chimney-side, after a long walk through green lanes. The men were drinking their tankards of ale and smoking their long clay pipes ; and they were talking about their dogs and horses, the crops, the hard times, and the prospect of bettering themselves by emigration to America. On this latter theme I was able to make myself

[1] 'Romeo and Juliet,' Act II., Sc. 4.

interesting, and acquaintance was thereupon easily established on a friendly footing. I led the conversation into the domain of folk-lore ; and this book is richer in illustration on many a page, in consequence. Among others, this tale was told :

On a certain farm in Glamorganshire lived Rowli Pugh, who was known far and wide for his evil luck. Nothing prospered that he turned his hand to ; his crops proved poor, though his neighbours' might be good ; his roof leaked in spite of all his mending ; his walls remained damp when every one else's walls were dry ; and above all, his wife was so feeble she could do no work. His fortunes at last seemed so hard that he resolved to sell out and clear out, no matter at what loss, and try to better himself in another country—not by going to America, for there was no America in those days. Well, and if there was, the poor Welshman didn't know it. So as Rowli was sitting on his wall one day, hard by his cottage, musing over his sad lot, he was accosted by a little man who asked him what was the matter. Rowli looked around in surprise, but before he could answer the ellyll said to him with a grin, ' There, there, hold your tongue, I know more about you than you ever dreamed of knowing. You're in trouble, and you're going away. But you may stay, now I've spoken to you. Only bid your good wife leave the candle burning when she goes to bed, and say no more about it.' With this the ellyll kicked up his heels and disappeared. Of course the farmer did as he was bid, and from that day he prospered. Every night Catti Jones, his wife,[1] set the candle out, swept the hearth, and went to bed ; and every night the fairies would come and do her

---

[1] Until recently, Welsh women retained their maiden names even after marriage.

baking and brewing, her washing and mending,
sometimes even furnishing their own tools and
materials. The farmer was now always clean of

ROWLI AND THE ELLYLL.

linen and whole of garb; he had good bread and
good beer; he felt like a new man, and worked
like one. Everything prospered with him now as
nothing had before. His crops were good, his barns

were tidy, his cattle were sleek, his pigs the fattest in the parish. So things went on for three years. One night Catti Jones took it into her head that she must have a peep at the fair family who did her work for her; and curiosity conquering prudence, she arose while Rowli Pugh lay snoring, and peeped through a crack in the door. There they were, a jolly company of ellyllon, working away like mad, and laughing and dancing as madly as they worked. Catti was so amused that in spite of herself she fell to laughing too; and at sound of her voice the ellyllon scattered like mist before the wind, leaving the room empty. They never came back any more; but the farmer was now prosperous, and his bad luck never returned to plague him.

The resemblance of this tale to many he has encountered will at once be noted by the student of comparative folk-lore. He will also observe that it trenches on the domain of another class in my own enumeration, viz., that of the Bwbach, or household fairy. This is the stone over which one is constantly stumbling in this field of scientific research. Mr. Baring-Gould's idea that all household tales are reducable to a primeval root (in the same or a similar manner that we trace words to their roots), though most ingeniously illustrated by him, is constantly involved in trouble of the sort mentioned. He encounters the obstacle which lies in the path of all who walk this way. His roots sometimes get inextricably gnarled and intertwisted with each other. But some effort of this sort is imperative, and we must do the best we can with our materials. Stories of the class of Grimm's Witchel-männer (Kinder und Hausmärchen) will be recalled by the legend of Rowli Pugh as here told. The German Hausmänner are elves of a domestic turn,

B

sometimes mischievous and sometimes useful, but usually looking for some material reward for their labours. So with the English goblin named by Milton in ' L'Allegro,' which drudges

To earn his cream-bowl duly set.

IV.

The Ellylldan is a species of elf exactly corresponding to the English Will-o'-wisp, the Scandinavian Lyktgubhe, and the Breton Sand Yan y Tad. The Welsh word dan means fire; dàn also means a lure; the compound word suggests a luring elf-fire. The Breton Sand Yan y Tad (St. John and Father)[1] is a double ignis fatuus fairy, carrying at its finger-ends five lights, which spin round like a wheel. The negroes of the southern seaboard states of America invest this goblin with an exaggeration of the horrible peculiarly their own. They call it Jack-muh-lantern, and describe it as a hideous creature five feet in height, with goggle-eyes and huge mouth, its body covered with long hair, and which goes leaping and bounding through the air like a gigantic grasshopper. This frightful apparition is stronger than any man, and swifter than any horse, and compels its victims to follow it into the swamp, where it leaves them to die.

Like all goblins of this class, the Ellylldan was, of course, seen dancing about in marshy grounds, into which it led the belated wanderer; but, as a distinguished resident in Wales has wittily said, the poor elf ' is now starved to death, and his breath is taken from him; his light is quenched for ever by the improving farmer, who has drained the bog; and, instead of the rank decaying vegetation of the

---

[1] Keightley. 'Fairy Mythology,' 441.

autumn, where bitterns and snipes delighted to secrete themselves, crops of corn and potatoes are grown.' [1]

A poetic account by a modern character, called Iolo the Bard, is thus condensed : 'One night, when the moon had gone down, as I was sitting on a hill-top, the Ellylldan passed by. I followed it into the valley. We crossed plashes of water where the tops of bulrushes peeped above, and where the lizards lay silently on the surface, looking at us with an unmoved stare. The frogs sat croaking and swelling their sides, but ceased as they raised a melancholy eye at the Ellylldan. The wild fowl, sleeping with their heads under their wings, made a low cackle as we went by. A bittern awoke and rose with a scream into the air. I felt the trail of the eels and leeches peering about, as I waded through the pools. On a slimy stone a toad sat sucking poison from the night air. The Ellylldan glowed bravely in the slumbering vapours. It rose airily over the bushes that drooped in the ooze. When I lingered or stopped, it waited for me, but dwindled gradually away to a speck barely perceptible. But as soon as I moved on again, it would shoot up suddenly and glide before. A bat came flying round and round us, flapping its wings heavily. Screech-owls stared silently at us with their broad eyes. Snails and worms crawled about. The fine threads of a spider's web gleamed in the light of the Ellylldan. Suddenly it shot away from me, and in the distance joined a ring of its fellows, who went dancing slowly round and round in a goblin dance, whch sent me off to sleep.' [2]

[1] Hon. W. O. Stanley, M.P., in 'Notes and Queries.'
[2] 'The Vale of Glamorgan.' (London, 1839.)

B 2

V.

Pwca, or Pooka, is but another name for the Ellyll-dan, as our Puck is another name for the Will-o'-wisp; but in both cases the shorter term has a more poetic flavour and a wider latitude. The name Puck was originally applied to the whole race of English fairies, and there still be few of the realm who enjoy a wider popularity than Puck, in spite of his mischievous attributes. Part of this popularity is due to the poets, especially to Shakspeare. I have alluded to the bard's accurate knowledge of Welsh folk-lore; the subject is really one of unique interest, in view of the inaccuracy charged upon him as to the English fairyland. There is a Welsh tradition to the effect that Shakspeare received his knowledge of the Cambrian fairies from his friend Richard Price, son of Sir John Price, of the priory of Brecon. It is even claimed that Cwm Pwca, or Puck Valley, a part of the romantic glen of the Clydach, in Breconshire, is the original scene of the 'Midsummer Night's Dream '—a fancy as light and airy as Puck himself.[1] Anyhow, there Cwm Pwca is, and in the sylvan days, before Frere and Powell's ironworks were set up there, it is said to have been as full of goblins as a Methodist's head is of piety. And there are in Wales other places bearing like names, where Pwca's pranks are well remembered by old inhabitants. The range given to the popular

---

[1] According to a letter written by the poet Campbell to Mrs. Fletcher, in 1833, and published in her Autobiography, it was thought Shakspeare went in person to see this magic valley. 'It is no later than yesterday,' wrote Campbell, 'that I discovered a probability—almost near a certainty—that Shakspeare visited friends in the very town (Brecon in Wales) where Mrs. Siddons was born, and that he there found in a neighbouring glen, called "The Valley of Fairy Puck," the principal machinery of his "Midsummer Night's Dream."'

fancy in Wales is expressed with fidelity by Shakspeare's words in the mouth of Puck:

> I'll follow you, I'll lead you about a round,
> Through bog, through bush, through brake, through brier,
> Sometime a horse I'll be, sometime a hound,
> A hog, a headless bear, sometime a fire;
> And neigh, and bark, and grunt, and roar, and burn,
> Like horse, hound, hog, bear, fire, at every turn.[1]

The various stories I have encountered bear out these details almost without an omission.

In his own proper character, however, Pwca has a sufficiently grotesque elfish aspect. It is stated that a Welsh peasant who was asked to give an

idea of the appearance of Pwca, drew the above figure with a bit of coal.

[1] 'Midsummer Night's Dream,' Act. III., Sc., 3.

A servant girl who attended to the cattle on the Trwyn farm, near Abergwyddon, used to take food to 'Master Pwca,' as she called the elf. A bowl of fresh milk and a slice of white bread were the component parts of the goblin's repast, and were placed on a certain spot where he ·got them. One night the girl, moved by the spirit of mischief, drank the milk and ate most of the bread, leaving for Master Pwca only water and crusts. Next morning she found that the fastidious fairy had left the food untouched. Not long after, as the girl was passing the lonely spot, where she had hitherto left Pwca his food, she was seized under the arm pits by fleshly hands (which, however, she could not see), and subjected to a castigation of a most mortifying character. Simultaneously there fell upon her ear in good set Welsh a warning not to repeat her offence on peril of still worse treatment. This story 'is thoroughly believed in there to this day.'[1]

I visited the scene of the story, a farm near Abergwyddon (now called Abercarne), and heard a great deal more of the exploits of that particular Pwca, to which I will refer again. The most singular fact of the matter is that although at least a century has elapsed, and some say several centuries, since the exploits in question, you cannot find a Welsh peasant in the parish but knows all about Pwca'r Trwyn.

VI.

The most familiar form of the Pwca story is one which I have encountered in several localities, varying so little in its details that each account would be interchangeable with another by the alteration of

[1] 'Archæologia Cambrensis,' 4th Se., vi., 175. (1875.)

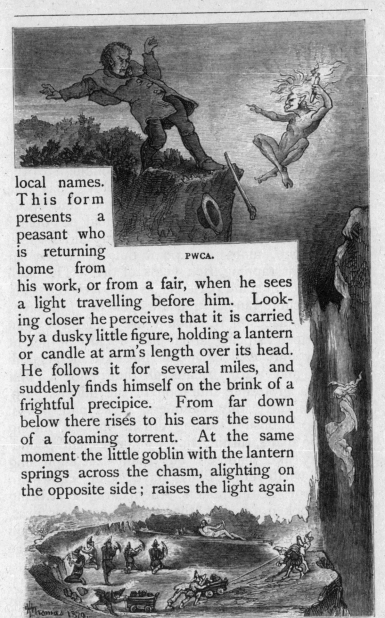

PWCA.

local names. This form presents a peasant who is returning home from his work, or from a fair, when he sees a light travelling before him. Looking closer he perceives that it is carried by a dusky little figure, holding a lantern or candle at arm's length over its head. He follows it for several miles, and suddenly finds himself on the brink of a frightful precipice. From far down below there rises to his ears the sound of a foaming torrent. At the same moment the little goblin with the lantern springs across the chasm, alighting on the opposite side; raises the light again

COBLYNAU.

high over its head, utters a loud and malicious laugh, blows out its candle and disappears up the opposite hill, leaving the awestruck peasant to get home as best he can.

VII.

Under the general title of Coblynau I class the fairies which haunt the mines, quarries and underground regions of Wales, corresponding to the cabalistic Gnomes. The word coblyn has the double meaning of knocker or thumper and sprite or fiend ; and may it not be the original of goblin? It is applied by Welsh miners to pigmy fairies which dwell in the mines, and point out, by a peculiar knocking or rapping, rich veins of ore. The faith is extended, in some parts, so as to cover the indication of subterranean treasures generally, in caves and secret places of the mountains. The coblynau are described as being about half a yard in height and very ugly to look upon, but extremely good-natured, and warm friends of the miner. Their dress is a grotesque imitation of the miner's garb, and they carry tiny hammers, picks and lamps. They work busily, loading ore in buckets, flitting about the shafts, turning tiny windlasses, and pounding away like madmen, but really accomplishing nothing whatever. They have been known to throw stones at the miners, when enraged at being lightly spoken of ; but the stones are harmless. Nevertheless, all miners of a proper spirit refrain from provoking them, because their presence brings good luck.

VIII.

Miners are possibly no more superstitious than other men of equal intelligence ; I have heard some

of their number repel indignantly the idea that they
are superstitious at all ; but this would simply be to
raise them above the level of our common humanity.
There is testimony enough, besides, to support my
own conclusions, which accredit a liberal share of
credulity to the mining class. The *Oswestry Adver-
tiser*, a short time ago, recorded the fact that, at
Cefn, 'a woman is employed as messenger at one
of the collieries, and as she commences her duty
early each morning she meets great numbers of
colliers going to their work. Some of them, we are
gravely assured, consider it a bad omen to meet a
woman first thing in the morning ; and not having
succeeded in deterring her from her work by other
means, they waited upon the manager and declared
that they should remain at home unless the woman
was dismissed.' This was in 1874. In June, 1878,
the *South Wales Daily News* recorded a superstition
of the quarrymen at Penrhyn, where some thousands
of men refused to work on Ascension Day. 'This
refusal did not arise out of any reverential feeling,
but from an old and wide-spread superstition, which
has lingered in that district for years, that if work
is continued on Ascension Day an accident will
certainly follow. A few years ago the agents
persuaded the men to break through the superstition, and there were accidents each year—a not
unlikely occurrence, seeing the extent of works
carried on, and the dangerous nature of the occupation of the men. This year, however, the men, one
and all, refused to work.' These are examples
dealing with considerable numbers of the mining
class, and are quoted in this instance as being more
significant than individual cases would be. Of these
last I have encountered many. Yet I should be

sorry if any reader were to conclude from all this that Welsh miners are not in the main intelligent, church-going, newspaper-reading men. They are so, I think, even beyond the common. Their superstitions, therefore, like those of the rest of us, must be judged as 'a thing apart,' not to be reconciled with intelligence and education, but co-existing with them. Absolute freedom from superstition can come only with a degree of scientific culture not yet reached by mortal man.

It can hardly be cause for wonder that the miner should be superstitious. His life is passed in a dark and gloomy region, fathoms below the earth's green surface, surrounded by walls on which dim lamps shed a fitful light. It is not surprising that imagination (and the Welsh imagination is peculiarly vivid) should conjure up the faces and forms of gnomes and coblynau, of phantoms and fairy men. When they hear the mysterious thumping which they know is not produced by any human being, and when in examining the place where the noise was heard they find there are really valuable indications of ore, the sturdiest incredulity must sometimes be shaken. Science points out that the noise may be produced by the action of water upon the loose stones in fissures and pot-holes of the mountain limestone, and does actually suggest the presence of metals.

In the days before a Priestley had caught and bottled that demon which exists in the shape of carbonic acid gas, when the miner was smitten dead by an invisible foe in the deep bowels of the earth it was natural his awe-struck companions should ascribe the mysterious blow to a supernatural enemy. When the workman was assailed suddenly by what we now call fire-damp, which hurled him and his companions right and left upon the dark rocks, scorching, burning, and killing, those who survived were not likely to question the existence of the mine fiend. Hence arose the superstition—now probably quite extinct—of basilisks in the mines, which destroyed with their terrible gaze. When the explanation came, that the thing which killed the miner was what he breathed, not what he saw ; and when chemistry took the fire-damp from the domain of faerie, the basilisk and the fire fiend had not a leg to stand on. The explanation of the Knockers is more recent, and less palpable and convincing.

IX.

The Coblynau are always given the form of dwarfs, in the popular fancy ; wherever seen or heard, they are believed to have escaped from the mines or the secret regions of the mountains. Their homes are hidden from mortal vision. When encountered, either in the mines or on the mountains, they have strayed from their special abodes, which are as spectral as themselves. There is at least one account extant of their secret territory having been revealed to mortal eyes. I find it in a quaint volume (of which I shall have more to say), printed at Newport, Monmouthshire, in 1813.[1] It relates that one William Evans, of Hafodafel, while crossing the Beacon Mountain very early in the morning, passed a fairy coal mine, where fairies were busily at work. Some were cutting the coal, some carrying it to fill the sacks, some raising the loads upon the

[1] 'A Relation of Apparitions of Spirits in the County of Monmouth and the Principality of Wales.' By Rev. Edmund Jones of the Tranch. (Newport, 1813.)

horses' backs, and so on; but all in the completest silence. He thought this 'a wonderful extra natural thing,' and was considerably impressed by it, for well he knew that there really was no coal mine at that place. He was a person of ' undoubted veracity,' and what is more, 'a great man in the world—above telling an untruth.'

That the Coblynau sometimes wandered far from home, the same chronicler testifies; but on these occasions they were taking a holiday. Egbert Williams, 'a pious young gentleman of Denbigh-shire, then at school,' was one day playing in a field called Cae Caled, in the parish of Bodfari, with three girls, one of whom was his sister. Near the stile beyond Lanelwyd House they saw a company of fifteen or sixteen coblynau engaged in dancing madly. They were in the middle of the field, about seventy yards from the spectators, and they danced something after the manner of Morris-dancers, but with a wildness and swiftness in their motions. They were clothed in red like British soldiers, and wore red handkerchiefs spotted with yellow wound round their heads. And a strange circumstance about them was that although they were almost as big as ordinary men, yet they had unmistakably the appearance of dwarfs, and one could call them nothing but dwarfs. Presently one of them left the company and ran towards the group near the stile, who were direfully scared thereby, and scrambled in great fright to go over the stile. Barbara Jones got over first, then her sister, and as Egbert Williams was helping his sister over they saw the coblyn close upon them, and barely got over when his hairy hand was laid on the stile. He stood leaning on it, gazing after them as they ran, with a grim copper-coloured countenance and a fierce look. The young people ran to Lanelwyd House and called the elders out, but though they hurried quickly to the field the dwarfs had already disappeared.

X.

The counterparts of the Coblynau are found in most mining countries. In Germany, the Wichtlein (little Wights) are little old long-bearded men, about three-quarters of an ell high, which haunt the mines of the southern land. The Bohemians call the Wichtlein by the name of Haus-schmiedlein, little House-smiths, from their sometimes making a noise as if labouring hard at the anvil. They are not so popular as in Wales, however, as they predict misfortune or death. They announce the doom of a miner by knocking three times distinctly, and when any lesser evil is about to befall him they are heard digging, pounding, and imitating other kinds of work. In Germany also the kobolds are rather troublesome than otherwise, to the miners, taking pleasure in frustrating their objects, and rendering their toil unfruitful. Sometimes they are downright malignant, especially if neglected or insulted, but sometimes also they are indulgent to individuals whom they take under their protection. 'When a miner therefore hit upon a rich vein of ore, the inference commonly was not that he possessed more skill, industry, or even luck than his fellow-workmen, but that the spirits of the mine had directed him to the treasure.'[1]

The intimate connection between mine fairies and the whole race of dwarfs is constantly met throughout the fairy mythology; and the connection of

[1] Scott, 'Demonology and Witchcraft,' 121.

the dwarfs with the mountains is equally universal. 'God,' says the preface to the Heldenbuch, 'gave the dwarfs being, because the land and the mountains were altogether waste and uncultivated, and there was much store of silver and gold and precious stones and pearls still in the mountains.' From the most ancient times, and in the oldest countries, down to our own time and the new world of America, the traditions are the same. The old Norse belief which made the dwarfs the current machinery of the northern Sagas is echoed in the Catskill Mountains with the rolling of the thunder among the crags where Hendrik Hudson's dwarfs are playing ninepins.

XI.

The Bwbach, or Boobach, is the good-natured goblin which does good turns for the tidy Welsh maid who wins its favour by a certain course of behaviour recommended by long tradition. The maid having swept the kitchen, makes a good fire the last thing at night, and having put the churn, filled with cream, on the whitened hearth, with a basin of fresh cream for the Bwbach on the hob, goes to bed to await the event. In the morning she finds (if she is in luck) that the Bwbach has emptied the basin of cream, and plied the churn-dasher so well that the maid has but to give a thump or two to bring the butter in a great lump. Like the Ellyll which it so much resembles, the Bwbach does not approve of dissenters and their ways, and especially strong is its aversion to total abstainers.

There was a Bwbach belonging to a certain estate in Cardiganshire, which took great umbrage at a Baptist preacher who was a guest in the house, and who was much fonder of prayers than of good ale. Now the Bwbach had a weakness in favour of people who sat around the hearth with their mugs of cwrw da and their pipes, and it took to pestering the preacher. One night it jerked the stool from under the good man's elbows, as he knelt pouring forth prayer, so that he fell down flat on his face. Another time it interrupted the devotions by jangling the fire-irons on the hearth ; and it was continually making the dogs fall a-howling during prayers, or frightening the farm-boy by grinning at him through the window, or throwing the maid into fits. At last it had the audacity to attack the preacher as he was crossing a field. The minister told the story in this wise : ' I was reading busily in my hymn-book as I walked on, when a sudden fear came over me and my legs began to tremble. A shadow crept upon me from behind, and when I turned round—it was myself!—my person, my dress, and even my hymn-book. I looked in its face a moment, and then fell insensible to the ground.' And there, insensible still, they found him. This encounter proved too much for the good man, who considered it a warning to him to leave those parts. He accordingly mounted his horse next day and rode away. A boy of the neighbourhood, whose veracity was, like that of all boys, unimpeachable, afterwards said that he saw the Bwbach jump up behind the preacher, on the horse's back. And the horse went like lightning, with eyes like balls of fire, and the preacher looking back over his shoulder at the Bwbach, that grinned from ear to ear.

XII.

The same confusion in outlines which exists regarding our own Bogie and-Hobgoblin gives the Bwbach a double character, as a household fairy and as a terrifying phantom. In both aspects it is ludicrous, but in the latter it has dangerous practices. To get into its clutches under certain circumstances is no trifling matter, for it has the power of whisking people off through the air. Its services are brought into requisition for this purpose by troubled ghosts who cannot sleep on account of hidden treasure they want removed ; and if they can succeed in getting a mortal to help them in removing the treasure, they employ the Bwbach to transport the mortal through the air.

This ludicrous fairy is in France represented by the gobelin. Mothers threaten children with him. 'Le gobelin vous mangera, le gobelin vous emportera.'[1] In the English 'hobgoblin' we have a word apparently derived from the Welsh hob, to hop, and coblyn, a goblin, which presents a hopping goblin to the mind, and suggests the Pwca (with which the Bwbach is also confused in the popular fancy at times), but should mean in English simply the goblin of the hob, or household fairy. In its bugbear aspect, the Bwbach, like the English bogie, is believed to be identical with the Slavonic 'bog,' and the 'baga' of the Cuneiform Inscriptions, both of which are names for the Supreme Being, according to Professor Fiske. 'The ancestral form of these epithets' is found in 'the old Aryan "Bhaga,"' which reappears unchanged in the Sanskrit of the

[1] Père l'Abbé, ' Etymologie,' i., 262.

Vedas, and has left a memento of itself in the surname of the Phrygian Zeus " Bagaios." It seems originally to have denoted either the unclouded sun, or the sky of noonday illuminated by the solar rays. . . . Thus the same name which to the Vedic poet, to the Persian of the time of Xerxes, and to the modern Russian, suggests the supreme majesty of deity, is in English associated with an ugly and ludicrous fiend, closely akin to that grotesque Northern Devil of whom Southey was unable to think without laughing.'[1]

[1] Fiske, ' Myths and Myth-makers, 105.

CHAPTER III.

I.

THE Gwragedd Annwn (literally, wives of the lower
world, or hell) are the elfin dames who dwell under
the water. I find no resemblance in the Welsh
fairy to our familiar mermaid, beyond the watery
abode, and the sometimes winning ways. The
Gwragedd Annwn are not fishy of aspect, nor do
they dwell in the sea. Their haunt is the lakes
and rivers, but especially the wild and lonely lakes
upon the mountain heights. These romantic sheets
are surrounded with numberless superstitions, which
will be further treated of. In the realm of faerie
they serve as avenues of communication between
this world and the lower one of annwn, the shadowy
domain presided over by Gwyn ap Nudd, king of
the fairies. This sub-aqueous realm is peopled by
those children of mystery termed Plant Annwn, and
the belief is current among the inhabitants of the
Welsh mountains that the Gwragedd Annwn still
occasionally visit this upper world of ours.[1] The

[1] 'Archæologia Cambrensis,' 2nd Se., iv., 253.

only reference to Welsh mermaids I have either read or heard is contained in Drayton's account of the Battle of Agincourt. There it is mentioned, among the armorial ensigns of the counties of Wales :

> As Cardigan, the next to them that went,
> Came with a mermaid sitting on a rock.[1]

II.

Crumlyn Lake, near the quaint village of Briton Ferry, is one of the many in Wales which are a resort of the elfin dames. It is also believed that a large town lies swallowed up there, and that the Gwragedd Annwn have turned the submerged walls to use as the superstructure of their fairy palaces. Some claim to have seen the towers of beautiful castles lifting their battlements beneath the surface of the dark waters, and fairy bells are at times heard ringing from these towers. The way the elfin dames first came to dwell there was this : A long, ay, a very long time ago, St. Patrick came over from Ireland on a visit to St. David of Wales, just to say ' Sut yr y'ch chwi ? ' (How d'ye do ?) ; and as they were strolling by this lake conversing on religious topics in a friendly manner, some Welsh people who had ascertained that it was St. Patrick, and being angry at him for leaving Cambria for Erin, began to abuse him in the Welsh language, his native tongue. Of course such an insult could not go unpunished, and St. Patrick caused his villifiers to be transformed into fishes ; but some of them being females, were converted into fairies instead. It is also related that the sun, on account of this insolence to so holy a man, never shed its life-giving rays upon the dark

---

[1] There is in ' Cymru Fu ' a mermaid story, but its mermaid feature is apparently a modern embellishment of a real incident, and without value here.

D

waters of this picturesque lake, except during one week of the year. This legend and these magical details are equally well accredited to various other lakes, among them Llyn Barfog, near Aberdovey, the town whose 'bells' are celebrated in immortal song.

III.

Llyn Barfog is the scene of the famous elfin cow's descent upon earth, from among the droves of the Gwragedd Annwn. This is the legend of the origin of the Welsh black cattle, as related to me in Carmarthenshire: In times of old there was a band of elfin ladies who used to haunt the neighbourhood of Llyn Barfog, a lake among the hills just back of Aberdovey. It was their habit to make their appearance at dusk clad all in green, accompanied by their milk-white hounds. Besides their hounds, the green ladies of Llyn Barfog were peculiar in the possession of droves of beautiful milk-white kine, called Gwartheg y Llyn, or kine of the lake. One day an old farmer, who lived near Dyssyrnant, had the good luck to catch one of these mystic cows, which had fallen in love with the cattle of his herd. From that day the farmer's fortune was made. Such calves, such milk, such butter and cheese, as came from the milk-white cow never had been seen in Wales before, nor ever will be seen again. The fame of the Fuwch Gyfeiliorn (which was what they called the cow) spread through the country round. The farmer, who had been poor, became rich; the owner of vast herds, like the patriarchs of old. But one day he took it into his silly noddle that the elfin cow was getting old, and that he had better fatten her for the market. His nefarious purpose thrived amazingly. Never, since beef steaks were invented, was seen such a fat cow as this cow grew to be. Killing day came, and the neighbours arrived from all about to witness the taking-off of this monstrously fat beast. The farmer had already counted up the gains from the sale of her, and the butcher had bared his red right arm. The cow was tethered, regardless of her mournful lowing and her pleading eyes ; the butcher raised his bludgeon and struck fair and hard between the eyes—when lo ! a shriek resounded through the air, awakening the echoes of the hills, as the butcher's bludgeon went through the goblin head of the elfin cow, and knocked over nine adjoining men, while the butcher himself went frantically whirling around trying to catch hold of something permanent. Then the astonished assemblage beheld a green lady standing on a crag high up over the lake, and crying with a loud voice :

> Dere di felen Einion,
> Cyrn Cyfeiliorn—braith y Llyn,
> A'r foel Dodin,
> Codwch, dewch adre.

> Come yellow Anvil, stray horns,
> Speckled one of the lake,
> And of the hornless Dodin,
> Arise, come home.

Whereupon not only did the elfin cow arise and go home, but all her progeny to the third and fourth generations went home with her, disappearing in the air over the hill tops and returning nevermore. Only one cow remained of all the farmer's herds, and she had turned from milky white to raven black. Whereupon the farmer in despair drowned himself in the lake of the green ladies, and the black cow became the progenitor of the existing race of Welsh black cattle.

This legend appears, in a slightly different form, in the ' Iolo MSS.,' as translated by Taliesin Williams, of Merthyr:[1] 'The milk-white milch cow gave enough of milk to every one who desired it; and however frequently milked, or by whatever number of persons, she was never found deficient. All persons who drank of her milk were healed of every illness; from fools they became wise; and from being wicked, became happy. This cow went round the world; and wherever she appeared, she filled with milk all the vessels that could be found, leaving calves behind her for all the wise and happy. It was from her that all the milch cows in the world were obtained. After traversing through the island of Britain, for the benefit and blessing of country and kindred, she reached the Vale of Towy; where, tempted by her fine appearance and superior condition, the natives sought to kill and eat her; but just as they were proceeding to effect their purpose, she vanished from between their hands, and was never seen again. A house still remains in the locality, called Y Fuwch Laethwen Lefrith (The Milk-white Milch Cow.)'

IV.

The legend of the Meddygon Myddfai again introduces the elfin cattle to our notice, but combines with them another and a very interesting form of this superstition, namely, that of the wife of supernatural race. A further feature gives it its name, Meddygon meaning physicians, and the legend professing to give the origin of certain doctors who were renowned in the thirteenth century. The legend relates that a farmer in the parish of Myddfai, Carmarthenshire, having bought some lambs in a neighbouring fair, led them to graze near Llyn y Fan Fach, on the Black Mountains. Whenever he visited these lambs three beautiful damsels appeared to him from

[1] Llandovery, published for the Welsh MSS. Society, 1848.

the lake, on whose shores they often made excursions. Sometimes he pursued and tried to catch them, but always failed ; the enchanting nymphs ran before him and on reaching the lake taunted him in these words :

> Cras dy fara,
> Anhawdd ein dala ;

which, if one must render it literally, means :

> Bake your bread,
> 'Twill be hard to catch us ;

but which, more poetically treated, might signify :

> Mortal, who eatest baken bread,
> Not for thee is the fairy's bed !

One day some moist bread from the lake came floating ashore. The farmer seized it, and devoured it with avidity. The following day, to his great delight, he was successful in his chase, and caught the nymphs on the shore. After talking a long time with them, he mustered up the courage to propose marriage to one of them. She consented to accept him on condition that he would distinguish her from her sisters the next day. This was a new and great difficulty to the young farmer, for the damsels were so similar in form and features, that he could scarcely see any difference between them. He noted, however, a trifling singularity in the strapping of the chosen one's sandal, by which he recognized her on the following day. As good as her word, the gwraig immediately left the lake and went with him to his farm. Before she quitted the lake she summoned therefrom to attend her, seven cows, two oxen, and one bull. She stipulated that she should remain with the farmer only until such time as he should strike her thrice without cause. For some years they dwelt peaceably together, and she bore him three sons, who were the celebrated Meddygon Myddfai. One day, when preparing for a fair in the neighbourhood, the farmer desired her to go to the field for his horse. She said she would, but being rather dilatory, he said to her humorously 'Dôs, dôs, dôs,' i.e., 'Go, go, go,' and at the same time slightly tapped her arm three times with his glove. . . . The blows were slight—but they were blows. The terms of the marriage contract were broken, and the dame departed, summoning with her her seven cows, her two oxen, and the bull. The oxen were at that moment ploughing in the field, but they immediately obeyed her call and dragged the plough after them to the lake. The furrow, from the field in which they were ploughing to the margin of the lake, is still to be seen—in several parts of that country—at the present day. After her departure, the gwraig annwn once met her three sons in the valley now called Cwm Meddygon, and gave them a magic box containing remedies of wonderful power, through whose use they became celebrated. Their names were Cadogan, Gruffydd and Einion, and the farmer's name was Rhiwallon. Rhiwallon and his sons, named as above, were physicians to Rhys Gryg, Lord of Dynevor, and son of the last native prince of Wales. They lived about 1230, and dying, left behind them a compendium of their medical practice. 'A copy of their works is in the Welsh School Library in Gray's Inn Lane.'[1]

V.

In a more polished and elaborate form this legend omits the medical features altogether, but substitutes a number of details so peculiarly Welsh that I cannot refrain from presenting them. This version relates

[1] 'Cambro Briton,' ii., 315.

that the enamoured farmer had heard of the lake
maiden, who rowed up and down the lake in a
golden boat, with a golden oar. Her hair was long
and yellow, and her face was pale and melancholy.
In his desire to see this wondrous beauty, the farmer
went on New Year's Eve to the edge of the lake,
and in silence awaited the coming of the first hour
of the new year. It came, and there in truth was
the maiden in her golden boat, rowing softly to and
fro. Fascinated, he stood for hours beholding her,
until the stars faded out of the sky, the moon sank
behind the rocks, and the cold gray dawn drew
nigh; and then the lovely gwraig began to vanish
from his sight. Wild with passion, and with the
thought of losing her for ever, he cried aloud to the
retreating vision, 'Stay! stay! Be my wife.' But
the gwraig only uttered a faint cry, and was gone.
Night after night the young farmer haunted the
shores of the lake, but the gwraig returned no more.
He became negligent of his person; his once robust
form grew thin and wan; his face was a map of
melancholy and despair. He went one day to
consult a soothsayer who dwelt on the mountain,
and this grave personage advised him to besiege
the damsel's heart with gifts of bread and cheese.
This counsel commending itself strongly to his
Welsh way of thinking, the farmer set out upon an
assiduous course of casting his bread upon the
waters—accompanied by cheese. He began on
Midsummer eve by going to the lake and dropping
therein a large cheese and a loaf of bread. Night
after night he continued to throw in loaves and
cheeses, but nothing appeared in answer to his
sacrifices. His hopes were set, however, on the
approaching New Year's eve. The momentous
night arrived at last. Clad in his best array, and

armed with seven white loaves and his biggest and handsomest cheese, he set out once more for the

THE GWRAIG OF THE GOLDEN BOAT.

lake. There he waited till midnight, and then slowly and solemnly dropped the seven loaves into the

water, and with a sigh sent the cheese to keep them
company.   His persistence was at length rewarded.
The magic skiff appeared ; the fair gwraig guided it
to where he stood ; stepped ashore, and accepted
him as her husband.   The before-mentioned stipulation was made as to the blows ; and she brought
her dower of cattle.   One day, after they had been
four years married, they were invited to a christening.
In the midst of the ceremony the gwraig burst into
tears.   Her husband gave her an angry look, and
asked her why she thus made a fool of herself.   She
replied, 'The poor babe is entering a world of sin
and sorrow ; misery lies before it.   Why should I
rejoice ?'   He pushed her pettishly away.   'I warn
you, husband,' said the gwraig ; 'you have struck
me once.'   After a time they were bidden to the
funeral of the child they had seen christened.   Now
the gwraig laughed, sang, and danced about.   The
husband's wrath again arose, and again he asked her
why she thus made a fool of herself.   She answered,
'The dear babe has escaped the misery that was
before it, and gone to be good and happy for ever.
Why should I grieve ?'   Again he pushed her from
him, and again she warned him ; he had struck her
twice.   Soon they were invited to a wedding ; the
bride was young and fair, the groom a tottering,
toothless, decrepit old miser.   In the midst of
the wedding feast the gwraig annwn burst into
tears, and to her husband's question why she
thus made a fool of herself she replied, 'Truth
is wedded to age for greed, and not for love—
summer and winter cannot agree—it is the diawl's
compact.'   The angry husband thrust her from him
for the third and last time.   She looked at him
with tender love and reproach, and said, 'The three
blows are struck—husband, farewell !'   He never

saw her more, nor any of the flocks and herds she had brought him for her dowry.

In its employment of the myth to preach a sermon, and in its introduction of cheese, this version of the legend is very Welsh indeed. The extent to which cheese figures in Cambrian folk-lore is surprising; cheese is encountered in every sort of fairy company; you actually meet cheese in the Mabinogion, along with the most romantic forms of beauty known in story. And herein again is illustrated Shakspeare's accurate knowledge of the Cambrian goblins. 'Heaven defend me from that Welsh fairy!' says Falstaff, 'lest he transform me to a piece of cheese!'[1] Bread is found figuring actively in the folk-lore of every country, especially as a sacrifice to water-gods; but cheese is, so far as I know, thus honoured only in Cambria.

VI.

Once more this legend appears, this time with a feature I have nowhere else encountered in fairy land, to wit, the father of a fairy damsel. The son of a farmer on Drws Coed farm was one foggy day looking after his father's sheep, when crossing a marshy meadow he beheld a little lady behind some rising ground. She had yellow hair, blue eyes and rosy cheeks. He approached her, and asked permission to converse; whereupon she smiled sweetly and said to him, 'Idol of my hopes, you have come at last!' They there and then began to 'keep company,' and met each other daily here and there along the farm meadows. His intentions were honourable; he desired her to marry him. He was sometimes absent for days together, no one knew where, and his friends whispered about that he had been witched. Around the Turf Lake (Llyn y

[1] 'Merry Wives of Windsor' Act. V., Sc. 5.

Dywarchen) was a grove of trees, and under one of these one day the fairy promised to be his. The consent of her father was now necessary. One moonlight night an appointment was made to meet in this wood. The father and daughter did not appear till the moon had disappeared behind the hill. Then they both came. The fairy father immediately gave his consent to the marriage, on one condition, namely, that her future husband should never hit her with iron. 'If ever thou dost touch her flesh with iron she shall be no more thine, but she shall return to her own.' They were married —a good-looking pair. Large sums of money were brought by her, the night before the wedding, to Drws Coed. The shepherd lad became wealthy, had several handsome children, and they were very happy. After some years, they were one day out riding, when her horse sank in a deep mire, and by the assistance of her husband, in her hurry to remount, she was struck on her knee by the stirrup of the saddle. Immediately voices were heard singing on the brow of the hill, and she disappeared, leaving all her children behind. She and her mother devised a plan by which she could see her beloved, but as she was not allowed to walk the earth with man, they floated a large turf on the lake, and on this turf she stood for hours at a time holding converse with her husband. This continued until his death.[1]

VII.

The didactic purpose again appears in the following legend, which, varying but little in phraseology, is current in the neighbourhood of a dozen different mountain lakes: In other days, before the Cymry had become reconciled to their Saxon foe, on every

[1] 'Cymru Fu,' 476.

New Year's morning a door was found open in a rock hard by the lake. Those mortals who had the curiosity and the resolution to enter this door were conducted by a secret passage to a small island in the middle of the lake. Here they found a most enchanting garden, stored with the choicest fruits and flowers, and inhabited by the Gwragedd Annwn, whose beauty could be equalled only by the courtesy and affability which they exhibited to those who pleased them. They gathered fruit and flowers for each of their guests, entertained them with the most exquisite music, disclosed to them many secrets of futurity, and invited them to stay as long as they liked. 'But,' said they, 'the island is secret, and nothing of its produce must be carried away.' The warning being heeded, all went well. But one day there appeared among the visitors a wicked Welshman, who, thinking to derive some magical aid therefrom, pocketed a flower with which he had been presented, and was about to leave the garden with his prize. But the theft boded him no good. As soon as he had touched unhallowed ground the flower vanished, and he lost his senses. However, of this abuse of their hospitality the Gwragedd Annwn took no notice at the time. They dismissed their guests with their accustomed courtesy, and the door was closed as usual. But their resentment was bitter; for though the fairies of the lake and their enchanted garden undoubtedly occupy the spot to this day, the door which led to the island has never been reopened.

VIII.

In all these legends the student of comparative folk-lore traces the ancient mythology, however overlain with later details. The water-maidens of every land doubtless originally were the floating clouds of the sky, or the mists of the mountain. From this have come certain fair and fanciful creations with which Indo-European folk-lore teems, the most familiar of which are Undine, Melusina, Nausicaa, and the classic Muse. In Wales, as in other lands, the myth has many forms. The dispersion of dark clouds from the mountains, by the beams of the rising sun, or the morning breezes, is localized in the legend of the Men of Ardudwy. These men make a raid on the maidens of the Vale of Clwyd, and are pursued and slaughtered by the latter's fathers and brothers. The maidens thereupon cast themselves headlong into the lake, which is thenceforth called the Maidens' Lake, or Llyn y Morwynion. In another legend, the river mist over the Cynwal is the spirit of a traitress who perished long ago in the lake. She had conspired with the sea-born pirates of the North (the ocean storms) to rob her Cambrian lord of his domains. She was defeated by the aid of a powerful enchanter (the sun), and fled up the river to the lake, accompanied by her maidens, who were drowned with her there.[1]

IX.

As the mermaid superstition is seemingly absent in Wales, so there are no fairy tales of maidens who lure mortals to their doom beneath the water, as the Dracæ did women and children, and as the Nymph of the Lurley did marriageable young men. But it is believed that there are several old Welsh families who are the descendants of the Gwragedd Annwn, as in the case of the Meddygon Myddfai. The familiar Welsh name of Morgan is sometimes thought to signify, 'Born of the Sea.' Certainly môr in Welsh

[1] 'Arch. Camb.,' 4th Se., vii., 251.

means sea, and gân a birth. It is curious, too, that a mermaid is called in Basse Bretagne 'Mary Morgan.' But the class of stories in which a mortal marries a water-maiden is large, and while the local details smack of the soil, the general idea is so like in lands far remote from each other as to indicate a common origin in pre-historic times. In Wales, where the mountain lakes are numerous, gloomy, lonely, and yet lovely; where many of them, too, show traces of having been inhabited in ancient times by a race of lake-dwellers, whose pile-supported villages vanished ages ago; and where bread and cheese are as classic as beer and candles, these particulars are localized in the legend. In the Faro Islands, where the seal is a familiar yet ever-mysterious object, with its human-like eyes, and glossy skin, the wife of supernatural race is a transformed seal. She comes ashore every ninth night, sheds her skin, leaves it on the shore, and dances with her fairy companions. A mortal steals her sealskin dress, and when day breaks, and her companions return to their abode in the sea, compels her to remain and be his wife. Some day he offends her; she recovers her skin and plunges into the sea. In China, the superstition appears in a Lew-chewan legend mentioned by Dr. Dennys,[1] which relates how a fairy in the guise of a beautiful woman is found bathing in a man's well. He persuades her to marry him, and she remains with him for nine years, at the end of which time, despite the affection she has for their two children, she 'glides upwards into a cloud' and disappears.

[1] 'Folk-Lore of China,' 99.

CHAPTER IV.

Mountain Fairies—The Gwyllion—The Old Woman of the Mountain —The Black Mountain Gwyll—Exorcism by Knife—Occult Intellectual Powers of Welsh Goats—The Legend of Cadwaladr's Goat.

I.

THE Gwyllion are female fairies of frightful characteristics, who haunt lonely roads in the Welsh mountains, and lead night-wanderers astray. They partake somewhat of the aspect of the Hecate of Greek mythology, who rode on the storm, and was a hag of horrid guise. The Welsh word gwyll is variously used to signify gloom, shade, duskiness, a hag, a witch, a fairy, and a goblin ; but its special application is to these mountain fairies of gloomy and harmful habits, as distinct from the Ellyllon of the forest glades and dingles, which are more often beneficent. The Gwyllion take on a more distinct individuality under another name—as the Ellyllon do in mischievous Puck—and the Old Woman of the Mountain typifies all her kind. She is very carefully described by the Prophet Jones,[1] in the guise in which she haunted Llanhyddel Mountain in Monmouthshire. This was the semblance of a poor old woman, with an oblong four-cornered hat, ash-coloured clothes, her apron thrown across her shoulder, with a pot or wooden can in her hand, such as poor people carry to fetch milk with, always going before the spectator, and sometimes crying ' Wow up !' This is an English form of a Welsh cry

[1] See p. 104.

of distress, 'Wwb!' or 'Ww-bwb!'[1] Those who saw this apparition, whether by night or on a misty day, would be sure to lose their way, though they might be perfectly familiar with the road. Sometimes they heard her cry, 'Wow up!' when they did not see her. Sometimes when they went out by night, to fetch coal, water, etc., the dwellers near that mountain would hear the cry very close to them, and immediately after they would hear it afar off, as if it were on the opposite mountain, in the parish of Aberystruth. The popular tradition in that district was that the Old Woman of the Mountain was the spirit of one Juan White, who lived time out of mind in those parts, and was thought to be a witch; because the mountains were not haunted in this manner until after Juan White's death.[2] When people first lost their way, and saw her before them, they used to hurry forward and try to catch her, supposing her to be a flesh-and-blood woman, who could set them right; but they never could overtake her, and she on her part never looked back; so that no man ever saw her face. She has also been seen in the Black Mountain in Breconshire. Robert Williams, of Langattock, Crickhowel, 'a substantial man and of undoubted veracity,' tells this tale: As he was travelling one night over part of the Black Mountain, he saw the Old Woman, and at the same time found he had lost his way. Not knowing her to be a spectre he hallooed to her to stay for him, but receiving no answer thought she was deaf. He then hastened

[1] Pronounced Wooboob.

[2] 'Juan (Shuï) White is an old acquaintance of my boyhood,' writes to me a friend who was born some thirty years ago in Monmouthshire. 'A ruined cottage on the Lasgarn hill near Pontypool was understood by us boys to have been her house, and there she appeared at 12 p.m., carrying her head under her arm.'

his steps, thinking to overtake her, but the faster he ran the further he found himself behind her, at which he wondered very much, not knowing the reason of it. He presently found himself stumbling in a marsh, at which discovery his vexation increased ; and then he heard the Old Woman laughing at him with a weird, uncanny, crackling old laugh. This set him to thinking she might be a gwyll ; and when he happened to draw out his knife for some purpose, and the Old Woman vanished, then he was sure of it ; for Welsh ghosts and fairies are afraid of a knife.

II.

Another account relates that John ap John, of Cwm Celyn, set out one morning before daybreak to walk to Caerleon Fair. As he ascended Milfre Mountain he heard a shouting behind him as if it were on Bryn Mawr, which is a part of the Black Mountain in Breconshire. Soon after he heard the shouting on his left hand, at Bwlch y Llwyn, nearer to him, whereupon he was seized with a great fright, and began to suspect it was no human voice. He had already been wondering, indeed, what any one could be doing at that hour in the morning, shouting on the mountain side. Still going on, he came up higher on the mountain, when he heard the shouting just before him, at Gilfach fields, to the right—and now he was sure it was the Old Woman of the Mountain, who purposed leading him astray. Presently he heard behind him the noise of a coach, and with it the special cry of the Old Woman of the Mountain, viz., 'Wow up !' Knowing very well that no coach could go that way, and still hearing its noise approaching nearer and nearer, he became thoroughly terrified, and running out of the road threw himself down upon the ground and buried his

E

face in the heath, waiting for the phantom to pass.
When it was gone out of hearing, he arose; and
hearing the birds singing as the day began to break,
also seeing some sheep before him, his fear went
quite off.   And this, says the Prophet Jones, was
'no profane, immoral man,' but 'an honest, peaceable, knowing man, and a very comely person' moreover.

III.

The exorcism by knife appears to be a Welsh
notion; though there is an old superstition of wide
prevalence in Europe that to give to or receive
from a friend a knife or a pair of scissors cuts friendship.   I have even encountered this superstition in
America; once an editorial friend at Indianapolis
gave me a very handsome pocket-knife, which
he refused to part with except at the price of one
cent, lawful coin of the realm, asserting that we
should become enemies without this precaution.   In
China, too, special charms are associated with
knives, and a knife which has slain a fellow-being is
an invaluable possession.   In Wales, according to
Jones, the Gwyllion often came into the houses of
the people at Aberystruth, especially in stormy
weather, and the inmates made them welcome—not
through any love they bore them, but through fear
of the hurts the Gwyllion might inflict if offended
—by providing clean water for them, and taking
especial care that no knife, or other cutting tool,
should be in the corner near the fire, where the
fairies would go to sit.   'For want of which care
many were hurt by them.'   While it was desirable
to exorcise them when in the open air, it was not
deemed prudent to display an inhospitable spirit
towards any member of the fairy world.   The cases
of successful exorcism by knife are many, and no-

thing in the realm of faerie is better authenticated. There was Evan Thomas, who, travelling by night over Bedwellty Mountain, towards the valley of Ebwy Fawr, where his house and estate were, saw the Gwyllion on each side of him, some of them dancing around him in fantastic fashion. He also heard the sound of a bugle-horn winding in the air, and there seemed to be invisible hunters riding by. He then began to be afraid, but recollected his having heard that any person seeing Gwyllion may drive them away by drawing out a knife. So he drew out his knife, and the fairies vanished directly. Now Evan Thomas was 'an old gentleman of such strict veracity that he' on one occasion 'did confess a truth against himself,' when he was 'like to suffer loss' thereby, and notwithstanding he 'was persuaded by some not to do it, yet he would persist in telling the truth, to his own hurt.'

Should we find, in tracing these notions back to their source, that they are connected with Arthur's sword Excalibur? If so, there again we touch the primeval world.

Jones says that the Old Woman of the Mountain has, since about 1800, (at least in South Wales,) been driven into close quarters by the light of the Gospel—in fact, that she now haunts mines—or in the preacher's formal words, 'the coal-pits and holes of the earth.'

IV.

Among the traditions of the origin of the Gwyllion is one which associates them with goats. Goats are in Wales held in peculiar esteem for their supposed occult intellectual powers. They are believed to be on very good terms with the Tylwyth Teg, and possessed of more knowledge than their appearance indicates. It is one of the peculiarities of the

E 2

Tylwyth Teg that every Friday night they comb the goats' beards to make them decent for Sunday. Their association with the Gwyllion is related in the legend of Cadwaladr's goat : Cadwaladr owned a very handsome goat, named Jenny, of which he was extremely fond ; and which seemed equally fond of him ; but one day, as if the very diawl possessed her, she ran away into the hills, with Cadwaladr tearing after her, half mad with anger and affright. At last his Welsh blood got so hot, as the goat eluded him again and again, that he flung a stone at her, which knocked her over a precipice, and she fell bleating to her doom. Cadwaladr made his way to the foot of the crag ; the goat was dying, but not dead, and licked his hand—which so affected the poor man that he burst into tears, and sitting on the ground took the goat's head on his arm. The moon rose, and still he sat there. Presently he found that the goat had become transformed to a beautiful young woman, whose brown eyes, as her head lay on his arm, looked into his in a very disturbing way. 'Ah, Cadwaladr,' said she, 'have I at last found you ?' Now Cadwaladr had a wife at home, and was much discomfited by this singular circumstance ; but when the goat—yn awr maiden—arose, and putting her black slipper on the end of a moonbeam, held out her hand to him, he put his hand in hers and went with her. As for the hand, though it looked so fair, it felt just like a hoof. They were soon on the top of the highest mountain in Wales, and surrounded by a vapoury company of goats with shadowy horns. These raised a most unearthly bleating about his ears. One, which seemed to be the king, had a voice that sounded above the din as the castle bells of Carmarthen used to do long ago above all the other bells in the town. This one rushed at Cadwaladr and butting him in the stomach sent him toppling over a crag as he had sent his poor nannygoat. When he came to himself, after his fall, the morning sun was shining on him and the birds were singing over his head. But he saw no more of either his goat or the fairy she had turned into, from that time to his death.

CHAPTER V.

Changelings—The Plentyn-newid—The Cruel Creed of Ignorance regarding Changelings—Modes of Ridding the House of the Fairy Child—The Legend of the Frugal Meal—Legend of the Place of Strife—Dewi Dal and the Fairies—Prevention of Fairy Kidnapping—Fairies caught in the Act by Mothers—Piety as an Exorcism.

I.

THE Tylwyth Teg have a fatal admiration for lovely children. Hence the abundant folk-lore concerning infants who have been stolen from their cradles, and a plentyn-newid (change-child—the equivalent of our changeling) left in its place by the Tylwyth Teg. The plentyn-newid has the exact appearance of the stolen infant, at first; but its aspect speedily alters. It grows ugly of face, shrivelled of form, ill-tempered, wailing, and generally frightful. It bites and strikes, and becomes a terror to the poor mother. Sometimes it is idiotic; but again it has a supernatural cunning, not only impossible in a mortal babe, but not even appertaining to the oldest heads, on other than fairy shoulders. The veracious Prophet Jones testifies to a case where he himself saw the plentyn-newid—an idiot left in the stead of a son of Edmund John William, of the Church Valley, Monmouthshire. Says Jones: 'I saw him myself. There was something diabolical in his aspect,' but especially in his motions. He 'made very disagreeable screaming sounds,' which used to frighten strangers greatly, but otherwise he was harmless. He was of a 'dark, tawny complexion.

He lived longer than such children usually lived in Wales in that day, (a not altogether pleasant intimation regarding the hard lot to which such children were subjected by their unwilling parents,) reaching the age of ten or twelve years. But the creed of ignorance everywhere as regards changelings is a very cruel one, and reminds us of the tests of the witchcraft trials. Under the pretence of proving whether the objectionable baby is a changeling or not, it is held on a shovel over the fire, or it is bathed in a solution of the fox-glove, which kills it; a case where this test was applied is said to have actually occurred in Carnarvonshire in 1857. That there is nothing specially Welsh in this, needs not to be pointed out. Apart from the fact that infanticide, like murder, is of no country, similar practices as to changelings have prevailed in most European lands, either to test the child's uncanny quality, or, that being admitted, to drive it away and thus compel the fairies to restore the missing infant. In Denmark the mother heats the oven, and places the changeling on the peel, pretending to put it in; or whips it severely with a rod; or throws it into the water. In Sweden they employ similar methods. In Ireland the hot shovel is used. With regard to a changeling which Martin Luther tells of in his 'Colloquia Mensalia,' the great reformer declared to the Prince of Anhalt, that if he were prince of that country he would 'venture *homicidium* thereon, and would throw it into the River Moldaw.' He admonished the people to pray devoutly to God to take away the devil, which 'was done accordingly; and the second year after the changeling died.' It is hardly probable that the child was very well fed during the two years that this pious process

was going on. Its starved ravenous appetite
indeed is indicated in Luther's description: It
'would eat as much as two threshers, would laugh
and be joyful when any evil happened in the house,
but would cry and be very sad when all went well.'

II.

A story, told in various forms in Wales, preserves
a tradition of an exceedingly frugal meal which was
employed as a means of banishing a plentyn-newid.
M. Villemarqué, when in Glamorganshire, heard
this story, which he found to be precisely the same
as a Breton legend, in which the changeling utters a
rhymed triad as follows :

> Gweliz vi ken guelet iar wenn,
> Gweliz mez ken gwelet gwezen.
> Gweliz mez ha gweliz gwial,
> Gweliz derven e Koat Brezal,
> Biskoaz na weliz kemend all.

In the Glamorgan story the changeling was heard
muttering to himself in a cracked voice: 'I have
seen the acorn before I saw the oak : I have seen
the egg before I saw the white hen : I have never
seen the like of this.'   M. Villemarqué found it
remarkable that these words form in Welsh a rhymed
triad nearly the same as in the Breton ballad, thus :

> Gweliz mez ken gwelet derven,
> Gweliz vi ken gwelet iar wenn,
> Erioez ne wiliz evelhenn.[1]

Whence he concluded that the story and the rhyme
are older than the seventh century, the epoch of the
separation of the Britons of Wales and Armorica.
And this is the story: A mother whose child had
been stolen, and a changeling left in its place, was
advised by the Virgin Mary to prepare a meal for

---

[1] Keightley, 'Fairy Mythology,' 437.

ten farm-servants in an egg-shell, which would make the changeling speak. This she did, and the changeling asked what she was about. She told him. Whereupon he exclaimed, 'A meal for ten, dear mother, in one egg-shell?' Then he uttered the exclamation given above, ('I have seen the acorn,' etc.,) and the mother replied, 'You have seen too many things, my son, you shall have a beating.' With this she fell to beating him, the child fell to bawling, and the fairy came and took him away, leaving the stolen child sleeping sweetly in the cradle. It awoke and said, 'Ah, mother, I have been a long time asleep!'

III.

I have encountered this tale frequently among the Welsh, and it always keeps in the main the likeness of M. Villemarqué's story. The following is a nearly literal version as related in Radnorshire (an adjoining county to Montgomeryshire), and which, like most of these tales, is characterised by the non-primitive tendency to give names of localities: 'In the parish of Trefeglwys, near Llanidloes, in the county of Montgomery, there is a little shepherd's cot that is commonly called the Place of Strife, on account of the extraordinary strife that has been there. The inhabitants of the cottage were a man and his wife, and they had born to them twins, whom the woman nursed with great care and tenderness. Some months after, indispensable business called the wife to the house of one of her nearest neighbours, yet notwithstanding that she had not far to go, she did not like to leave her children by themselves in their cradle, even for a minute, as her house was solitary, and there were many tales of goblins, or the Tylwyth Teg,

haunting the neighbourhood. However, she went
and returned as soon as she could;' but on her
way back she was 'not a little terrified at seeing,
though it was midday, some of the old elves of the
blue petticoat.' She hastened home in great
apprehension; but all was as she had left it, so
that her mind was greatly relieved. 'But after
some time had passed by, the good people began
to wonder that the twins did not grow at all, but
still continued little dwarfs. The man would have
it that they were not his children; the woman said
they must be their children, and about this arose
the great strife between them that gave name to
the place. One evening when the woman was
very heavy of heart, she determined to go and
consult a conjuror, feeling assured that everything
was known to him. . . . Now there was to be a
harvest soon of the rye and oats, so the wise man
said to her, "When you are preparing dinner for the
reapers, empty the shell of a hen's egg, and boil
the shell full of pottage, and take it out through
the door as if you meant it for a dinner to the
reapers, and then listen what the twins will say;
if you hear the children speaking things above the
understanding of children, return into the house,
take them and throw them into the waves of Llyn
Ebyr, which is very near to you; but if you don't
hear anything remarkable do them no injury." And
when the day of the reaping came, the woman did
as her adviser had recommended to her; and as
she went outside the door to listen she heard one
of the children say to the other:

> Gwelais fesen cyn gweled derwen ;
> Gwelais wy cyn gweled iâr ;
> Erioed ni welais ferwi bwyd i fedel
> Mewn plisgyn wy iâr !

> Acorns before oak I knew ;
> An egg before a hen ;
> Never one hen's egg-shell stew
> Enough for harvest men !

'On this the mother returned to her house and took the two children and threw them into the Llyn ; and suddenly the goblins in their blue trousers came to save their dwarfs, and the mother had her own children back again ; and thus the strife between her and her husband ended.'[1]

IV.

This class of story is not always confined to the case of the plentyn-newid, as I have said. It is applied to the household fairy, when the latter, as in the following instance, appears to have brought a number of extremely noisy friends and acquaintances to share his shelter. Dewi Dal was a farmer, whose house was over-run with fairies, so that he could not sleep of nights for the noise they made. Dewi consulted a wise man of Taiar, who entrusted Dewi's wife to do certain things, which she did carefully, as follows : 'It was the commencement of oat harvest, when Cae Mawr, or the big field, which it took fifteen men to mow in a day, was ripe for the harvesters. "I will prepare food for the fifteen men who are going to mow Cae Mawr to-morrow," said Eurwallt, the wife, aloud. "Yes, do," replied Dewi, also aloud, so that the fairies might hear, "and see that the food is substantial and sufficient for the hard work before them." Said Eurwallt, "The fifteen men shall have no reason to complain upon that score. They shall be fed according to our means." Then when evening was come Eurwallt prepared food for the harvesters' sustenance upon the following day. Having procured a sparrow,

[1] 'Cambrian Quarterly,' ii., 86.

she trussed it like a fowl, and roasted it by the kitchen fire. She then placed some salt in a nut-shell, and set the sparrow and the salt, with a small piece of bread, upon the table, ready for the fifteen men's support while mowing Cae Mawr. So when the fairies beheld the scanty provision made for so many men, they said "Let us quickly depart from this place, for alas! the means of our hosts are exhausted. Who before this was ever so reduced in circumstances as to serve up a sparrow for the day's food of fifteen men?" So they departed upon that very night. And Dewi Dal and his family lived, ever afterwards, in comfort and peace.'[1]

V.

The Welsh fairies have several times been detected in the act of carrying off a child; and in these cases, if the mother has been sufficiently energetic in her objections, they have been forced to abandon their purpose. Dazzy Walter, the wife of Abel Walter, of Ebwy Fawr, one night in her husband's absence awoke in her bed and found her baby was not at her side. In great fright she sought for it, and caught it with her hand upon the boards above the bed, which was as far as the fairies had succeeded in carrying it. And Jennet Francis, of that same valley of Ebwy Fawr, one night in bed felt her infant son being taken from her arms; whereupon she screamed and hung on, and, as she phrased it, 'God and me were too hard for them.' This son subsequently grew up and became a famous preacher of the gospel.

There are special exorcisms and preventive mea-sures to interfere with the fairies in their quest of infants. The most significant of these, throughout

[1] Rev. T. R. Lloyd (Estyn), in 'The Principality.'

Cambria, is a general habit of piety. Any pious exclamation has value as an exorcism; but it will not serve as a preventive. To this end you must put a knife in the child's cradle when you leave it

JENNET FRANCIS STRUGGLES WITH THE
FAIRIES FOR HER BABY.

alone, or you must lay a pair of tongs across the cradle. But the best preventive is baptism; it is usually the unbaptised infant that is stolen. So in Friesland, Germany, it is considered a protection against the fairies who deal in changelings, to lay a Bible under the child's pillow. In Thuringia it is deemed an infallible preventive to hang the father's breeches against the wall. Anything

more trivial than this, as a matter for the consideration of grave and scholarly men, one could hardly
imagine; but it is in precisely these trivial or seemingly trivial details that the student of comparative
folk-lore finds his most extraordinary indices. Such
a superstition in isolation would suggest nothing; but
it is found again in Scotland,[1] and other countries,
including China, where 'a pair of the trousers of
the child's father are put on the frame of the bed-
stead in such a way that the waist shall hang downward or be lower than the legs. On the trousers
is stuck a piece of red paper, having four words
written upon it intimating that all unfavourable
influences are to go into the trousers instead of
afflicting the babe.'[2]

[1] Henderson, 'Notes on the Folk-Lore of the Northern Counties,' 6.
[2] See Doolittle's 'Social Life of the Chinese.'

CHAPTER VI.

I.

CLOSELY akin to the subject of changelings is that of
adults or well-grown children being led away to live
with the Tylwyth Teg. In this field the Welsh
traditions are innumerable, and deal not only with
the last century or two, but distinctly with the
middle ages. Famed among British goblins are
those fairies which are immortalised in the Tale of
Elidurus. This tale was written in Latin by Giraldus
Cambrensis (as he called himself, after the pedantic
fashion of his day), a Welshman, born at Pembroke
Castle, and a hearty admirer of everything Welsh,
himself included. He was beyond doubt a man of
genius, and of profound learning. In 1188 he made
a tour through Wales, in the interest of the crusade
then in contemplation, and afterwards wrote his
book—a fascinating picture of manners and customs
in Wales in the twelfth century.

The scene of the tale is that Vale of Neath, already
named as a famous centre of fairyland. Elidurus,
when a youth of twelve years, 'in order to avoid the
severity of his preceptor,' ran away from school,

'and concealed himself under the hollow bank of a river.' After he had fasted in that situation for two days, 'two little men of pigmy stature appeared to him,' and said, ' If 'you will go with us, we will lead you into a country full of delights and sports.' Assenting, Elidurus rose up and 'followed his guides through a path at first subterraneous and dark, into a most beautiful country, but obscure and not illuminated with the full light of the sun.' All the days in that country 'were cloudy, and the nights extremely dark.' The boy was brought before the king 'of the strange little people, and introduced to him in the presence of his Court. Having examined Elidurus for a long time, the king delivered him to his son, that prince being then a boy. The men of this country, though of the smallest stature, were very well proportioned, fair-complexioned, and wore long hair. 'They had horses and greyhounds adapted to their size. They neither ate flesh nor fish, but lived on milk-diet, made up into messes with saffron. As often as they returned from our hemisphere, they reprobated our ambition, infidelities, and inconstancies; and though they had no form of public worship, were, it seems, strict lovers and reverers of truth. The boy frequently returned to our hemisphere, sometimes by the way he had gone, sometimes by others; at first in company, and afterwards alone; and made himself known only to his mother, to whom he described what he had seen. Being desired by her to bring her a present of gold, with which that country abounded, he stole, whilst at play with the king's son, a golden ball with which he used to divert himself, and brought it in haste to his mother, but not unpursued; for, as he entered the house of his father, he stumbled at the threshold; the ball fell, 'and two pigmies seizing it, departed, showing

the boy every mark of contempt and derision. Notwithstanding every attempt for the space of a year,
he never again could find the track to the subterraneous passage.' He had made himself acquainted
with the language of his late hosts, 'which was very
conformable to the Greek idiom. When they asked
for water, they said *Udor udorum;* when they want
salt, they say *Halgein udorum.*' [1]

II.

Exactly similar to this medieval legend in spirit,
although differing widely in detail, is the modern
story of Shuï Rhys, told to me by a peasant in
Cardiganshire. Shuï was a beautiful girl of seven-
teen, tall and fair, with a skin like ivory, hair black
and curling, and eyes of dark velvet. She was but
a poor farmer's daughter, notwithstanding her beauty,
and among her duties was that of driving up the
cows for the milking. Over this work she used to
loiter sadly, to pick flowers by the way, or chase
the butterflies, or amuse herself in any agreeable
manner that fortune offered. For her loitering she
was often chided ; indeed, people said Shuï's mother
was far too sharp with the girl, and that it was for
no good the mother had so bitter a tongue. After
all the girl meant no harm, they said. But when
one night Shuï never came home till bed-time,
leaving the cows to care for themselves, dame Rhys
took the girl to task as she never had done before.
'Ysgwaetheroedd, mami,' said Shuï, 'I couldn't
help it ; it was the Tylwyth Teg.' The dame was
aghast at this, but she could not answer it—for well
she knew the Tylwyth Teg were often seen in the
woods of Cardigan. Shuï was at first shy about
talking of the fairies, but finally confessed they were

[1] See Sir R. C. Hoare's Translation of Giraldus.

little men in green coats, who danced around her and made music on their tiny harps; and they talked to her in language too beautiful to be re-

SHUI RHYS AND THE TYLWYTH TEG.

peated; indeed she couldn't understand the words, though she knew well enough what the fairies meant. Many a time after that Shuï was late;

but now nobody chided her, for fear of offending the fairies. At last one night Shuï did not come home at all. In alarm the woods were searched; there was no sign of her; and never was she seen in Cardigan again. Her mother watched in the fields on the Teir-nos Ysprydion, or three nights of the year when goblins are sure to be abroad; but Shuï never returned. Once indeed there came back to the neighbourhood a wild rumour that Shuï Rhys had been seen in a great city in a foreign land— Paris, perhaps, or London, who knows? but this tale was in no way injurious to the sad belief that the fairies had carried her off; they might take her to those well-known centres of idle and sinful pleasure, as well as to any other place.

III.

An old man who died in St. Dogmell's parish, Pembrokeshire, a short time since (viz., in 1860), nearly a hundred years old, used to say that that whole neighbourhood was considered 'fou.' It was a common experience for men to be led astray there all night, and after marvellous adventures and un-tellable trampings, which seemed as if they would be endless, to find when day broke that they were close to their own homes. In one case, a man who was led astray chanced to have with him a number of hoop-rods, and as he wandered about under the influence of the deluding phantom, he was clever enough to drop the rods one by one, so that next day he might trace his journeyings. When day-light came, and the search for the hoop-rods was entered on, it was found they were scattered over miles upon miles of country. Another time, a St. Dogmell's fisherman was returning home from a wedding at Moelgrove, and it being very dark, the fairies led him astray, but after a few hours he had the good luck (which Sir John Franklin might have envied him) to 'discover the North Pole,' and by this beacon he was able to steer his staggering barque to the safe port of his own threshold. It is even gravely stated that a severe and dignified clerical person, no longer in the frisky time of life, but advanced in years, was one night forced to join in the magic dance of St. Dogmell's, and keep it up till nearly daybreak. Specific details in this instance are wanting; but it was no doubt the Ellyllon who led all these folk astray, and put a cap of oblivion on their heads, which prevented them from ever telling their adventures clearly.

IV.

Dancing and music play a highly important part in stories of this class. The Welsh fairies are most often dancing together when seen. They seek to entice mortals to dance with them, and when any-one is drawn to do so, it is more than probable he will not return to his friends for a long time. Edmund William Rees, of Aberystruth, was thus drawn away by the fairies, and came back at the year's end, looking very bad. But he could not give a very clear account of what he had been about, only said he had been dancing. This was a common thing in these cases. Either they were not able to, or they dared not, talk about their experiences.

Two farm servants named Rhys and Llewellyn were one evening at twilight returning home from their work, when Rhys cried out that he heard the fairy music. Llewellyn could hear nothing, but Rhys said it was a tune to which he had danced a hundred times, and would again, and at once. 'Go

on,' says he, 'and I'll soon catch you up again.'
Llewellyn objected, but Rhys stopped to hear no
more ; he bounded away and left Llewellyn to go
home alone, which he did, believing Rhys had
merely gone off on a spree, and would come home
drunk before morning. But the morning came, and
no Rhys. In vain search was made, still no Rhys.
Time passed on ; days grew into months ; and at
last suspicion fell on Llewellyn, that he had murdered
Rhys. He was put in prison. A farmer learned
in fairy-lore, suspecting how it was, proposed that
he and a company of neighbours should go with
poor Llewellyn to the spot where he had last seen
Rhys. Agreed. Arrived at the spot, 'Hush,' cried
Llewellyn, 'I hear music! I hear the sweet music
of the harps !' They all listened, but could hear
nothing. 'Put your foot on mine, David,' says
Llewellyn to one of the company ; his own foot
was on the outward edge of a fairy ring as he
spoke. David put his foot on Llewellyn's, and so
did they all, one after another ; and then they heard
the sound of many harps, and saw within a circle
about twenty feet across, great numbers of little
people dancing round and round. And there was
Rhys, dancing away like a madman ! As he came
whirling by, Llewellyn caught him by his smock-
frock and pulled him out of the circle. 'Where
are the horses ? where are the horses ?' cried
Rhys in an excited manner. 'Horses, indeed !'
sneered Llewellyn, in great disgust ; 'wfft ! go home.
Horses !' But Rhys was for dancing longer, declaring he had not been there five minutes. 'You've
been there,' says Llewellyn, 'long enough to come
near getting me hanged, anyhow.' They got him
home finally, but he was never the same man
again, and soon after he died.

V.

In the great majority of these stories the hero dies immediately after his release from the thraldom of the fairies—in some cases with a suddenness and a completeness of obliteration as appalling as dramatic. The following story, well known in Carmarthenshire, presents this detail with much force : There was a certain farmer who, while going early one morning to fetch his horses from the pasture, heard harps playing. Looking carefully about for the source of this music, he presently saw a company of Tylwyth Teg footing it merrily in a corelw. Resolving to join their dance and cultivate their acquaintance, the farmer stepped into the fairy ring. Never had man his resolution more thoroughly carried out, for having once begun the reel he was not allowed to finish it till years had elapsed. Even then he might not have been released, had it not chanced that a man one day passed by the lonely spot, so close to the ring that he saw the farmer dancing. 'Duw catto ni!' cried the man, 'God save us! but this is a merry one. Hai, holo! man, what, in Heaven's name, makes you so lively?' This question, in which the name of Heaven was uttered, broke the spell which rested on the farmer, who spoke like one in a dream : 'O dyn!' cried he, 'what's become of the horses?' Then he stepped from the fairy circle and instantly crumbled away and mingled his dust with the earth.

A similar tale is told in Carnarvon, but with the fairy dance omitted and a pious character substituted, which helps to indicate the antiquity of this class of legend, by showing that it was one of the monkish adoptions of an earlier story. Near Clynog, in Carnarvonshire, there is a place called **Llwyn y Nef,** (the Bush of Heaven,) which thus received its name : In Clynog lived a monk of most devout life, who longed to be taken to heaven. One evening, whilst walking without the monastery by the riverside, he sat down under a green tree and fell into a deep reverie, which ended in sleep ; and he slept for thousands of years. At last he heard a voice calling unto him, 'Sleeper, awake and be up.' He awoke. All was strange to him except the old monastery, which still looked down upon the river. He went to the monastery, and was made much of. He asked for a bed to rest himself on and got it. Next morning when the brethren sought him, they found nothing in the bed but a handful of ashes.[1]

So in the monkish tale of the five saints, who sleep in the cave of Caio, reappears the legend of Arthur's sleeping warriors under Craig-y-Ddinas.

VI.

A tradition is current in Mathavarn, in the parish of Llanwrin, and the Cantref of Cyfeillioc, concerning a certain wood called Ffridd yr Ywen, (the Forest of the Yew,) that it is so called on account of a magical yew-tree which grows exactly in the middle of the forest. Under that tree there is a fairy circle called The Dancing Place of the Goblin. There are several fairy circles in the Forest of the Yew, but the one under the yew-tree in the middle has this legend connected with it : Many years ago, two farm-servants, whose names were Twm and Iago, went out one day to work in the Forest of the Yew. Early in the afternoon the country became covered with so dense a mist that the youths thought the sun was setting, and they prepared to go home ; but when they came to the

[1] 'Cymru Fu,' 188.

yew-tree in the middle of the forest, suddenly they found all light around them. They now thought it too early to go home, and concluded to lie down under the yew-tree and have a nap. By-and-by Twm awoke, to find his companion gone. He was much surprised at this, but concluded Iago had gone to the village on an errand of which they had been speaking before they fell asleep. So Twm went home, and to all inquiries concerning Iago, he answered, 'Gone to the cobbler's in the village.'

PLUCKED FROM THE FAIRY CIRCLE.

But Iago was still absent next morning, and now Twm was cross-questioned severely as to what had become of his fellow-servant. Then he confessed that they had fallen asleep under the yew where the fairy circle was, and from that moment he had seen nothing more of Iago. They searched the whole forest over, and the whole country round, for many days, and finally Twm went to a gwr cyfar-wydd (or conjuror), a common trade in those days,

says the legend.   The conjuror gave him this advice :
' Go to the same place where you and the lad slept.
Go there exactly a year after the boy was lost.   Let
it be on the same day of the year and at the same
time of the day ; but take care that you do not step
inside the fairy ring.   Stand on the border of the
green circle you saw there, and the boy will come
out with many of the goblins to dance.   When you
see him so near to you that you may take hold of
him, snatch him out of the ring as quickly as you can.'
These instructions were obeyed.   Iago appeared,
dancing in the ring with the Tylwyth Teg, and was
promptly plucked forth.   ' Duw ! Duw !' cried Tom,
' how wan and pale you look !   And don't you feel
hungry too ? '   ' No,' said the boy, ' and if I did,
have I not here in my wallet the remains of my
dinner that I had before I fell asleep ?'   But when
he looked in his wallet, the food was not there.
' Well, it must be time to go home,' he said, with a
sigh ; for he did not know that a year had passed
by.   His look was like a skeleton, and as soon as
he had tasted food, he mouldered away.

VII.

Taffy ap Sion, the shoemaker's son, living near
Pencader, Carmarthenshire, was a lad who many
years ago entered the fairy circle on the mountain
hard by there, and having danced a few minutes,
as he supposed, chanced to step out.   He was then
astonished to find that the scene which had been
so familiar was now quite strange to him.   Here
were roads and houses he had never seen, and in
place of his father's humble cottage there now stood
a fine stone farmhouse.   About him were lovely
cultivated fields instead of the barren mountain he
was acccustomed to.   ' Ah,' thought he, ' this is

some fairy trick to deceive my eyes. It is not ten minutes since I stepped into that circle, and now when I step out they have built my father a new house! Well, I only hope it is real; anyhow, I'll go and see.' So he started off by a path he knew instinctively, and suddenly struck against a very solid hedge. He rubbed his eyes, felt the hedge with his fingers, scratched his head, felt the hedge again, ran a thorn into his fingers and cried out, 'Wbwb! this is no fairy hedge anyhow, nor, from the age of the thorns, was it grown in a few minutes' time.' So he climbed over it and walked on. 'Here was I born,' said he, as he entered the farmyard, staring wildly about him, 'and not a thing here do I know!' His mystification was complete when there came bounding towards him a huge dog, barking furiously. 'What dog is this? Get out, you ugly brute! Don't you know I'm master here? —at least, when mother's from home, for father don't count.' But the dog only barked the harder. 'Surely,' muttered Taffy to himself, 'I have lost my road and am wandering through some unknown neighbourhood; but no, yonder is the Careg Hir!' and he stood staring at the well-known erect stone thus called, which still stands on the mountain south of Pencader, and is supposed to have been placed there in ancient times to commemorate a victory. As Taffy stood thus looking at the Long Stone, he heard footsteps behind him, and turning, beheld the occupant of the farmhouse, who had come out to see why his dog was barking. Poor Taffy was so ragged and wan that the farmer's Welsh heart was at once stirred to sympathy. 'Who are you, poor man?' he asked. To which Taffy answered, 'I know who I was, but I do not know who I *am now*. 'I was the son of a shoemaker who lived in this place, this morning; for that rock, though it is changed a little, I know too well.' 'Poor fellow,' said the farmer, 'you have lost your senses. This house was built by my great-grandfather, repaired by my grandfather; and that part there, which seems newly built, was done about three years ago at my expense. You must be deranged, or have missed the road; but come in and refresh yourself with some victuals, and rest.' Taffy was half persuaded that he had overslept himself and lost his road, but looking back he saw the rock before mentioned, and exclaimed, 'It is but an hour since I was on yonder rock robbing a hawk's nest.' 'Where have you been since?' Taffy related his adventure. 'Ah,' quoth the farmer, 'I see how it is—you have been with the fairies. Pray, who was your father?' 'Sion Evan y Crydd o Glanrhyd,' was the answer. 'I never heard of such a man,' said the farmer, shaking his head, 'nor of such a place as Glanrhyd, either: but no matter, after you have taken a little food we will step down to Catti Shon, at Pencader, who will probably be able to tell us something.' With this he beckoned Taffy to follow him, and walked on; but hearing behind him the sound of footsteps growing weaker and weaker, he turned round, when to his horror he beheld the poor fellow crumble in an instant to about a thimbleful of black ashes. The farmer, though much terrified at this sight, preserved his calmness sufficiently to go at once and see old Catti, the aged crone he had referred to, who lived at Pencader, near by. He found her crouching over a fire of faggots, trying to warm her old bones. 'And how do you do the day, Catti Shon?' asked the farmer. 'Ah,' said old Catti, 'I'm wonderful well, farmer, considering how old I am.' 'Yes, yes, you're very old. Now, since you are so old, let me ask you—do you remember anything about Sion y Crydd o Glanrhyd? Was there ever such a man, do you know?' 'Sion Glanrhyd? O! I have some faint recollection of hearing my grandfather, old Evan Shenkin, Penferdir, relate that Sion's son was lost one morning, and they never heard of him afterwards, so that it was said he was taken by the fairies. His father's cot stood somewhere near your house.' 'Were there many fairies about at that time?' asked the farmer. 'O yes; they were often seen on yonder hill, and I was told they were lately seen in Pant Shon Shenkin, eating flummery out of egg-shells, which they had stolen from a farm hard by.' 'Dir anwyl fi!' cried the farmer; 'dear me! I recollect now—I saw them myself!'

Pant Shon[1] Shenkin, it must be here remarked, was a famous place for the Carmarthenshire fairies. The traditions thereabout respecting them are numerous. Among the strangest is, that a woman once actually caught a fairy on the mountain near Pant Shon Shenkin, and that it remained long in her custody, retaining still the same height and size, but at last made its escape.

Another curious tradition relates that early one Easter Monday, when the parishioners of Pencarreg and Caio were met to play at football, they saw a numerous company of Tylwyth Teg dancing. Being so many in number, the young men were not intimidated at all, but proceeded in a body towards the puny tribe, who, perceiving them, removed to

---

[1] Sion and Shon are the same word, just as are our Smith and Smyth. Where there are so few personal names as in Wales, while I would not myself change a single letter in order to render the actors in a tale more distinct, it is perhaps as well to encourage any eccentricities of spelling which we are so lucky as to find on the spot.

another place. The young men followed, whereupon the little folks suddenly appeared dancing at the first place. Seeing this, the men divided and surrounded them, when they immediately became invisible, and were never more seen there.

VIII.

Ignorance of what transpired in the fairy circle is not an invariable feature of legends like those we have been observing. In the story of Tudur of Llangollen, preserved by several old Welsh writers, the hero's experiences are given with much liveliness of detail. The scene of this tale is a hollow near Llangollen, on the mountain side half-way up to the ruins of Dinas Bran Castle, which hollow is to this day called Nant yr Ellyllon. It obtained its name, according to tradition, in this wise : A young man, called Tudur ap Einion Gloff, used in old times to pasture his master's sheep in that hollow. One summer's night, when Tudur was preparing to return to the lowlands with his woolly charge, there suddenly appeared, perched upon a stone near him, ' a little man in moss breeches with a fiddle under his arm. He was the tiniest wee specimen of humanity imaginable. His coat was made of birch leaves, and he wore upon his head a helmet which consisted of a gorse flower, while his feet were encased in pumps made of beetle's wings. He ran his fingers over his instrument, and the music made Tudur's hair stand on end. " Nos da'ch', nos da'ch'," said the little man, which means " Good-night, good-night to you," in English. " Ac i chwithau," replied Tudur; which again, in English, means " The same to you." Then continued the little man, " You are fond of dancing, Tudur ; and if you but tarry awhile you shall behold some of the best dancers in Wales, and I am the musician." Quoth Tudur, "Then where is your harp? A Welshman even cannot dance without a harp." "Oh," said the little man, "I can discourse better dance music upon my fiddle." "Is it a fiddle you call that stringed wooden spoon in your hand?" asked Tudur, for he had never seen such an instrument before. And now Tudur beheld through the dusk hundreds of pretty little sprites converging towards the spot where they stood, from all parts of the mountain. Some were dressed in white, and some in blue, and some in pink, and some carried glow-worms in their hands for torches. And so lightly did they tread that not a blade nor a flower was crushed beneath their weight, and every one made a curtsey or a bow to Tudur as they passed, and Tudur doffed his cap and moved to them in return. Presently the little minstrel drew his bow across the strings of his instrument, and the music produced was so enchanting that Tudur stood transfixed to the spot.' At the sound of the sweet melody, the Tylwyth Teg ranged themselves in groups, and began to dance. Now of all the dancing Tudur had ever seen, none was to be compared to that he saw at this moment going on. He could not help keeping time with his hands and feet to the merry music, but he dared not join in the dance, 'for he thought within himself that to dance on a mountain at night in strange company, to perhaps the devil's fiddle, might not be the most direct route to heaven.' But at last he found there was no resisting this bewitching strain, joined to the sight of the capering Ellyllon. '"Now for it, then," screamed Tudur, as he pitched his cap into the air under the excitement of delight. "Play away, old devil; brimstone and water, if you like!" No sooner were the words uttered than everything underwent a change. The gorse-blossom cap vanished from the minstrel's head, and a pair of goat's horns branched out instead. His face turned as black as soot; a long tail grew out of his leafy coat, while cloven feet replaced the beetle-wing pumps. Tudur's heart was heavy, but his heels were light. Horror was in his bosom, but the impetus of motion was in his feet. The fairies changed into a variety of forms. Some became goats, and some became dogs, some assumed the shape of foxes, and others that of cats. It was the strangest crew that ever surrounded a human being. The dance became at last so furious that Tudur could not distinctly make out the forms of the dancers. They reeled around him with such rapidity that they almost resembled a wheel of fire. Still Tudur danced on. He could not stop, the devil's fiddle was too much for him, as the figure with the goat's horns kept pouring it out with unceasing vigour, and Tudur kept reeling around in spite of himself. Next day Tudur's master ascended the mountain in search of the lost shepherd and his sheep. He found the sheep all right at the foot of the Fron, but fancy his astonishment when, ascending higher, he saw Tudur spinning like mad in the middle of the basin now known as Nant yr Ellyllon.' Some pious words of the master broke the charm, and restored Tudur to his home in Llangollen, where he told his adventures with great gusto for many years afterwards.[1]

IX.

Polly Williams, a good dame who was born in Trefethin parish, and lived at the Ship Inn, at Pontypool, Monmouthshire, was wont to relate that, when a child, she danced with the Tylwyth Teg. The first time was one day while coming home from

[1] Rev. T. R. Lloyd (Estyn), in ' The Principality.'

school. She saw the fairies dancing in a pleasant, dry place, under a crab-tree, and, thinking they were children like herself, went to them, when they induced her to dance with them. She brought them into an empty barn and they danced there together. After that, during three or four years, she often met and danced with them, when going to or coming from school. She never could hear the sound of their feet, and having come to know that they were fairies, took off her ffollachau (clogs), so that she, too, might make no noise, fearful that the clattering of her clog-shodden feet was displeasing to them. They were all dressed in blue and green aprons, and, though they were so small, she could see by their mature faces that they were no children. Once when she came home barefoot, after dancing with the fairies, she was chided for going to school in that condition ; but she held her tongue about the fairies, for fear of trouble, and never told of them till after she grew up. She gave over going with them to dance, however, after three or four years, and this displeased them. They tried to coax her back to them, and, as she would not come, hurt her by dislocating 'one of her walking members,'[1] which, as a euphemism for legs, surpasses anything charged against American prudery.

X.

Contrasting strongly with this matter-of-fact account of a modern witness is the glowing description of fairy life contained in the legend of the Fairies of Frennifawr. About ten miles south of Cardigan is the Pembrokeshire mountain called Frennifawr, which is the scene of this tale : A shepherd's lad was tending his sheep on the small

[1] Jones, 'Apparitions.'

mountains called Frennifach one fine morning in June. Looking to the top of Frennifawr to note what way the fog hung—for if the fog on that mountain hangs on the Pembrokeshire side, there will be fair weather, if on the Cardigan side, storm —he saw the Tylwyth Teg, in appearance like tiny soldiers, dancing in a ring. He set out for the scene of revelry, and soon drew near the ring where, in a gay company of males and females, they were footing it to the music of the harp. Never had he seen such handsome people, nor any so enchantingly cheerful. They beckoned him with laughing faces to join them as they leaned backward almost falling, whirling round and round with joined hands. Those who were dancing never swerved from the perfect circle; but some were clambering over the old cromlech, and others chasing each other with surprising swiftness and the greatest glee. Still others rode about on small white horses of the most beautiful form ; these riders were little ladies, and their dresses were indescribably elegant, surpassing the sun in radiance, and varied in colour, some being of bright whiteness, others the most vivid scarlet. The males wore red tripled caps, and the ladies a light fantastic headdress which waved in the wind. All this was in silence, for the shepherd could not hear the harps, though he saw them. But now he drew nearer to the circle, and finally ventured to put his foot in the magic ring. The instant he did this, his ears were charmed with strains of the most melodious music he had ever heard. Moved with the transports this seductive harmony produced in him, he stepped fully into the ring. He was no sooner in than he found himself in a palace glittering with gold and pearls. Every form of beauty surrounded him, and every variety of pleasure was offered him. He was

G

made free to range whither he would, and his every movement was waited on by young women of the most matchless loveliness. And no tongue can tell the joys of feasting that were his ! Instead of the tatws-a-llaeth (potatoes and butter-milk) to which he had hitherto been accustomed, here were birds and meats of every choice description, served on plates of silver. Instead of home-brewed cwrw, the only bacchic beverage he had ever tasted in real life, here were red and yellow wines of wondrous enjoyableness, brought in golden goblets richly inlaid with gems. The waiters were the most beautiful virgins, and everything was in abundance. There was but one restriction on his freedom : he must not drink, on any consideration, from a certain well in the garden, in which swam fishes of every colour, including the colour of gold. Each day new joys were provided for his amusement, new scenes of beauty were unfolded to him, new faces presented themselves, more lovely if possible than those he had before encountered. Everything was done to charm him ; but one day all his happiness fled in an instant. Possessing every joy that mortal could desire, he wanted the one thing forbidden—like Eve in the garden, like Fatima in the castle ; curiosity undid him. He plunged his hand into the well : the fishes all disappeared instantly. He put the water to his mouth : a confused shriek ran through the garden. He drank : the palace and all vanished from his sight, and he stood shivering in the night air, alone on the mountain, in the very place where he had first entered the ring.[1]

[1] 'Cambrian Superstitions,' 148. (This is a small collection of Welsh stories printed at Tipton in 1831, and now rare ; its author was W. Howells, a lad of nineteen, and his work was drawn out by a small prize offered by Archdeacon Beynon through a Carmarthen newspaper in 1830. Its English requires rehandling, but its material is of value.)

XI.

Comment on the resemblances borne by these tales to the more famous legends of other lands, is perhaps unnecessary; they will occur to every reader

THE FATAL DRAUGHT.

who is at all familiar with the subject of folk-lore. To those who are not, it is sufficient to say that these resemblances exist, and afford still further testimony to the common origin of such tales in a remote past. The legend last given embodies the curiosity feature which is familiar through the story of Bluebeard,

G 2

but has its root in the story of Psyche. She was forbidden to look upon her husband Eros, the god of love ; she disobeyed the injunction, and the beautiful palace in which she had dwelt with him vanished in an instant, leaving her alone in a desolate spot. Ages older than the Psyche story, however, is the legend embodying the original Aryan myth. The drop of oil which falls upon the shoulder of the sleeping prince and wakes him, revealing Psyche's curiosity and destroying her happiness, is paralleled among the Welsh by the magic ointment in the legend of the Fiend Master. This legend, it may be premised, is also familiar to both France and Germany, where its details differ but little from those here given : A respectable young Welshwoman of the working class, who lived with her parents, went one day to a hiring fair. Here she ' was addressed by a very noble-looking gentleman all in black, who asked her if she would be a nurse-maid, and undertake the management of his children. She replied that she had no objection ; when he promised her immense wages, and said he would take her home behind him, but that she must, before they started, consent to be blindfolded. This done, she mounted behind him on a coal-black steed, and away they rode at a great rate. At length they dismounted, when her new master took her by the hand and led her on, still blindfolded, for a considerable distance. The handkerchief was then removed, when she beheld more grandeur than she had ever seen before ; a beautiful palace lighted up by more lights than she could count, and a number of little children as beautiful as angels ; also many noble-looking ladies and gentlemen. The children her master put under her charge, and gave her a box containing ointment, which she was to put on

their eyes. At the same time he gave her strict
orders always to wash her hands immediately after
using the ointment, and be particularly careful never
to let a bit of it touch her own eyes. These
injunctions she strictly followed, and was for some
time very happy; yet she sometimes thought it odd
that they should always live by candle-light; and
she wondered, too, that grand and beautiful as the
palace was, such fine ladies and gentlemen as were
there should never wish to leave it. But so it was;
no one ever went out but her master. One morning,
while putting the ointment on the eyes of the
children, her own eye itched, and forgetting the
orders of her master she touched one corner of it
with her finger which was covered with ointment.
Immediately, with the vision of that corner of her
eye, she saw herself surrounded by fearful flames;
the ladies and gentlemen looked like devils, and
the children appeared like the most hideous imps of
hell. Though with the other parts of her eyes she
beheld all grand and beautiful as before, she could
not help feeling much frightened at all this; but
having great presence of mind she let no one see
her alarm. However, she took the first opportunity
of asking her master's leave to go and see her
friends. He said he would take her, but she must
again consent to be blindfolded. Accordingly a
handkerchief was put over her eyes; she was again
mounted behind her master, and was soon put
down in the neighbourhood of her own house. It
will be believed that she remained quietly there, and
took good care not to return to her place; but
very many years afterwards, being at a fair, she
saw a man stealing something from a stall, and with
one corner of her eye beheld her old master pushing
his elbow. Unthinkingly she said, " How are you,

master ? how are the children ?"   He said, " How
did you see me ?"   She answered, " With the corner
of my left eye."   From that moment she was blind
of her left eye, and lived many years with only her
right.' [1]   An older legend preserving this mythical
detail is the story of Taliesin.   Gwion Bach's eyes
are opened by a drop from Caridwen's caldron
falling upon his finger, which he puts in his mouth.

XII.

A Carmarthenshire tradition names among those
who lived for a period among the Tylwyth Teg no
less ·a person than the translator into Welsh of
Bunyan's 'Pilgrim's Progress.'   He was called
Iago ap Dewi, and lived in the parish of Llan-
llawddog, Carmarthenshire, in a cottage situated in
the wood of Llangwyly.   He was absent from the
neighbourhood for a long period, and the universal
belief among the peasantry was that Iago ' got out
of bed one night to gaze on the starry sky, as he
was accustomed (astrology being one of his favourite
studies), and whilst thus occupied the fairies (who
were accustomed to resort in a neighbouring
wood), passing by, carried him away, and he
dwelt with them seven years.   Upon his return
he was questioned by many as to where he had
been, but always avoided giving them a reply.'

XIII.

The wide field of interest opened up in tales of
this class is a fascinating one to the students of
fairy mythology.   The whole world seems to be
the scene of such tales, and collectors of folk-lore
in many lands have laid claim to the discovery of

[1] 'Camb. Sup.,' 349.

' the original ' on which the story of Rip van Winkle is based. It is an honour to American genius, to which I cannot forbear a passing allusion, that of all these legends, none has achieved so wide a fame as that which Washington Irving has given to our literature, and Joseph Jefferson to our stage. It is more than probable that Irving drew his inspiration from Grimm, and that the Catskills are indebted to the Hartz Mountains of Germany for their romantic fame. But the legends are endless in which occur this unsuspected lapse of time among supernatural beings, and the wandering back to the old home to find all changed. In Greece, it is Epimenides, the poet, who, while searching for a lost sheep, wanders into a cave where he slumbers forty-seven years. The Gaelic and Teutonic legends are well known. But our wonder at the vitality of this myth is greatest when we find it in both China and Japan. In the Japanese account a young man fishing in his boat on the ocean is invited by the goddess of the sea to her home beneath the waves. After three days he desires to see his old mother and father. On parting she gives him a golden casket and a key, but begs him never to open it. At the village where he lived he finds that all is changed, and he can get no trace of his parents until an aged woman recollects having heard of their names. He finds their graves a hundred years old. Thinking that three days could not have made such a change, and that he was under a spell, he opens the casket. A white vapour rises, and under its influence the young man falls to the ground. His hair turns grey, his form loses its youth, and in a few moments he dies of old age. The Chinese legend relates how two friends wandering amongst the ravines of their native mountains in search of herbs for medicinal purposes, come to a fairy bridge where two maidens of more than earthly beauty are on guard. They invite them to the fairy land which lies on the other side of the bridge, and the invitation being accepted, they become enamoured of the maidens, and pass what to them seems a short though blissful period of existence with the fairy folk. At length they desire to revisit their earthly homes and are allowed to return, when they find that seven generations have lived and died during their apparently short absence, they themselves having become centenarians.[1] In China, as elsewhere, the legend takes divers forms.

[1] Dennys, ' Folk-Lore of China,' 98.

CHAPTER VII.

Fairy Music—Birds of Enchantment—The Legend of Shon ap Shenkin —Harp-Music in Welsh Fairy Tales—Legend of the Magic Harp —Songs and Tunes of the Tylwyth Teg—The Legend of Iolo ap Hugh—Mystic Origin of an old Welsh Air.

I.

IN those rare cases where it is not dancing which holds the victim of Tylwyth Teg in its fatal fascination, the seducer is music. There is a class of stories still common in Wales, in which is preserved a wondrously beautiful survival of the primitive mythology. In the vast middle ground between our own commonplace times and the pre-historic ages we encounter more than once the lovely legend of the Birds of Rhiannon, which sang so sweetly that the warrior knights stood listening entranced for eighty years. This legend appears in the Mabinogi of 'Branwen, daughter of Llyr,' and, as we read it there, is a medieval tale ; but the medieval authors of the Mabinogion as we know them were working over old materials—telling again the old tales which had come down through unnumbered centuries from father to son by tradition. Cambrian poets of an earlier age often allude to the birds of Rhiannon ; they are mentioned in the Triads. In the Mabinogi, the period the warriors listened is seven years. Seven men only had escaped from a certain battle with the Irish, and they were bidden by their dying chief to cut off his head and bear it to London and bury it with the face towards France. Various were the adventures they encountered while obeying this injunction. At Harlech they stopped to rest, and sat down to eat and drink. 'And there came three birds, and began singing unto them a certain song, and all the songs they had ever heard were unpleasant compared thereto; and the birds seemed to them to be at a great distance from them over the sea, yet they appeared as distinct as if they were close by; and at this repast they continued seven years.'[1] This enchanting fancy reappears in the local story of Shon ap Shenkin, which was related to me by a farmer's wife near the reputed scene of the legend. Pant Shon Shenkin has already been mentioned as a famous centre for Carmarthenshire fairies. The story of Taffy ap Sion and this of Shon ap Shenkin were probably one and the same at some period in their career, although they are now distinct. Shon ap Shenkin was a young man who lived hard by Pant Shon Shenkin. As he was going afield early one fine summer's morning he heard a little bird singing, in a most enchanting strain, on a tree close by his path. Allured by the melody he sat down under the tree until the music ceased, when he arose and looked about him. What was his surprise at observing that the tree, which was green and full of life when he sat down, was now withered and barkless! Filled with astonishment he returned to the farmhouse which he had left, as he supposed, a few minutes before; but it also was changed, grown older, and covered with ivy. In the doorway stood an old man whom he had never before seen; he at once asked the old man what he wanted there. 'What do I want here?' ejaculated the old man, reddening angrily; 'that's a pretty question! Who

[1] Lady Charlotte Guest's 'Mabinogion,' 381.

are you that dare to insult me in my own house?'
'In your own house?' How is this? where's my

SHON AP SHENKIN RETURNS HOME.

father and mother, whom I left here a few minutes
since, whilst I have been listening to the charming

music under yon tree, which, when I rose, was withered and leafless?' 'Under the tree!—music! what's your name?' Shon ap Shenkin.' 'Alas, poor Shon, and is this indeed you!' cried the old man. 'I often heard my grandfather, your father, speak of you, and long did he bewail your absence. Fruitless inquiries were made for you; but old Catti Maddock of Brechfa said you were under the power of the fairies, and would not be released until the last sap of that sycamore tree would be dried up. Embrace me, my dear uncle, for you are my uncle —embrace your nephew.' With this the old man extended his arms, but before the two men could embrace, poor Shon ap Shenkin crumbled into dust on the doorstep.

II.

The harp is played by Welsh fairies to an extent unknown in those parts of the world where the harp is less popular among the people. When any instrument is distinctly heard in fairy cymmoedd it is usually the harp. Sometimes it is a fiddle, but then on close examination it will be discovered that it is a captured mortal who is playing it; the Tylwyth Teg prefer the harp. They play the bugle on specially grand occasions, and there is a case or two on record where the drone of the bagpipes was heard; but it is not doubted that the player was some stray fairy from Scotland or elsewhere over the border. On the top of Craig-y-Ddinas thousands of white fairies dance to the music of many harps. In the dingle called Cwm Pergwm, in the Vale of Neath, the Tylwyth Teg make music behind the waterfall, and when they go off over the mountains the sounds of their harps are heard dying away as they recede. The story which presents the Cambrian equivalent of the

Magic Flute substitutes a harp for the (to Welsh-men) less familiar instrument. As told to me this story runs somewhat thus: A company of fairies which frequented Cader Idris were in the habit of going about from cottage to cottage in that part of Wales, in pursuit of information concerning the degree of benevolence possessed by the cottagers. Those who gave these fairies an ungracious wel-come were subject to bad luck during the rest of their lives, but those who were good to the little folk became the recipients of their favour. Old Morgan ap Rhys sat one night in his own chimney corner making himself comfortable with his pipe and his pint of cwrw da. The good ale having melted his soul a trifle, he was in a more jolly mood than was natural to him, when there came a little rap at the door, which reached his ear dully through the smoke of his pipe and the noise of his own voice—for in his merriment Morgan was singing a roystering song, though he could not sing any better than a haw—which is Welsh for a donkey. But Morgan did not take the trouble to get up at sound of the rap; his manners were not the most refined; he thought it was quite enough for a man on hospitable purposes bent to bawl forth in ringing Welsh, 'Gwaed dyn a'i gilydd! Why don't you come in when you've got as far as the door?' The welcome was not very polite, but it was sufficient. The door opened, and three travellers entered, looking worn and weary. Now these were the fairies from Cader Idris, disguised in this manner for purposes of observation, and Morgan never suspected they were other than they appeared. 'Good sir,' said one of the travellers, 'we are worn and weary, but all we seek is a bite of food to put in our wallet, and then we will go on our way.'

'Waw, lads! is that all you want? Well, there, look you, is the loaf and the cheese, and the knife lies by them, and you may cut what you like, and fill your bellies as well as your wallet, for never shall it be said that Morgan ap Rhys denied bread and cheese to a fellow creature.' The travellers proceeded to help themselves, while Morgan continued to drink and smoke, and to sing after his fashion, which was a very rough fashion indeed. As they were about to go, the fairy travellers turned to Morgan and said, 'Since you have been so generous we will show that we are grateful. It is in our power to grant you any one wish you may have; therefore tell us what that wish may be.' 'Ho, ho!' said Morgan, 'is that the case? Ah, I see you are making sport of me. Wela, wela, the wish of my heart is to have a harp that will play under my fingers no matter how ill I strike it; a harp that will play lively tunes, look you; no melancholy music for me!' He had hardly spoken, when to his astonishment, there on the hearth before him stood a splendid harp, and he was alone. 'Waw!' cried Morgan, 'they're gone already.' Then looking behind him he saw they had not taken the bread and cheese they had cut off, after all. ''Twas the fairies, perhaps,' he muttered, but sat serenely quaffing his beer, and staring at the harp. There was a sound of footsteps behind him, and his wife came in from out doors with some friends. Morgan feeling very jolly, thought he would raise a little laughter among them by displaying his want of skill upon the harp. So he commenced to play—oh, what a mad and capering tune it was! 'Waw!' said Morgan, 'but this is a harp. Holo! what ails you all?' For as fast as he played his neighbours danced, every man, woman, and child of them all footing it like mad creatures. Some of them bounded up against the roof of the cottage till their heads cracked again; others spun round and round, knocking over the furniture; and, as Morgan went on thoughtlessly playing, they began to pray to him to stop before they should be jolted to pieces. But Morgan found the scene too amusing to want to stop; besides, he was enamoured of his own suddenly developed skill as a musician; and he twanged the strings and laughed till his sides ached and the tears rolled down his cheeks, at the antics of his friends. Tired out at last he stopped, and the dancers fell exhausted on the floor, the chairs, the tables, declaring the diawl himself was in the harp. 'I know a tune worth two of that,' quoth Morgan, picking up the harp again; but at sight of this motion all the company rushed from the house and escaped, leaving Morgan rolling merrily in his chair. Whenever Morgan got a little tipsy after that, he would get the harp and set everybody round him to dancing; and the consequence was he got a bad name, and no one would go near him. But all their precautions did not prevent the neighbours from being caught now and then, when Morgan took his revenge by making them dance till their legs were broken, or some other damage was done them. Even lame people and invalids were compelled to dance whenever they heard the music of this diabolical telyn. In short, Morgan so abused his fairy gift that one night the good people came and took it away from him, and he never saw it more. The consequence was he became morose, and drank himself to death—a warning to all who accept from the fairies favours they do not deserve.

III.

The music of the Tylwyth Teg has been variously described by people who claim to have heard it; but as a rule with much vagueness, as of a sweet intangible harmony, recalling the experience of Caliban:

> The isle is full of noises;
> Sounds, and sweet airs, that give delight, and hurt not.
> Sometimes a thousand twangling instruments
> Will hum about mine ears.[1]

One Morgan Gwilym, who saw the fairies by Cylepsta Waterfall, and heard their music dying away, was only able to recall the last strain, which he said sounded something like this:

Edmund Daniel, of the Arail, 'an honest man and a constant speaker of truth,' told the Prophet Jones that he often saw the fairies after sunset crossing the Cefn Bach from the Valley of the Church towards Hafodafel, leaping and striking in the air, and making a serpentine path through the air, in this form:

The fairies were seen and heard by many persons in that neighbourhood, and sometimes by several persons together. They appeared more often by night than by day, and in the morning and evening more often than about noon. Many heard their music, and said of it that it was low and pleasant; but that it had this peculiarity: no one could ever

---

[1] 'Tempest,' Act III., Sc. 2.

learn the tune. In more favoured parts of the Principality, the words of the song were distinctly heard, and under the name of the 'Cân y Tylwyth Teg' are preserved as follows:

> Dowch, dowch, gyfeillion mân,
> O blith marwolion byd,
>   Dowch, dowch, a dowch yn lân.
> Partowch partowch eich pibau cân,
> Gan ddawnsio dowch i gyd,
>   Mae yn hyfryd heno i hwn.

One is reluctant to turn into bald English this goblin song, which in its native Welsh is almost as impressive as 'Fi Fo Fum.' Let it suffice that the song is an invitation to the little ones among the dead of earth to come with music and dancing to the delights of the night revel.

IV.

In the legend of Iolo ap Hugh, than which no story is more widely known in Wales, the fairy origin of that famous tune 'Ffarwel Ned Pugh' is shown. It is a legend which suggests the Enchanted Flute fancy in another form, the instrument here being a fiddle, and the victim and player one under fairy control. In its introduction of bread and cheese and candles it smacks heartily of the soil. In North Wales there is a famous cave which is said to reach from its entrance on the hill-side 'under the Morda, the Ceiriog, and a thousand other streams, under many a league of mountain, marsh and moor, under the almost unfathomable wells that, though now choked up, once supplied Sycharth, the fortress of Glyndwrdwy, all the way to Chirk Castle.' Tradition said that whoever went within five paces of its mouth would be drawn into it and lost. That the peasants dwelling near it had a thorough respect for this tradition, was proved by

H

the fact that all around the dangerous hole 'the grass grew as thick and as rank as in the wilds of America or some unapproached ledge of the Alps.' Both men and animals feared the spot : 'A fox, with a pack of hounds in full cry at his tail,' once turned short round on approaching it, 'with his hair all bristled and fretted like frostwork with terror,' and ran into the middle of the pack, 'as if anything earthly—even an earthly death—was a relief to his supernatural perturbations.' And the dogs in pursuit of this fox all declined to seize him, on account of the phosphoric smell and gleam of his coat. Moreover, 'Elias ap Evan, who happened one fair night to stagger just upon the rim of the forbidden space,' was so frightened at what he saw and heard that he arrived at home perfectly sober, 'the only interval of sobriety, morning, noon, or night, Elias had been afflicted with for upwards of twenty years.' Nor ever after that experience— concerning which he was wont to shake his head solemnly, as if he might tell wondrous tales an' he dared—could Elias get tipsy, drink he never so faithfully to that end. As he himself expressed it, 'His shadow walked steadily before him, that at one time wheeled around him like a pointer over bog and stone.' One misty Hallow E'en, Iolo ap Hugh, the fiddler, determined to solve the mysteries of the Ogof, or Cave, provided himself with 'an immense quantity of bread and cheese and seven pounds of candles,' and ventured in. He never returned ; but long, long afterwards, at the twilight of another Hallow E'en, an old shepherd was passing that—as he called it—'Land-Maelstrom of Diaboly,' when he heard a faint burst of melody dancing up and down the rocks above the cave. As he listened, the music gradually 'moulded itself in something like a tune, though it was a tune the shepherd had never heard before.' And it sounded as if it were being played by some jolting fiend, so rugged was its rhythm, so repeated its discordant groans. Now there appeared at the mouth of the Ogof a figure well known to the shepherd by remembrance. It was dimly visible; but it was Iolo ap Hugh, one could see that at once. He was capering madly to the music of his own fiddle, with a lantern dangling at his breast. 'Suddenly the moon shone full on the cave's yellow mouth, and the shepherd saw poor Iolo for a single moment—but it was distinctly and horribly. His face was pale as marble, and his eyes stared fixedly and deathfully, whilst his head dangled loose and unjointed on his shoulders. His arms seemed to keep his fiddlestick in motion without the least sympathy from their master. The shepherd saw him a moment on the verge of the cave, and then, still capering and fiddling, vanish like a shadow from his sight; but the old man was heard to say he seemed as if he slipped into the cave in a manner quite different from the step of a living and a willing man; 'he was dragged inwards like the smoke up the chimney, or the mist at sunrise.' Years elapsed; 'all hopes and sorrows connected with poor Iolo had not only passed away, but were nearly forgotten; the old shepherd had long lived in a parish at a considerable distance amongst the hills. One cold December Sunday evening he and his fellow-parishioners were shivering in their seats as the clerk was beginning to light the church, when a strange burst of music, starting suddenly from beneath the aisle, threw the whole congregation into confusion, and then it passed faintly along to the farther end of the church, and died gradually away till at last it was impossible to distinguish it

H 2

from the wind that was careering and wailing through almost every pillar of the old church.' The shepherd immediately recognised this to be the tune Iolo had played at the mouth of the Ogof. The parson of the parish—a connoisseur in music—took it down from the old man's whistling; and to this day, if you go to the cave on Hallow eve and put your ear to the aperture, you may hear the tune 'Ffarwel Ned Pugh' as distinctly as you may hear the waves roar in a sea-shell. 'And it is said that in certain nights in leap-year a star stands opposite the farther end of the cave, and enables you to view all through it and to see Iolo and its other inmates.'[1]

[1] 'Camb. Quarterly,' i., 45.

FFARWEL NED PUGH.

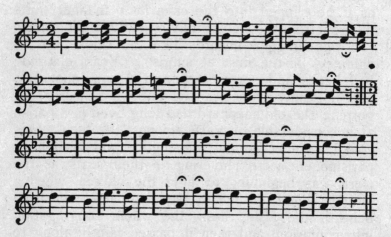

CHAPTER VIII.

Fairy Rings—The Prophet Jones and his Works—The Mysterious Language of the Tylwyth Teg—The Horse in Welsh Folk-Lore—Equestrian Fairies—Fairy Cattle, Sheep, Swine, etc.—The Flying Fairies of Bedwellty—The Fairy Sheepfold at Cae'r Cefn.

I.

THE circles in the grass of green fields, which are commonly called fairy rings, are numerous in Wales, and it is deemed just as well to keep out of them, even in our day. The peasantry no longer believe that the fairies can be seen dancing there, nor that the cap of invisibility will fall on the head of one who enters the circle; but they do believe that the fairies, in a time not long gone, made these circles with the tread of their tripping feet, and that some misfortune will probably befall any person intruding upon this forbidden ground. An old man at Peterstone-super-Ely told me he well remembered in his childhood being warned by his mother to keep away from the fairy rings. The counsel thus given him made so deep an impression on his mind, that he had never in his life entered one. He remarked further, in answer to a question, that he had never walked under a ladder, because it was unlucky to walk under a ladder. This class of superstitions is a very large one, and is encountered the world over; and the fairy rings seem to fall into this class, so far as present-day belief in Wales is concerned.

II.

Allusion has been made in the preceding pages to the Prophet Jones, and as some account of this personage is imperatively called for in a work treating of Welsh folk-lore, I will give it here, before citing his remarks respecting fairy circles. Edmund Jones, 'of the Tranch,' was a dissenting minister, noted in Monmouthshire in the first years of the present century for his fervent piety and his large credulity with regard to fairies and all other goblins. He was for many years pastor of the congregation of Protestant Dissenters at the Ebenezer Chapel, near Pontypool, and lived at a place called 'The Tranch,' near there. He wrote and published two books, one an 'Account of the Parish of Aberystruth,' printed at Trevecca; the other a 'Relation of Apparitions of Spirits in the County of Monmouth and the Principality of Wales,' printed at Newport; and they have been referred to by most writers on folk-lore who have attempted any account of Welsh superstitions during the past half-century; but the books are extremely rare, and writers who have quoted from them have generally been content to do so at second-hand. Keightley,[1] quoting from the 'Apparitions,' misprints the author's name 'Edward Jones of the Tiarch,' and accredits the publication to 'the latter half of the eighteenth century,' whereas it was published in 1813. Keightley's quotations are taken from Croker, who himself had never seen the book, but heard of it through a Welsh friend. It is not in the library of the British Museum, and I know of but a few copies in Wales; the one I saw is at Swansea. The author of these curious volumes was called the Prophet Jones, because of his gift of prophecy—

[1] 'Fairy Mythology,' 412.

so a Welshman in Monmouthshire told me. In my informant's words, 'He was noted in his district for foretelling things. He would, for instance, be asked to preach at some anniversary, or quarterly meeting, and he would answer, "I cannot, on that day; the rain will descend in torrents, and there will be no congregation." He would give the last mite he possessed to the needy, and tell his wife, "God will send a messenger with food and raiment at nine o'clock to-morrow." And so it would be.' He was a thorough-going believer in Welsh fairies, and full of indignant scorn toward all who dared question their reality. To him these phantoms were part and parcel of the Christian faith, and those who disbelieved in them were denounced as Sadducees and infidels.

III.

With regard to the fairy rings, Jones held that the Bible alludes to them, Matt. xii. 43: 'The fairies dance in circles in dry places; and the Scripture saith that the walk of evil spirits is in dry places.' They favour the oak-tree, and the female oak especially, partly because of its more wide-spreading branches and deeper shade, partly because of the 'superstitious use made of it beyond other trees' in the days of the Druids. Formerly, it was dangerous to cut down a female oak in a fair dry place. 'Some were said to lose their lives by it, by a strange aching pain which admitted of no remedy, as one of my ancestors did; but now that men have more knowledge and faith, this effect follows not.' William Jenkins was for a long time the schoolmaster at Trefethin church, in Monmouthshire, and coming home late in the evening, as he usually did, he often saw the fairies under an oak within two or three fields from the church. He saw them more often on Friday evenings than

any other. At one time he went to examine the
ground about this oak, and there he found the
reddish circle wherein the fairies danced, 'such as
have often been seen under the female oak, called
Brenhin-bren.' They appeared more often to an
uneven number of persons, as one, three, five, &c.;
and oftener to men than to women. Thomas
William Edmund, of Hafodafel, 'an honest pious
man, who often saw them,' declared that they
appeared with one bigger than the rest going before
them in the company. They were also heard talking
together in a noisy, jabbering way; but no one
could distinguish the words. They seemed, however, to be a very disputatious race; insomuch,
indeed, that there was a proverb in some parts of
Wales to this effect: 'Ni chytunant hwy mwy na
Bendith eu Mammau,' (They will no more agree
than the fairies).

IV.

This observation respecting the mysterious language used by fairies recalls again the medieval
story of Elidurus. The example of fairy words
there given by Giraldus is thought by the learned
rector of Llanarmon[1] to be 'a mixture of Irish and
Welsh. The letter U, with which each of the
words begins, is, probably, no more than the repre-
sentative of an indistinct sound like the E mute of
the French, and which those whose language and
manners are vulgar often prefix to words indifferently.
If, then, they be read dor dorum, and halgein
dorum, dor and halgein are nearly dwr (or, as it is
pronounced, door) and halen, the Welsh words for
water and salt respectively. Dorum therefore is
equivalent to "give me," and the Irish expression for
"give me" is thorum; the Welsh dyro i mi. The

Rev. Peter Roberts, 'Cambrian Popular Antiquities,' 195. (1815.)

order of the words, however, is reversed. The order should be thorum dor, and thorum halen in Irish, and in Welsh dyro i mi ddwr, and dyro i mi halen, but was, perhaps, reversed intentionally by the narrator, to make his tale the more marvellous.'[1]

V.

The horse plays a very active part in Welsh fairy tales. Not only does his skeleton serve for Mary Lwyds[2] and the like, but his spirit flits. The Welsh fairies seem very fond of going horseback. An old woman in the Vale of Neath told Mrs. Williams, who told Thomas Keightley, that she had seen fairies to the number of hundreds, mounted on little white horses, not bigger than dogs, and riding four abreast. This was about dusk, and the fairy equestrians passed quite close to her, in fact less than a quarter of a mile away. Another old woman asserted that her father had often seen the fairies riding in the air on little white horses; but he never saw them come to the ground. He heard their music sounding in the air as they galloped by. There is a tradition among the Glamorgan peasantry of a fairy battle fought on the mountain between Merthyr and Aberdare, in which the pigmy combatants were on horseback. There appeared to be two armies, one of which was mounted on milk-white steeds, and the other on horses of jet-black. They rode at each other with the utmost fury, and their swords could be seen flashing in the air like so many penknife blades. The army on the white horses won the day, and drove the black-mounted force from the field. The whole scene then disappeared in a light mist.

[1] Supra, p. 67.   [2] See Index.

VI.

In the agricultural districts of Wales, the fairies are accredited with a very complete variety of useful animals; and Welsh folk-lore, both modern and medieval, abounds with tales regarding cattle, sheep, horses, poultry, goats, and other features of rural life. Such are the marvellous mare of Teirnyon, which foaled every first of May, but whose colt was always spirited away, no man knew whither; the Ychain Banog, or mighty oxen, which drew the water-monster out of the enchanted lake, and by their lowing split the rocks in twain; the lambs of St. Melangell, which at first were hares, and ran frightened under the fair saint's robes; the fairy cattle which belong to the Gwraig Annwn; the fairy sheep of Cefn Rhychdir, which rose up out of the earth and vanished into the sky; even fairy swine, which the hay-makers of Bedwellty beheld flying through the air. To some of these traditions reference has already been made; others will be mentioned again. Welsh mountain sheep will run like stags, and bound from crag to crag like wild goats; and as for Welsh swine, they are more famed in Cambrian romantic story than almost any other animal that could be named. Therefore the tale told by Rev. Roger Rogers, of the parish of Bedwellty, sounds much less absurd in Wales than it might elsewhere. It relates to a very remarkable and odd sight, seen by Lewis Thomas Jenkin's two daughters, described as virtuous and good young women, their father a substantial freeholder; and seen not only by them but by the man-servant and the maid-servant, and by two of the neighbours, viz., Elizabeth David, and Edmund Roger. All these six people were on a certain day making hay in a field called Y Weirglodd Fawr Dafolog, when they plainly beheld a company of fairies rise up out of the earth in the shape of a flock of sheep; the same being about a quarter of a mile distant, over a hill, called Cefn Rhychdir; and soon the fairy flock went out of sight, as if they vanished in the air. Later in the day they all saw this company of fairies again, but while to two of the haymakers the fairies appeared as sheep, to others they appeared as greyhounds, and to others as swine, and to others as naked infants. Whereupon the Rev. Roger remarks: 'The sons of infidelity are very unreasonable not to believe the testimonies of so many witnesses.'[1]

VII.

The Welsh sheep, it is affirmed, are the only beasts which will eat the grass that grows in the fairy rings; all other creatures avoid it, but the sheep eat it greedily—hence the superiority of Welsh mutton over any mutton in the wide world. The Prophet Jones tells of the sheepfold of the fairies, which he himself saw—a circumstance to be accorded due weight, the judicious reader will at once perceive, because as a habit Mr. Jones was not specially given to seeing goblins on his own account. He believes in them with all his heart, but it is usually a friend or acquaintance who has seen them. In this instance, therefore, the exception is to be noted sharply. He thus tells the tale: 'If any think I am too credulous in these relations, and speak of things of which I myself have had no experience, I must let them know they are mistaken. For when a very young boy, going with my aunt, early in the morning, but after sun-rising, from Hafodafel towards my father's house at Pen-y-

[1] Jones, 'Apparitions,' 24.

Llwyn, at the end of the upper field of Cae'r Cefn, . . . I saw the likeness of a sheepfold, with the door towards the south, . . . and within the fold a company of many people. Some sitting down, and some going in, and coming out, bowing their heads as they passed under the branch over the door. . . . I well remember the resemblance among them of a fair woman with a high-crown hat and a red jacket, who made a better appearance than the rest, and whom I think they seemed to honour. I still have a pretty clear idea of her white face and well-formed countenance. The men wore white cravats. . . . I wondered at my aunt, going before me, that she did not look towards them, and we going so near them. As for me, I was loth to speak until I passed them some way, and then told my aunt what I had seen, at which she wondered, and said I dreamed. . . . There was no fold in that place. There is indeed the ruins of some small edifice in that place, most likely a fold, but so old that the stones are swallowed up, and almost wholly crusted over with earth and grass.'

This tale has long been deemed a poser by the believers in Cambrian phantoms; but there is something to be said on the side of doubt. Conceding that the Reverend Edmund Jones, the dissenting minister, was an honest gentleman who meant to tell truth, it is still possible that Master Neddy Jones, the lad, could draw a long bow like another boy; and that having seen, possibly, some gypsy group (or possibly nothing whatever) he embellished his tale to excite wonderment, as boys do. Telling a fictitious tale so often that one at last comes to believe it oneself, is a well-known mental phenomenon.

VIII.

The only other instance given by the Prophet Jones as from the depths of his own personal experience, is more vague in its particulars than the preceding, and happened when he had presumably grown to years of discretion. He was led astray, it appears, by the Old Woman of the Mountain, on Llanhiddel Bryn, near Pontypool—an eminence with which he was perfectly well acquainted, and which 'is no more than a mile and a half long and about half a mile broad.' But as a result of his going astray, he came to a house where he had never been before; and being deeply moved by his uncanny experience, 'offered to go to prayer, which they admitted. . . . I was then about twenty-three years of age and had begun to preach the everlasting gospel. They seemed to admire that a person so young should be so warmly disposed; few young men of my age being religious in this country then. Much good came into this house and still continues in it. . . . So the old hag got nothing by leading me astray that time.'

CHAPTER IX.

Piety as a Protection from the Seductions of the Tylwyth Teg—
　　Various Exorcisms—Cock-crowing—The Name of God—Fencing
　　off the Fairies—Old Betty Griffith and her Eithin Barricade—
　　Means of Getting Rid of the Tylwyth Teg—The Bwbach of the
　　Hendrefawr Farm—The Pwca'r Trwyn's Flitting in a Jug of Barm.

I.

THE extreme piety of his daily walk and conversation may have been held as an explanation why the
Prophet Jones saw so few goblins himself, and consequently why most of his stories of the fairies are
related as coming from other people. The value of a
general habit of piety, as a means of being rid of
fairies, has already been mentioned.　The more
worldly exorcisms, such as the production of a black-
handled knife, or the turning one's coat wrongside out,
are passed over by the Prophet as trivial ; but by the
student of comparative folk-lore, they are not deemed
unimportant.　The last-mentioned exorcism, by the
way, is current among the Southern negroes of the
United States.　The more spiritual exorcisms are
not less interesting than the others, however.　First
among these is ranked the pronunciation of God's
name ; but the crowing of a cock is respectfully mentioned, in connection with the story of our Saviour.
Jones gives many accounts which terminate in the
manner of the following : Rees John Rosser, born at
Hendy, in the parish of Llanhiddel, 'a very religious
young man,' went one morning very early to feed
the oxen in a barn called Ysgubor y Llan, and having

fed them lay himself upon the hay to rest. While he lay there he heard the sound of music approaching, and presently a large company of fairies came into the barn. They wore striped clothes, some in gayer colours than the others, but all very gay ; and they all danced to the music. He lay there as quiet as he could, thinking they would not see him, but he was espied by one of them, a woman, who brought a striped cushion with four tassels, one at each corner of it, and put it under his head. After some time the cock crew at the house of Blaen y Cwm, hard by, upon which they appeared as if they were surprised and displeased ; the cushion was hastily whisked from under his head, and the fairies vanished. 'The spirits of darkness do not like the crowing of the cock, because it gives notice of the approach of day, for they love darkness rather than light. . . . And it hath been several times observed that these fairies cannot endure to hear the name of God.' A modern Welsh preacher (but one whose opinions contrast most decidedly with those of Jones) observes : 'The cock is wonderfully well versed in the circumstances of the children of Adam ; his shrill voice at dawn of day is sufficient intimation to every spirit, coblyn, wraith, elf, bwci, and apparition to flee into their illusive country for their lives, before the light of day will show them to be an empty nothingness, and bring them to shame and reproach.'[1] Shakspeare introduces this superstition in Hamlet :

> *Ber.* It was about to speak, when the cock crew.
> *Hor.* And then it started like a guilty thing
> Upon a fearful summons.[2]

But the opinion that spirits fly away at cock-crow

[1] Rev. Robert Ellis, in 'Manion Hynafiaethol.' (Treherbert, 1873.)
[2] 'Hamlet,' Act I., Sc. 1.

is of extreme antiquity. It is mentioned by the Christian poet Prudentius (fourth century) as a tradition of common belief.[1] As for the effect of the name of God as an exorcism, we still encounter this superstition, a living thing in our own day, and in every land where modern 'spiritualism' finds believers. The mischief produced at 'spiritual seances' by 'bad spirits' is well-known to those who have paid any attention to this subject. The late Mr. FitzHugh Ludlow once related to me, with dramatic fervour, the result of his attempts to exorcise a bad spirit which was in possession of a female 'medium,' by trying to make her pronounce the name of Christ. She stumbled and stammered over this test in a most embarrassing way, and finally emerged from her trance with the holy name unspoken ; the bad spirit had fled. This was in New York, in 1867. Like many others who assert their unbelief in spiritualism, Mr. Ludlow was intensely impressed by this phenomenon.

Students of comparative folk-lore class all such manifestations under a common head, whether related of fairies or spirit mediums. They trace their origin to the same source whence come the notions of propitiating the fairies by euphemistic names. The use of such names as Jehovah, the Almighty, the Supreme Being, etc., for the terrible and avenging God of the Jewish theology, being originally an endeavour to avoid pronouncing the name of God, it is easy to see the connection with the exorcising power of that name upon all evil spirits, such as fairies are usually held to be. Here also, it is thought, is presented the ultimate source of that horror of profane language which prevails among the Puritanic peoples of England and America. The name of the devil is

---

[1] Brand, 'Popular Antiquities,' ii., 31.

similarly provided with euphemisms, some of which —such as the Old Boy—are not of a sort to offend that personage's ears ; and until recently the word devil was deemed almost as offensive as the word God, when profanely used.

II.

A popular protection from the encroachments of fairies is the eithin, or prickly furze, common in Wales. It is believed that the fairies cannot penetrate a fence or hedge composed of this thorny shrub. An account illustrating this, and otherwise curious in its details, was given in 1871 by a prominent resident of Anglesea:[1] 'One day, some thirty years ago, Mrs. Stanley went to one of the old houses to see an old woman she often visited. It was a wretched hovel ; so unusually dark when she opened the door, that she called to old Betty Griffith, but getting no answer she entered the room. A little tiny window of one pane of glass at the further side of the room gave a feeble light. A few cinders alight in the miserable grate also gave a glimmer of light, which enabled her to see where the bed used to be, in a recess. To her surprise she saw it entirely shut out by a barricade of thick gorse, so closely packed and piled up that no bed was to be seen. Again she called Betty Griffith ; no response came. She looked round the wretched room ; the only symptom of life was a plant of the Wandering Jew (*Saxifraga tricolor*), so called by the poor people, and dearly loved to grace their windows. It was planted in a broken jar or teapot on the window, trailing its long tendrils around, with here and there a new formed plant seeming to derive sustenance from the air alone.

[1] Hon. W. O. Stanley, in ' Notes and Queries.'

I

As she stood, struck with the miserable poverty of the human abode, a faint sigh came from behind the gorse. She went close and said, " Betty, where are you ? " Betty instantly recognised her voice, and ventured to turn herself round from the wall. Mrs. Stanley then made a small opening in the gorse barricade, which sadly pricked her fingers ; she saw Betty in her bed and asked her, " Are you not well ? are you cold, that you are so closed up ? " " Cold ! no. It is not cold, Mrs. Stanley ; it is the Tylwyth Teg ; they never will leave me alone, there they sit making faces at me, and trying to come to me." " Indeed ! oh how I should like to see them, Betty." " Like to see them, is it ? Oh, don't say so." " Oh but Betty, they must be so pretty and good." " Good ? they are not good." By this time the old woman got excited, and Mrs. Stanley knew she should hear more from her about the fairies, so she said, " Well, I will go out ; they never will come if I am here." Old Betty replied sharply, " No, do not go. You must not leave me. I will tell you all about them. Ah ! they come and plague me sadly. If I am up they will sit upon the table ; they turn my milk sour and spill my tea ; then they will not leave me at peace in my bed, but come all round me and mock at me." " But Betty, tell me what is all this gorse for ? It must have been great trouble for you to make it all so close." " Is it not to keep them off ? They cannot get through this, it pricks them so bad, and then I get some rest." So she replaced the gorse and left old Betty Griffith happy in her device for getting rid of the Tylwyth Teg.'

III.

A common means of getting rid of the fairies is to change one's place of residence ; the fair folk

will not abide in a house which passes into new
hands. A story is told of a Merionethshire farmer
who, being tormented beyond endurance by a
Bwbach of a mischievous turn, reluctantly resolved
to flit. But first consulting a wise woman at
Dolgelly, he was advised to make a pretended
flitting, which would have the same effect; he need
only give out that he was going to move over the
border into England, and then get together his cattle
and his household goods, and set out for a day's
drive around the Arenig. The fairy would surely
quit the house when the farmer should quit it, and
especially would it quit the premises of a born Cymro
who avowed his purpose of settling in the foreign
land of the Sais. So then he could come back to
his house by another route, and he would find the
obnoxious Bwbach gone. The farmer did as he
was told, and set out upon his journey, driving his
cattle and sheep before him, and leading the cart
upon which his furniture was piled, while his wife
and children trudged behind. When he reached
Rhyd-y-Fen, a ford so called from this legend,
they met a neighbour, who exclaimed, 'Holo, Dewi,
are you leaving us for good?' Before the farmer
could answer there was a shrill cry from inside the
churn on the cart, 'Yes, yes, we are flitting from
Hendrefawr to Eingl-dud, where we've got a new
home.' It was the Bwbach that spoke. He was
flitting with the household gods, and the farmer's
little plan to be rid of him was a complete failure.
The good man sighed as he turned his horses about
and went back to Hendrefawr by the same road he
had come.

IV.

The famous Pwca of the Trwyn Farm, in
Mynyddyslwyn parish, came there from his first

abode, at Pantygasseg, in a jug of barm. One of the farm-servants brought the jug to Pantygasseg, and as she was being served with the barm in the jug, the Pwca was heard to say, 'The Pwca is going away now in this jug of barm, and he'll never come back;' and he was never heard at Pantygasseg again. Another story tells that a servant let fall a ball of yarn, over the ledge of the hill whose base is washed by the two fishponds between Hafod-yr-Ynys and Pontypool, and the Pwca said, 'I am going in this ball, and I'll go to the Trwyn, and never come back,'—and directly the ball was seen to roll down the hill-side, and across the valley, ascending the hill on the other side, and trundling along briskly across the mountain top to its new abode.

CHAPTER X.

Fairy Money and Fairy Gifts in General—The Story of Gitto Bach, or Little Griffith—The Penalty of Blabbing—Legends of the Shepherds of Cwm Llan—The Money Value of Kindness—Ianto Llewellyn and the Tylwyth Teg—The Legend of Hafod Lwyddog —Lessons inculcated by these Superstitions.

I.

'This is fairy gold, boy, and 'twill prove so,' says the old shepherd in 'Winter's Tale;' sagely adding, ' Up with it, keep it close; home, home, the next way. We are lucky, boy, and to be so still, requires nothing but secrecy.'[1] Here we have the traditional belief of the Welsh peasantry in a nut-shell. Fairy money is as good as any, so long as its source is kept a profound secret; if the finder relate the particulars of his good fortune, it will vanish. Sometimes—especially in cases where the money has been spent—the evil result of tattling consists in there being no further favours of the sort. The same law governs fairy gifts of all kinds. A Breconshire legend tells of the generosity of the Tylwyth Teg in presenting the peasantry with loaves of bread, which turned to toadstools next morning; it was necessary to eat the bread in darkness and silence to avoid this transformation. The story of Gitto Bach, a familiar one in Wales, is a picturesque example. Gitto Bach (little Griffith), a good little farmer's boy of Glamorganshire, used often to ramble to the top of the mountain to look after his father's sheep.

[1] ' Winter's Tale,' Act III., Sc. 3.

On his return he would show his brothers and sisters pieces of remarkably white paper, like crown pieces, with letters stamped upon them, which he said were given to him by the little children with whom he played on the mountain. One day he did not return. For two years nothing was heard of him. Meantime other children occasionally got like crown-pieces of paper from the mountains. One morning when Gitto's mother opened the door there he sat—the truant!—dressed exactly as he was when she saw him last, two years before. He had a little bundle under his arm. 'Where in the world have you been all this time?' asked the mother. 'Why, it's only yesterday I went away!' quoth Gitto. 'Look at the pretty clothes the children gave me on the mountain, for dancing with them to the music of their harps.' With this he opened his bundle, and showed a handsome dress; and behold, it was only paper, like the fairy money.

II.

But usually, throughout Wales, it is simply a dis-continuance of fairy favour which follows blabbing. A legend is connected with a bridge in Anglesea, of a lad who often saw the fairies there, and profited by their generosity. Every morning, while going to fetch his father's cows from pasture, he saw them, and after they were gone he always found a groat on a certain stone of Cymmunod Bridge. The boy's having money so often about him excited his father's suspicion, and one Sabbath day he cross-questioned the lad as to the manner in which it was obtained. Oh, the meddlesomeness of fathers! Of course the poor boy confessed that it was through the medium of the fairies, and of course, though he often went after this to the field, he never found any money on the bridge, nor saw the offended Tylwyth Teg again. Through his divulging the secret their favour was lost.

Jones tells a similar story of a young woman named Anne William Francis, in the parish of Bassalleg, who on going by night into a little grove of wood near the house, heard pleasant music, and saw a company of fairies dancing on the grass. She took a pail of water there, thinking it would gratify them. The next time she went there she had a shilling given her, 'and so had for several nights after, until she had twenty-one shillings.' But her mother happening to find the money, questioned her as to where she got it, fearing she had stolen it. At first the girl would not tell, but when her mother 'went very severe on her,' and threatened to beat her, she confessed she got the money from the fairies. After that they never gave her any more. The Prophet adds : ' I have heard of other places where people have had money from the fairies, sometimes silver sixpences, but most commonly copper coin. As they cannot make money, it certainly must be money lost or concealed by persons.' The Euhemerism of this is hardly like the wonder-loving Jones.

III.

In the legends of the two shepherds of Cwm Llan and their experience with the fairies, the first deals with the secrecy feature, while the second reproduces the often-impressed lesson concerning the money value of kindness. The first is as follows : One evening a shepherd, who had been searching for his sheep on the side of Nant y Bettws, after crossing Bwlch Cwm Llan, espied a number of little people singing and dancing, and some of the prettiest damsels he ever set eyes on preparing a feast. He went to them and partook of the meal, and thought he had never tasted anything to equal those dishes. When it became dusk they pitched their tents, and the shepherd had never seen before such beautiful things as they had about them there. They provided him with a soft feather-bed and sheets of the finest linen, and he retired, feeling like a prince. But on the morrow, lo and behold! his bed was but a bush of bulrushes, and his pillow a tuft of moss. He however found in his shoes some pieces of silver, and afterwards, for a long time, he continued to find once a week a piece of silver placed between two stones near the spot where he had lain. One day he divulged his secret to another, and the weekly coin was never placed there again.

There was another shepherd near Cwm Llan, who heard some strange noise in a crevice of a rock, and turning to see what it was, found there a singular creature who wept bitterly. He took it out and saw it to be a fairy child, but whilst he was looking at it compassionately, two middle-aged men came to him and thanked him courteously for his kindness, and on leaving him presented him with a staff as a token of remembrance of the occasion. The following year every sheep he possessed bore two ewe lambs. They continued to thus breed for years to come; but one very dark and stormy night, having stayed very late in the village, in crossing the river that comes down from Cwm Llan, there being a great flood sweeping everything before it, he dropped his staff into the river and saw it no more. On the morrow he found that nearly all his sheep and lambs, like his staff, had been swept away by the flood. His wealth had departed from him in the same way as it came—with the staff which he had received from the guardians of the fairy child.

IV.

A Pembrokeshire Welshman told me this story as a tradition well known in that part of Wales. Ianto Llewellyn was a man who lived in the parish of Llanfihangel, not more than fifty or eighty years ago, and who had precious good reason to believe in the fairies. He used to keep his fire of coal balls burning all night long, out of pure kindness of heart, in case the Tylwyth Teg should be cold. That they came into his kitchen every night he was well aware; he often heard them. One night when they were there as usual, Ianto was lying wide awake and heard them say, 'I wish we had some good bread and cheese this cold night, but the poor man has only a morsel left; and though it's true that would be a good meal for us, it is but a mouthful to him, and he might starve if we took it.' At this Ianto cried out at the top of his voice, 'Take anything I've got in my cupboard and welcome to you!' Then he turned over and went to sleep. The next morning, when he descended into the kitchen, he looked in his cupboard, to see if by good luck there might be a bit of crust there. He had no sooner opened the cupboard door than he cried out, 'O'r anwyl! what's this?' for there stood the finest cheese he had ever seen in his life, with two loaves of bread on top of it. 'Lwc dda i ti!' cried Ianto, waving his hand toward the wood where he knew the fairies lived; 'good luck to you! May you never be hungry or penniless!' And he had not got the words out of his mouth when he saw—what do you think?—a shilling on the hob! But that was the lucky shilling. Every morning after this, when Ianto got up, there was the shilling on the hob—another one, you mind, for he'd spent the first for beer and tobacco to go with his bread and cheese. Well, after that, no man in the parish was better supplied with money than Ianto Llewellyn, though he never did a stroke of work. He had enough to keep his wife in ease and comfort, too, and he got the name of Lucky Ianto. And lucky he might have been to the day of his death but for the curiosity of woman. Betsi his wife was determined to know where all this money came from, and gave the poor man no peace. 'Wel, naw wfft!' she cried—which means in English, 'Nine shames on you'—'to have a bad secret from your own dear wife!' 'But you know, Betsi, if I tell you I'll never get any more money.' 'Ah,' said she, 'then it's the fairies!' 'Drato!' said he—and that means 'Bother it all'—'yes—the fairies it is.' With that he thrust his hands down in his breeches pockets in a sullen manner and left the house. He had had seven shillings in his pockets up to that minute, and he went feeling for them with his fingers, and found they were gone. In place of them were some pieces of paper fit only to light his pipe. And from that day the fairies brought him no more money.

V.

The lesson of generosity is taught with force and simplicity in the legend of Hafod Lwyddog, and the necessity for secrecy is quite abandoned. Again it is a shepherd, who dwelt at Cwm Dyli, and who went every summer to live in a cabin by the Green Lake (Llyn Glas) along with his fold. One morning on awaking from sleep he saw a good-looking damsel dressing an infant close by his side. She had very little in which to wrap the babe, so he threw her an old shirt of his own, and bade her place it about the child. She thanked him and departed. Every night thereafter the shepherd found a piece of silver placed in an old clog in his cabin. Years and years this good luck continued, and Meirig the shepherd became immensely wealthy. He married a lovely girl, and went to the Hafod Lwyddog to live. Whatever he undertook prospered—hence the name Hafod Lwyddog, for Lwydd means prosperity. The fairies paid nightly visits to the Hafod. No witch or evil sprite could harm this people, as Bendith y Mammau was poured down upon the family, and all their descendants.[1]

VI.

The thought will naturally occur that by fostering belief in such tales as some of the foregoing, roguery might make the superstition useful in silencing inquiry as to ill-gotten gains. But on the other hand the virtues of hospitality and generosity were no doubt fostered by the same influences. If any one was favoured by the fairies in this manner, the immediate explanation was, that he had done a good turn to them, generally without suspecting who they were. The virtues of neatness, in young girls and servants, were encouraged by the like notions; the belief that a fairy will leave money only on a clean-kept hob, could tend to nothing more directly. It was also made a condition of pleasing the Tylwyth Teg that the hearth should be carefully swept and the pails left full of water. Then the fairies would come at midnight, continue their revels till daybreak, sing the well-known strain of 'Toriad y Dydd,' or 'The Dawn,' leave a piece of money on the hob, and disappear. Here is seen a precaution against fire in the clean-swept hearth and the provision of filled water-pails. That the promised reward did not always arrive, was not evidence it would never arrive; and so the virtue of perseverance was also fostered.

[1] 'Cymru Fu,' 472.

Superstitions of this class are widely prevalent among Aryan peoples. The 'Arabian Nights' story of the old rogue whose money turned to leaves will be recalled. In Danish folk-lore, the fairy money bestowed on the boors turns sometimes to pebbles, and sometimes grows hot and burns their fingers, so that they drop it, when it sinks into the earth.

TORIAD Y DYDD.

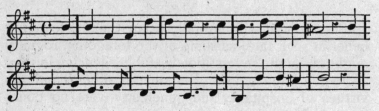

CHAPTER XI.

Origins of Welsh Fairies—The Realistic Theory—Legend of the Baron's Gate—The Red Fairies—The Trwyn Fairy a Proscribed Nobleman—The Theory of hiding Druids—Colour in Welsh Fairy Attire—The Green Lady of Caerphilly—White the favourite Welsh Hue—Legend of the Prolific Woman—The Poetico-Religious Theory—The Creed of Science.

I.

CONCERNING the origin of the Tylwyth Teg, there are two popular explanations, the one poetico-religious in its character, the other practical and realistic. Both are equally wide of the truth, the true origin of fairies being found in the primeval mythology; but as my purpose is to avoid enlarging in directions generally familiar to the student, I have only to present the local aspects of this, as of the other features of the subject.

The realistic theory of the origin of the Tylwyth Teg must be mentioned respectfully, because among its advocates have been men of culture and good sense. This theory presumes that the first fairies were men and women of mortal flesh and blood, and that the later superstitions are a mere echo of tales which first were told of real beings. In quasi-support of this theory, there is a well-authenticated tradition of a race of beings who, in the middle of the sixteenth century, inhabited the Wood of the Great Dark Wood (Coed y Dugoed Mawr) in Merionethshire, and who were called the Red Fairies. They lived in dens in the ground, had fiery red hair and long strong arms, and stole sheep and cattle by night. There are cottages in Cemmaes parish, near the Wood of the Great Dark Wood, with scythes in the chimneys, which were put there to keep these terrible beings out. One Christmas eve a valiant knight named Baron Owen headed a company of warriors who assailed the Red Fairies, and found them flesh and blood. The Baron hung a hundred of them; but spared the women, one of whom begged hard for the life of her son. The Baron refused her prayer, whereupon she opened her breast and shrieked, 'This breast has nursed other sons than he, who will yet wash their hands in thy blood, Baron Owen!' Not very long thereafter, the Baron was waylaid at a certain spot by the sons of the 'fairy' woman, who washed their hands in his warm and reeking blood, in fulfilment of their mother's threat. And to this day that spot goes by the name of Llidiart y Barwn (the Baron's Gate); any peasant of the neighbourhood will tell you the story, as one told it to me. There is of course no better foundation for the fairy features of it than the fancies of the ignorant mind, but the legend itself is—very nearly in this shape—historical. The beings in question were a band of outlaws, who might naturally find it to their interest to foster belief in their supernatural powers.

II.

The so-called Pwca'r Trwyn, which haunted the farm-house in the parish of Mynyddyslwyn, is sometimes cited as another case in which a fairy was probably a being of flesh and blood; and if this be true, it of course proves nothing but the adoption of an ancient superstition by a proscribed Welsh nobleman. There is a tradition that this fairy had a name, and that this name was 'yr Arglwydd

Hywel,' which is in English 'Lord Howell.' And it is argued that this Lord, in a contest with the forces of the English king, was utterly worsted, and driven into hiding ; that his tenants at Panty-gasseg and the Trwyn Farm, loving their Lord, helped to hide him, and to disseminate the belief that he was a household fairy, or Bwbach. It is related that he generally spoke from his own room in this farm-house, in a gentle voice which 'came down between the boards' into the common room beneath. One day the servants were comparing their hands, as to size and whiteness, when the fairy was heard to say, ' The Pwca's hand is the fairest and smallest.' The servants asked if the fairy would show its hand, and immediately a plank overhead was moved and a hand appeared, small, fair and beautifully formed, with a large gold ring on the little finger.

III.

Curiously interesting is the hypothesis concerning the realistic origin of the Tylwyth Teg, which was put forth at the close of the last century by several writers, among them the Rev. Peter Roberts, author of the 'Collectanea Cambrica.' This hypothesis precisely accounts for the fairies anciently as being the Druids, in hiding from their enemies, or if not they, other persons who had such cause for living concealed in subterraneous places, and venturing forth only at night. 'Some conquered aborigines,' thought Dr. Guthrie ; while Mr. Roberts fancied that as the Irish had frequently landed hostilely in Wales, 'it was very possible that some small bodies of that nation left behind, or unable to return, and fearing discovery, had hid themselves in caverns during the day, and sent their children out at night, fantastically dressed, for food and exercise, and thus secured themselves.' But there were objections to this presumption, and the Druidical theory was the favourite one. Says Mr. Roberts: 'The fairy customs appeared evidently too systematic, and too general, to be those of an accidental party reduced to distress. They are those of a consistent and regular policy instituted to prevent discovery, and to inspire fear of their power, and a high opinion of their beneficence. Accordingly tradition notes, that to attempt to discover them was to incur certain destruction. "They are fairies," says Falstaff: "he that looks on them shall die." They were not to be impeded in ingress or egress; a bowl of milk was to be left for them at night on the hearth; and, in return, they left a small present in money when they departed, if the house was kept clean; if not, they inflicted some punishment on the negligent, which, as it was death to look on them, they were obliged to suffer, and no doubt but many unlucky tricks were played on such occasions. Their general dress was green, that they might be the better concealed; and, as their children might have betrayed their haunts, they seem to have been suffered to go out only in the night time, and to have been entertained by dances on moonlight nights. These dances, like those round the May-pole, have been said to be performed round a tree; and on an elevated spot, mostly a tumulus, beneath which was probably their habitation, or its entrance. The older persons, probably, mixed as much as they dared with the world; and, if they happened to be at any time recognised, the certainty of their vengeance was their safety. If by any chance their society was thinned, they appear to have stolen children, and changed feeble for strong infants. The stolen children, if beyond infancy, being brought into their subterraneous dwellings, seem to have had a soporific given them, and to have been carried to a distant part of the country; and, being there allowed to go out merely by night, mistook the night for the day, and probably were not undeceived until it could be done securely. The regularity and generality of this system shows that there was a body of people existing in the kingdom distinct from its known inhabitants, and either confederated, or obliged to live or meet mysteriously; and their rites, particularly that of dancing round a tree, probably an oak, as Herne's, etc., as well as their character for truth and probity, refer them to a Druidic origin. If this was the case, it is easy to conceive, as indeed history shows, that, as the Druids were persecuted by the Romans and Christians, they used these means to preserve themselves and their families, and whilst the country was thinly peopled, and thickly wooded, did so successfully; and, perhaps, to a much later period than is imagined: till the increase of population made it impossible. As the Druidical was one of the most ancient religions, so it must have been one of the first persecuted, and forced to form a regular plan of security, which their dwelling in caves may have suggested, and necessity improved.'

IV.

It will be observed that one of the points in this curious speculation rests on the green dress of the fairies. I do not call attention to it with any Quixotic purpose of disputing the conclusion it assists; it is far more interesting as one feature of the general subject of fairies' attire. The Welsh fairies are described with details as to colour in costume not commonly met with in fairy tales, a fact to which I

have before alluded. In the legend of the Place of
Strife, the Tylwyth Teg encountered by the women
are called 'the old elves of the blue petticoat.'
A connection with the blue of the sky has here
been suggested. It has also been pointed out
that the sacred Druidical dress was blue. The
blue petticoat fancy seems to be local to North
Wales. In Cardiganshire, the tradition respecting
an encampment called Moyddin, which the fairies
frequented, is that they were always in green
dresses, and were never seen there but in the
vernal month of May. There is a Glamorganshire goblin called the Green Lady of Caerphilly,
the colour of whose dress is indicated by her title.
She haunts the ruin of Caerphilly Castle at night,
wearing a green robe, and has the power of turning herself into ivy and mingling with the ivy
growing on the wall. A more ingenious mode of
getting rid of a goblin was perhaps never invented.
The fairies of Frennifawr, in Pembrokeshire, were
on the contrary gorgeous in scarlet, with red caps,
and feathers waving in the wind as they danced.
But others were in white, and this appears to be the
favourite hue of modern Welsh fairy costume, when
the Tylwyth Teg are in holiday garb. These various
details of colour are due to the fervour of the Welsh
fancy, of course, and perhaps their variety may in
part be ascribed to a keener sense of the fitness of
things among moderns than was current in earlier
times. White, to the Welsh, would naturally be
the favourite colour for a beautiful creature, dancing
in the moonlight on the velvet sward. The most
popular pet name for a Welsh lass is to-day exactly
what it has been for centuries, viz., Gwenny, the dimi-
nutrive of Gwenllian (Anglicised into Gwendoline)—a
name which means simply white linen ; and the white

costume of the favourite fairies undoubtedly signifies a dress of white linen. This fabric, common as it is in our day, was in ancient times of inestimable value. In the Mabinogion, linen is repeatedly particularised in the gorgeous descriptions of fabled splendour in princely castles—linen, silk, satin, velvet, gold-lace, and jewels, are the constantly-recurring features of sumptuous attire. In his account of the royal tribes of Wales, Yorke mentions that linen was so rare in the reign of Charles VII. of France (i.e., in the fifteenth century) 'that her majesty the queen could boast of only two shifts of that commodity.' The first cause of the fairies' robes being white is evidently to be discerned here; and in Wales the ancient sentiment as to whiteness remains. The Welsh peasantry, coarsely and darkly clad themselves, would make white a purely holiday colour, and devise some other hue for such commoner fairies as the Bwbach and his sort :

> The coarse and country fairy,
> That doth haunt the hearth and dairy.[1]

So the Bwbach is usually brown, often hairy ; and the Coblynau are black or copper-coloured in face as well as dress.

V.

A local legend of the origin of fairies in Anglesea mingles the practical and the spiritual in this manner : 'In our Saviour's time there lived a woman whose fortune it was to be possessed of nearly a score of children, . . . and as she saw our blessed Lord approach her dwelling, being ashamed of being so prolific, and that He might not see them all, she concealed about half of them closely, and after his departure, when she went in search of them, to her

[1] Jonson, Masque of ' Oberon.'

K 2

great surprise found they were all gone. They never afterwards could be discovered, for it was supposed that as a punishment from heaven for hiding what God had given her, she was deprived of them; and it is said these her offspring have generated the race called fairies.'[1]

VI.

The common or popular theory, however, is in Wales the poetico-religious one. This is, in a word, the belief that the Tylwyth Teg are the souls of dead mortals not bad enough for hell nor good enough for heaven. They are doomed to live on earth, to dwell in secret places, until the resurrection day, when they will be admitted into paradise. Meantime they must be either incessantly toiling or incessantly playing, but their toil is fruitless and their pleasure unsatisfying. A variation of this general belief holds these souls to be the souls of the ancient Druids, a fancy which is specially impressive, as indicating the duration of their penance, and reminds us of the Wandering Jew myth. It is confined mainly to the Coblynau, or dwellers in mines and caves. Another variation considers the fairies bad spirits of still remoter origin—the same in fact who were thrown over the battlements of heaven along with Satan, but did not fall into hell —landed on the earth instead, where they are permitted to tarry till doomsday as above. A detail of this theory is in explanation of the rare appearance of fairies nowadays; they are refraining from mischief in view of the near approach of the judgment, with the hope of thus conciliating heaven.

The Prophet Jones, in explaining why the fairies have been so active in Wales, expounds the poetico-religious theory in masterly form. After stating that

[1] 'Camb. Sup,' 118.

some in Monmouthshire were so ignorant as to think the fairies happy spirits, because they had music and dancing among them, he proceeds to assert, in the most emphatic terms, that the Tylwyth Teg are nothing else, 'after all the talking about them,' but the disembodied spirits of men who lived and died without the enjoyment of the means of grace and salvation, as Pagans and others, and whose punishment therefore is far less severe than that of those who have enjoyed the means of salvation. 'But some persons may desire to know why these fairies have appeared in Wales more than in some other countries? to which I answer, that I can give no other reason but this, that having lost the light of the true religion in the eighth and ninth centuries of Christianity, and received Popery in its stead, it became dark night upon them; and then these spirits of darkness became more bold and intruding; and the people, as I said before, in their great ignorance seeing them like a company of children in dry clean places, dancing and having music among them, thought them to be some happy beings, . . . and made them welcome in their houses. . . . The Welsh entered into familiarity with the fairies in the time of Henry IV., and the evil then increased; the severe laws of that prince enjoining, among other things, that they were not to bring up their children to learning, etc., by which a total darkness came upon them; which cruel laws were occasioned by the rebellion of Owen Glandwr, and the Welsh which joined with him; foolishly thinking to shake off the Saxon yoke before they had repented of their sins.'

Whatever their locally accepted causes of being may be, it is beyond any question that in the fairy folk-lore of Wales, as of other lands, are to be found the *débris* of ancient mythology—scintillant fragments of those magic constellations which glow in the darkness of primeval time, grand and majestic as the vast Unknown out of which they were evolved by barbaric fancy. Through the aid of modern scientific research, 'those ages which the myths of centuries have peopled with heroic shadows'[1] are brought nearer to us, and the humble Welsh Tylwyth Teg may reach back and shake hands with the Olympian gods.

[1] Marquis of Bute, address before the Royal Archæological Institute, Cardiff meeting.

" The humble 'Tylwyth Teg' shake hands with the Olympian Gods"

BOOK II.

THE SPIRIT-WORLD.

Where the wan spectres walk eternal rounds.

POPE.

Miranda. What is't ? a spirit ?
Lord, how it looks about ! Believe me, sir,
It carries a brave form :—But 'tis a spirit.
SHAKESPEARE : *Tempest.*

———◆———

CHAPTER I.

Modern Superstition regarding Ghosts—American ' Spiritualism'—
Welsh Beliefs—Classification of Welsh Ghosts—Departed Mortals
— Haunted Houses — Lady Stradling's Ghost — The Haunted
Bridge—The Legend of Catrin Gwyn—Didactic Purpose in
Cambrian Apparitions — An Insulted Corpse— Duty-performing
Ghosts—Laws of the Spirit-World—Cadogan's Ghost.

I.

IN an age so given to mysticism as our own, it is
unnecessary to urge that the Welsh as a people are
not more superstitious regarding spirits than other
peoples. Belief in the visits to earth of disembodied
spirits is common to all lands. There are no doubt
differences in the degree of this belief, as there are
differences in matters of detail. Where or how
these spirits exist are questions much more difficult
to the average faith than why they exist. They
exist for the moral good of man ; of this there
prevails no 'doubt. The rest belongs to the still

unsettled science of the Unknowable. That form of mysticism called 'spiritualism' by its disciples is dignified to the thoughtful observer by being viewed as a remnant of the primeval philosophy. When we encounter, in wandering among the picturesque ghosts of the Welsh spirit-world, last-century stories displaying details exactly similar to those of modern spiritualism, our interest is strongly aroused. The student of folk-lore finds his materials in stories and beliefs which appear to be of a widespread family, rather than in stories and beliefs which are unique; and the spirit of inquiry is constantly on the alert, in following the details of a good old ghost story, however fascinating it may be in a poetic sense. The phantoms of the Welsh spirit-world are always picturesque; they are often ghastly; sometimes they are amusing to the point of risibility; but besides, they are instructive to him whose purpose in studying is, to know.

That this age is superstitious with regard to ghosts, is not wonderful; all ages have been so; the wonder is that this age should be so and yet be the possessor of a scientific record so extraordinary as its own. An age which has brought forth the magnetic telegraph, steamships and railway engines, sewing-machines, mowing-machines, gas-light, and innumerable discoveries and inventions of marvellous utility—not to allude to those of our own decade— should have no other use for ghostology than a scientific one. But it would be a work as idle as that of the Coblynau themselves, to point out how universal among the most civilised nations is the superstition that spirits walk. The 'controls' of the modern spiritualistic seance have the world for their audience. The United States, a land generally deemed—at least by its inhabitants—to be the most advanced in these directions of any on God's footstool, gave birth to modern spiritualism. Its disciples there compose a vast body of people, respectable and worthy people in the main (as the victims of superstition usually are), among whom are many men of high intellectual ability. With the masses, some degree of belief in the spirits is so nearly universal that I need hardly qualify the adjective. In a country where there is practically no such class as that represented in Europe by the peasantry, the rampancy of such a belief is a phenomenon deserving close and curious study. The present work affords no scope for this study, of course. But I may here mention in further illustration of my immediate theme, the constant appearance, in American communities, of ghosts of the old-fashioned sort. Especially in the New England states, which are notable for their enlightenment, are ghost-stories still frequent—such as that of the haunted school-house at Newburyport, Mass., where a disembodied spirit related its own murder ; of the ghost of New Bedford, which struck a visitor in the face, so that he yet bears the marks of the blow ; of the haunted house at Cambridge, in the classic shadow of Harvard College. It is actually on record in the last-named case, that the house fell to decay on account of its ghastly reputation, as no one would live in it ; that a tenant who ventured to occupy it in 1877 was disturbed by the spirit of a murdered girl who said her mortal bones were buried in his cellar ; and that a party of men actually dug all night in that cellar in search of those bones, while the ghost waltzed in a chamber overhead. The more common form of spirit peculiar to our time appears constantly in various parts of the country ; it is continually turning up in the American newspapers, rapping on walls, throwing stones,

tipping over tables, etc. 'Mediums' of every grade
of shrewdness and stupidity, and widely differing
degrees of education and ignorance, flourish abundantly. Occasionally, where revelations of murder
have been made to a mortal by a spirit, the police
have taken the matter in hand. It is to be observed
as a commendable practice in such cases, that the
mortal is promptly arrested by the police if there has
really been a murder; and when the fact appears,
as it sometimes does, that the mortal had need of no
ghost to tell him what he knows, he is hanged.

II.

The Welsh dearly love to discuss questions of a
spiritual and religious nature, and there are no
doubt many who look upon disbelief herein as something approaching paganism. That one should
believe in God and a future life, and yet be utterly
incredulous as to the existence of a mundane spirit-
world, seems to such minds impossible. It is not
many years since the clergy taught a creed of this
sort. One must not only believe in a spiritual
existence, but must believe in that existence here
below—must believe that ghosts walked, and
meddled, and made disagreeable noises. Our friend
the Prophet Jones taught this creed with energy.
In his relation of apparitions in Monmouthshire, he
says : ' Enough is said in these relations to satisfy
any reasonable sober-minded person, and to confute
this ancient heresy, now much revived and spreading,
especially among the gentry, and persons much
estranged from God and spiritual things ; and such
as will not be satisfied with things plainly proved
and well designed ; are, in this respect, no better
than fools, and to be despised as such. . . . They are
chiefly women and men of weak and womanish

understandings, who speak against the accounts of
spirits and apparitions. In some women this comes
from a certain proud fineness, excessive delicacy,
and a superfine disposition which cannot bear to
be disturbed with what is strange and disagreeable
to a vain spirit.' Nor does the Prophet hesitate to
apply the term 'Sadducees' to all doubters of his
goblins. His warrant for this is found in Wesley
and Luther. That Luther saw apparitions, or
believed he did, is commonly known. Wesley's
beliefs in this direction, however, are of a nearer
century, and strike us more strangely; though it
must be said that the Prophet Jones, in our own
century, believed more than either of his eminent
prototypes. 'It is true,' wrote Wesley, 'that the
English in general, and indeed most of the men in
Europe, have given up all accounts of witches and
apparitions as mere old wives' fables. I am sorry
for it, and I willingly take this opportunity of
entering my solemn protest against this violent
compliment which so many that believe the Bible
pay to those who do *not* believe it. . . . They well
know, whether Christians know it or not, that the
giving up witchcraft is, in effect, giving up the Bible.
And they know, on the other hand, that if but one
account of the intercourse of men with separate
spirits be admitted, their whole castle in the air
—deism, atheism, materialism—falls to the ground.'

III.

The ghosts of Wales present many well-defined
features. It is even possible to classify them, after
a fashion. Of course, as with all descriptions of
phantoms, the vagueness inevitable in creatures of
the imagination is here; but the ghosts of Welsh
tradition are often so old, and have been handed

down so cleanly through successive generations,
that in our day they have almost acquired definite outlines, as in the case of images arising
from the perceptions. Always bearing in mind
the risk of being lost in the labyrinthine eccentricities of popular fancy, compared to which the
Arsinoë of Herodotus was unperplexing, I venture
to classify the inhabitants of the Welsh spirit-world
thus : 1. Departed Mortals ; 2. Goblin Animals ;
3. Spectres of Natural Objects ; 4. Grotesque
Ghosts ; 5. Familiar Spirits ; 6. Death Omens.

IV.

The ghosts of departed mortals are usually the
late personal acquaintances of the people who see
them. But sometimes they are strangers whom
nobody knows, and concerning whom everybody is
curious. Two such ghosts haunted the streets of
Ebbw Vale, in Glamorganshire, in January, 1877.
One was in the shape of an old woman, the other in
that of a girl child. Timid people kept indoors
after nightfall, and there were many who believed
thoroughly in the ghostly character of the mysterious
visitors. Efforts were made to catch them, but they
eluded capture. It was hinted by materialists that
they were thieves ; by unbelievers in spiritualism
that they had perhaps escaped from a seance in
some adjoining town. These ghosts, however, are
not very interesting. A cultivated moderner can
have no satisfaction in forming the acquaintance of
a seance ghost ; it is quite otherwise in the case of
a respectable old family goblin which has haunted
a friend's house in the most orthodox manner for
centuries. Such ghosts are numerous in Wales, and
quite faithfully believed in by selected individuals.
Indeed one of the highest claims to a dignified

antiquity that can be put in by a Welsh family mansion, is the possession of a good old-fashioned blood-curdling spectre—like that, for example, which has haunted Duffryn House, a handsome stone manse near Cardiff, for the past two hundred years and more. This is the ghost of the doughty admiral Sir Thomas Button, famed in his day as an Arctic navigator. Since his death he has faithfully haunted (so the local farm folk say) the cellar and the garden of Duffryn House, where he lived, when he did live, which was in the 17th century. He has never been known to appear in hall or chamber of the mansion, within the memory of man, but has been seen hovering over the beer butt or tun in the cellar, commemorated in his name, and walking in the flower-garden of a fine windy night.

It is noteworthy that in Wales it is by no means necessary that a house should be tenantless, mortally speaking, merely because a ghost haunts it. The dreary picture of desolation drawn by Hood, the all-sufficient explanation of which was—

> . . . the place is haunted !

would not recall the smug tidiness of Duffryn House, whose clean-cut lawns and well-trimmed hedges are fit surroundings of a mansion where luxurious comfort reigns. A ghost which confines itself to the cellar and the garden need disturb neither the merrymaking nor the slumbers of the guests.

St. Donat's Castle is down on the southern coast of Glamorganshire, in a primitive region not yet profaned by railroads, nor likely to be perhaps for many years to come. It is owned and inhabited by a worthy gentleman whose ancestors for seven centuries sleep in the graveyard under the old castle wall. Its favourite ghost—for to confine this or any other ancient Welsh castle to a single ghost would be almost disrespectful—is that of Lady Stradling, who was done away with by some of her family in those wicked old times when families did not always dwell in peace together. This ghost makes a practice of appearing when any mishap is about to befall a member of the house of Stradling—the direct line of which is, however, extinct, a fact not very well apprehended among the neighbouring peasantry. She wears high-heeled shoes and a long trailing gown of the finest silk. In this guise doth she wander up and down the long majestic halls and chambers, and, while she wanders, the castle hounds refuse to rest, but with their howlings raise all the dogs of the village under the hill.

V.

Ghosts of this sort are vague and purposeless in character, beyond a general blood-curdling office which in all ghosts doth dwell. They haunt not only castles and family mansions, but bridges, rocks, and roads, objectless but frightful. The ghost of Pont Cwnca Bach, near Yscanhir, in Carmarthenshire, frightens people off the bridge into the rivulet. Many belated peasants have had this dire experience at the little bridge, afterwards wandering away in a dazed condition, and finding themselves on recovering at some distance from home, often in the middle of a bog. In crossing this bridge people were seized with 'a kind of *cold dread*,' and felt 'a peculiar sensation' which they could not describe, but which the poorest fancy can no doubt imagine. Another purposeless spectre exists in the legend of Catrin Gwyn, told in Cardiganshire. The ruin of a shepherd's cottage, standing on a mountain waste near the river Rheidol, is the haunt of this spectre.

A peasant who was asked to escort a stranger up
the narrow defile of rocks by the ruin, in horror exclaimed, 'Yn enw y daioni, peidiwch,' (in the name
of heaven, sir, don't go!) 'or you'll meet White
Catti of the Grove Cave.' 'And what's that?'
'An evil spirit, sir.' And the superstitious peasant
would neither be laughed nor reasoned out of his
fears. Catrin was the bride of a young shepherd
living near Machynlleth in 1705. One day she
went to market with a party of other peasants, who
separated from her on the return way at a point two
miles from Gelli Gogo. She was never more seen
alive. A violent storm arose in the night, and next
day a scrap of her red cloak was found on the edge
of a frightful bog, in which she is believed to have
disappeared in the darkness and storm. The husband went mad; their cottage fell to decay; and
to this day the shepherds declare that Catti's ghost
haunts the spot. It is most often seen, and in its
most terrific shape, during howling storms, when it
rides on the gale, shrieking as it goes.[1]

VI.

Few Cambrian spirits are devoid of a didactic
purpose. Some teach reverence for the dead,—a
lesson in great request among the rising generation
in Wales and elsewhere. The church at Tregaron,
Cardiganshire, was being rebuilt in 1877, and certain
skulls were turned up by the diggers in making new
foundations. The boys of Tregaron amused themselves playing ball with the skulls, picking out their
teeth, banging them against the wall to see if they
would break, and the like.[2] They probably never
heard the story told by Mrs. Morgan of Newport

---

[1] 'Camb. Quarterly,' i., 452.
[2] 'Western Mail,' Dec. 14, 1877.

to the Prophet Jones: of some people who were drinking at an inn there, 'two of them officers of excise,' when one of the men, to show his courage, declared he was afraid of no ghosts, and dared go to the charnel house and fetch a skull from that ghastly place. This bold and dangerous thing he did, and the men debated, over their beer, whether it was a male or a female skull, and concluded it was a woman's, 'though the grave nearly destroys the difference between male and female before the bones are turned to dust, and the difference then quite destroyed and known only to God.' After a jolly hour over the skull, the bold one carried it back and left it where he got it; but as he was leaving the church, suddenly a tremendous blast like a whirlwind seized him, and so mauled and hauled him that his teeth chattered in his head and his knees knocked together, and he ever after swore that nothing should tempt him to such a deed again. He was still more convinced that the ghost of the original owner of the skull had been after him, when he got home, and his wife told him that his cane, which hung in the room, had been beating against the wall in a dreadful manner.

VII.

As a rule, the motive for the reappearance on earth of a spirit lately tenanting a mortal body, is found in some neglected duty. The spirit of a suicide is morally certain to walk: a reason why suicides are so unpopular as tenants of graveyards. It is a brave man who will go to the grave of a suicide and play ' Hob y deri dando ' on the ysturmant (jew's-harp), without missing a note. Many are the tales displaying the motive, on the ghost's part, of a duty to perform—sometimes clearly defining it, sometimes vaguely suggesting it, as in the story of Noe. 'The evening was far gone when a traveller of the name of Noe arrived at an inn in Pembrokeshire, and called for refreshment. After remaining some time he remarked that he must proceed on his journey. "Surely," said the astonished landlord, " you will not travel at night, for it is said that a ghost haunts that road, crying out, The days are long and the nights are cold to wait for Noe." " O, I am the man sought for," said he, and immediately departed; but strange to say, neither Noe nor the ghost was ever heard of afterwards.'[1]

The ghost of a weaver, which appeared to Walter John Harry, had a very clear idea of the duty he must perform : Walter John Harry was a Quaker, a harmless, honest man, and by trade a farrier, who lived in the romantic valley of Ebwy Fawr. The house he lived in was haunted by the ghost of Morgan Lewis, a weaver, who had died in that house. One night, while lying awake in his bed, with his wife sleeping by his side, Harry saw a light slowly ascending the stairs, and being somewhat afraid, though he was naturally a fearless man, strove to awake his wife by pinching her, but could not awake her. So there he lay in great fear, and with starting eyes beheld the ghost of the weaver come up the stairs, bearing a candle in its hand, and wearing a white woollen cap on its head, with other garments usual to the weaver when alive. The ghost came near the farrier's bed, who then mustered up courage to speak to it. 'Morgan Lewis,' said Harry, 'why dost thou walk this earth?' The ghost replied with great solemnity, that its reason for so doing was that there were some 'bottoms of wool' hidden in the wall of this house, and until these

[1] 'Camb. Sup.' 31.

L

said bottoms were removed from the wall it could
not sleep. The ghost did not say this wool had
been stolen, but such was the inference. However,
the harmless farrier spoke severely to the ghost,
saying, ' I charge thee, Morgan Lewis, in the name
of God, that thou trouble my house no more.'
Whereupon the ghost vanished, and the house
ceased thereafter to be haunted.

The motives animating ghosts are much the same
the world over, and these details have no greater
novelty than that of the local colouring. European
peoples are familiar with the duty-compelled ghost ;
but it is odd to encounter the same spectre in China.
The most common form of Chinese ghost-story is
that wherein the ghost seeks to bring to justice the
murderer who shuffled off its mortal coil. The
ghosts of suicides are also especially obnoxious
there. The spectres which are animated by a sense
of duty are more frequently met than any others :
now they seek to serve virtue in distress, now they
aim to restore wrongfully-held treasure.[1]

VIII.

The laws governing the Welsh spirit-world are
clear and explicit. 'A ghost on duty bent has no
power of speech until first spoken to. Its persist-
ency in haunting is due to its eager desire to speak,
and tell its urgent errand, but the person haunted
must take his courage in both hands and put the
question to the issue. Having done so, he is booked
for the end of the business, be it what it may. The
mode of speech adopted must not vary, in address-
ing a spirit ; in the name of the Father, Son, or
Holy Ghost it must be addressed, and not otherwise.
Its business must be demanded ; three times the

[1] Dennys, ' Folk-Lore of China,' 73.

question must be repeated, unless the ghost answer earlier. When it answers, it speaks in a low and hollow voice, stating its desire; and it must not be interrupted while speaking, for to interrupt it is dangerous in the extreme. At the close of its remarks, questions are in order. They must be promptly delivered, however, or the ghost will vanish. They must bear on the business in hand: it is offended if asked as to its state, or other idle questions born of curiosity. Neglect to obey the ghost's injunctions will lead to much annoyance, and eventually to dire results. At first the spirit will appear with a discontented visage, next with an angry one, and finally with a countenance distorted with the most ferocious rage. Obedience is the only method of escape from its revenge. Such is a *resumé* of the laws. The illustrations thereof are generally consistent in their details.

The story of Cadogan's ghost is one of many in kind. Thomas Cadogan was the owner of a large estate in the parish of Llanvihangel Llantarnam, and being a covetous man did wickedly remove his landmarks in such a way as to absorb to himself part of the land of a widow his neighbour. After his death this injustice troubled him, and as a certain woman was going home one night, at a stile she passed over she met Cadogan's ghost. By a strange forgetfulness, this woman for the moment lost sight of the fact that Cadogan was now a ghost; she had momentarily forgotten that Cadogan was dead. ' Mr. Cadogan,' said she, with ungrammatical curiosity, ' what does you here this time o' night ?' To which the ghost answered, ' I was obliged to come.' It then explained the matter of the landmarks, and begged the woman to request a certain person (whom it mentioned) to remove them back to their proper places; and then the ghost vanished. At this unexpected termination of the interview, the woman suddenly recollected Cadogan's death, and fell into a state of extreme terror. She however did as the ghost had bidden her, and Cadogan walked no more.

CHAPTER II.

Household Ghosts and Hidden Treasures—The Miser of St. Donat's—
Anne Dewy's Ghost—The Ghost on Horseback—Hidden Objects
of Small Value—Transportation through the Air—From Breconshire to Philadelphia, Pa., in Thirty-Six Hours—Sir David Llwyd,
the Magician — The Levitation of Walter Jones—Superstitions
regarding Hares — The Legend of Monacella's Lambs — Aerial
Transportation in Modern Spiritualism—Exorcising Household
Ghosts—The Story of Haunted Margaret.

I.

THE majority of stories of this class turn on the
subject of hidden treasures. The popular belief is
that if a person die while any hoarded money—or
indeed metal of any kind, were it nothing more than
old iron—is still hidden secretly, the spirit of that
person cannot rest. Its perturbation can only be
relieved by finding a human hand to take the hidden
metal, and throw it down the stream of a river. To
throw it up the stream, will not do. The Ogmore
is the favourite river for this purpose in lower
Glamorganshire. The spirit selects a particular
person as the subject of its attentions, and haunts
that person till asked what it wants, when it prefers
its request. Some say it is only ill-gotten treasure
which creates this disturbance of the grave's repose.
A tailor's wife at Llantwit Major, who had been a
stout and jolly dame, was thus haunted until she was
worn to the semblance of a skeleton, 'for not
choosing to take a hoard honestly to the Ogmore.'
But flesh and blood could not resist for ever, and so
—this is her story : ' I at last consented, for the sake

of quiet, to take the treasure to the river; and the
spirit wafted me through the air so high that I saw
below me the church loft, and all the houses, as if I
leaned out of a balloon. When I took the treasure
to throw it into the river, in my flurry I flung it up
stream instead of down: and on this the spirit,
with a savage look, tossed me into a whirlwind, and
however I got back to my home I know not.' The
bell-ringers found her lying insensible in the church
lane, as they were going home from church late in
the evening.

II.

There was an old curmudgeon of a money-hoarder
who lived in a cottage on the side of the cwm, or
dingle, at St. Donat's, not far from the Castle. His
housekeeper was an antique dame of quaint aspect.
He died, and the dame lived there alone; but she
began to grow so gaunt and grizzly that people
wondered at it, and the children ran frightened from
her. Some one finally got from her the confession
that she was haunted by the miser's ghost. To
relieve her of its presence the Methodists resolved to
hold a prayer-meeting in the haunted house. While
they were there singing and praying the old woman
suddenly jumped up and screamed, 'There he is!
there he is!' The people grew silent. Then some
one said, 'Ask it what it wants.' 'What do you
want?' quavered the old woman. No one heard
the reply, except the dame, who presently said:
'Where is it?' Then the old woman, nodding and
staring as if obeying an invisible mandate, groped
her way to the chimney, thrust her gaunt arm up,
and drew down a bag of money. With this she
cried out, 'Let me go! let me go!' which, no one
preventing her, she did, as quickly as a flash of light.
Some young men by the door followed her, and, it

being a bright moonlight night, beheld her whisk over the stile without touching it, and so off up the road towards the Ogmore. The people now resumed their praying and singing. It was an hour before the old woman got back, and then she was found to be spattered with mud and bedraggled with wet, as if she had been having a terrific time. She had indeed, as she confessed, been to the Ogmore, and thrown the bag of money down the stream; the ghost had then taken off its hat, made a low bow, and vanished, to trouble her no more.

III.

A young man from Llywel parish, who was courting a lass who lodged at the house of Thomas Richard, in the vale of Towy, found himself haunted as he went to and fro by the ghost of Anne Dewy, a woman who had hanged herself. She would not only meet him in the road, and frighten him, but she would come to his bedside, and so scare him that he fell ill. While he was ill his cousin came to see him, and thinking his illness was due to his being crossed in love, rallied him, saying, 'Wfft! thou'rt sick because thy cariad has refused thee.' But being gravely answered, and told of Anne Dewy's ghost, this cousin advised the haunted man to speak to her. 'Speak to her,' said he, 'or thou wilt have no quiet. I will go with thee, and see thou shalt have no harm.' So they went out, and called at Tafarn y Garreg, an inn not far off; but the haunted man could not drink, and often looked towards the door. 'What ails the man?' asked the tap-room loungers. He continued to be uneasy, and finally went out, his cousin following him, and then he saw the ghost again. 'Oh God, here she is!' he cried out, his teeth chattering and his eyes rolling.

'This is a sad thing,' said his cousin: 'I know not what to think of thee; but come, I will go with thee, go where thou wilt.' They returned to the ale-house, and after a while the haunted man started up, saying he was called, but when others offered to go with him he said no, he must go alone. He did go alone, and spoke to the ghost, who said, 'Fear nothing; follow me.' She led him to a spot behind the house where she had lived when in the flesh, and where she had hanged herself, and bade him take from the wall a small bag. He did so. The bag contained 'a great sum of money,' in pieces of gold; he guessed it might be 200*l.* or more. But the ghost, greatly to his regret, bade him go and cast it into the river. He obeyed, against his better judgment. The next day, and for many a day thereafter, people looked for that money where he had thrown it in the river, but it never could be found. The Rev. Thomas Lewis, a dissenting minister in those parts, saw the place in the wall where the money had been hid, in the haunted house, and wondered how the young man could reach it, it being so very high; but thought it likely he was assisted by the ghost.

IV.

This same Rev. Thomas Lewis was well acquainted with a man who was similarly employed by a perturbed spirit, and was at the man's bedside when he died. This ghost was in appearance a clergyman, dressed in black clothes, with a white wig on. As the man was looking out of an ale-house window one night, he saw this ghost on horseback, and went out to him. The ghost bowed and silently offered him drink; but this was declined. Thereupon the ghost lifted his hat, crooked his elbow, and said in a hollow tone, 'Attoch chwi, syr,' (towards you, sir). But others who were there could see nothing and hear nothing. The ghost then said, 'Go to Clifford Castle, in Radnorshire, take out some money which lies hidden there, and throw it into the river. Do this, I charge thee, or thou shalt have no rest.' Further and more explicit directions were then given, and the unhappy man set out, against his will, for Clifford Castle, which is the castle in which was born Fair Rosamond, King Henry II.'s beautiful favourite. No one but himself was allowed to enter the castle, although he was permitted to have a friend's company to the ruined gate thereof. It was dark when they came to the castle, but he was guided to the place where the money was, and ran with it and flung it into the river. After that he was haunted no more.

An old house at Ty'n-y-Twr, in Carnarvonshire, was haunted by a ghost whose troubles were a reversal of the rule. A new tenant, who took possession of the house a few years ago, was so bothered by this spectre that he resolved to question it. He did so and got for answer the information that if he would deposit a particular sum of money in a specified place, his ghostship would cease to walk. The man actually did this, and it acted like magic. The money disappeared with promptitude, and the ghost came there no more.

A man at Crumlyn, Monmouthshire, was haunted by a ghost whose trouble related to a hidden object of small value. Nevertheless the spectre was so importunate that the man set out one night to accompany it to the scene of perturbation. In due time they came to a huge stone, which the ghost bade its friend lift up, who replied that he had not sufficient strength, it being a pretty large rock he was thus requested to move. 'But try,' said the ghost. So he tried, and lo! it was lifted as if it had been a feather. He drew forth a pike, or mattock; 'and the light,' the man afterwards related, 'was as great as if the sun shone; and in the snow there was no impression of the feet of either of us.' They went to the river, and by the ghost's command the man threw the pike over his head into the water, standing with his back to the flood. The ghost then conducted him home, and never troubled him more. But for a long time after he was out of his senses.

This was an illustration, according to the popular belief, of the wickedness of hiding anything, however trifling its value—a practice strongly condemned by the Welsh peasantry.

There is a Glamorganshire story about a certain young man who, returning late at night from courting his sweetheart, felt tired, and sitting down fell asleep. He had not slept long when he was aroused by a strange noise, and looking up recognised the ghost of his departed grandfather. Enquiring the cause of the old gentleman's visit to this scene of trials, he got his answer: 'Under the corner of the thatch of your roof, look and you will find a pair of silver spurs, surreptitiously obtained by me when in the flesh, and hidden there. Throw them into the river Taff, and I shall be at peace.' The young man obeyed these instructions, and found the spurs accordingly; and although many persons were present when he climbed to the roof and fumbled under the thatch, and saw him in the very act, not one among them could see the spurs, which were to them invisible. They said, however, that when the purloined spurs had been thrown into the river, a bright flame was seen to flash along the watre.

V.

A large proportion of these stories of ghostly perturbation concerning hidden treasure include a further feature of great interest, relating to transportation through the air. I have mentioned that ghosts sometimes employ the services of the fairy Boobach in thus carrying mortals from place to place. The fairies of Wales are indeed frequently found to be on the best of terms with the ghosts. Their races have much in common, and so many of their practices are alike that one is not always absolutely sure whether he is dealing with a fairy or a spectre, until some test-point crops up. However, in transporting a mortal through the air, ghost and fairy work together. The Boobach being set his task, complaisantly gives the mortal the choice of being transported above wind, amid wind, or below wind. The value of knowing beforehand what to expect, was never better illustrated than in this place. The mortal who, with a natural reluctance to get into an unpleasantly swift current, avoids travelling mid-wind, misses a pleasant journey, for mid-wind is the only agreeable mode of being borne by a Boobach. Should you choose to go above wind, you are transported so high that you skim the clouds and are in danger of being frightened to death. But choosing the below-wind course is even worse, for then you are dragged through bush, through briar, in a way to impress upon you the advice of Apollo to Phaeton, and teach you the value of the golden mean. *In medio tutissimus ibis.*

VI.

In the parish of Ystradgynlais, in Breconshire, Thomas Llewellyn, an innkeeper's son, was often troubled by the spirit of a well-dressed woman, who used to stand before him in narrow lanes, as if to bar his passage, but he always got by her, though in great alarm. One night he mustered up courage to speak to her, and ask her what she wanted with him. To which she replied, 'Be not afraid; I will not hurt thee.' Then she told him he must go to 'Philadelphia in Pennsylvania,' and take a box from a house there, (which she described,) in which there was a sum of 200*l*. But as he did not know how to go to that far-off place, he said as much. 'Meet me here next Friday night,' said the phantom; 'meet me, I charge thee.' She then vanished. The young man went home and told this story to his neighbours and friends. They held a consultation with the curate of the parish, who promptly appointed a prayer-meeting for that Friday night, to which the young man was bidden, and by which it was hoped the purpose of the ghost to spirit him off to Philadelphia might be circumvented. The meeting continued until midnight, and when it broke up the young man's friends stayed with him; but they had no sooner got beyond the parson's stables than he was taken from among them. His subsequent adventures are thus related by himself: 'The apparition carried me away to a river, and threw me into it, chiding me for telling the people of our appointed meeting and for not coming to meet her as she had charged me; but bade me be not' afraid, that 'she would not hurt me, because she had not charged me to be silent on the subject; nevertheless I had done wrong to go to the parson's house. Now, said she, we begin the journey. I was then lifted up and carried away I know not how. When I came to the place,' (in Philadelphia,) 'I was taken into a house, and conducted to a fine room. The spirit then bade me lift up a board, which I did. I then saw the box, and took it. Then the spirit said I must go three miles and cast it into the black sea. We went, as I thought, to a lake of clear water, where I was commanded to throw the box into it ; which when I did there was such a noise as if all about was going to pieces. From thence I was taken up and carried to the place where I was first taken up. I then asked her, Am I free now ? She said I was ; and then she told me a secret, which she strictly charged me to tell no person.' Extensive and ingenious guessing was indulged in by all Ystradgynlais, as to what this secret might be ; and one woman made herself popular by remembering that there was a certain Elizabeth Gething in other days who had gone from this neighbourhood to Pennsylvania, and the conclusion was eagerly arrived at, that this was the woman whose phantom the young man saw, and that the secret she told him was her name when alive. They questioned him as to her appearance, and he said she was largely made, very pale, her looks severe, and her voice hollow, different from a human voice. This was considered by the Ystradgynlaisians, with many nods to each other, as a most accurate description of what Elizabeth Gething would probably be, after having shuffled off this mortal coil. The time occupied in this mysterious transportation and ghostly enterprise was three days and three nights ; that is, from Friday night to Monday night ; and when the voyager came home he could scarcely speak.

VII.

Sir David Llwyd, the Welsh magician, was once at Lanidloes town, in Montgomeryshire, and as he was going home late at night, saw a boy there from his neighbourhood. He asked the lad if he would like to ride home behind him, and receiving an affirmative reply, took the boy up behind on the horse's back. They rode so swiftly that they were home in no time, and the boy lost one of his garters in the journey. The next day, seeing something hanging in the ash-tree near the church, he climbed up to learn what it was, and to his great surprise found it was the garter he had lost. 'Which shows they rode home in the air,' observes the Prophet Jones in telling the story. Mr. Jones has a number of extraordinary narratives of this class—*e.g.*, the following, which I condense :

Henry Edmund, of Hafodafel, was one night visiting Charles Hugh, the conjuror of Aberystruth, and they walked together as far as Lanhiddel, where Hugh tried to persuade his companion to stay all night with him at a public house. Edmund refused, and said he would go home. 'You had *better* stay,' said Hugh in a meaning tone. But Edmund went out into the street, when he was seized by invisible hands and borne through the air to Landovery, in Carmarthenshire, a distance of fully fifty miles as the crow flies. There he was set down at a public house where he had before been, and talked with people who knew him. He then went out into the street, when he was seized again and borne back to Lanhiddel, arriving there the next morning at daybreak. The first man he met was the conjuror Charles Hugh, who said, 'Did I not tell you you had better stay with me?'

VIII.

The landlord of the inn at Langattock Crickhowel, in Brcconshire, was a man called Richard the Tailor. He was more than suspected of resorting to the company of faries, and of practising infernal arts.

One day a company of gentlemen were hunting in that vicinity, when the hounds started a hare, which ran so long and so hard that everybody was prostrated with fatigue ; and this hare disappeared from view at the cellar window of the inn kept by Richard the Tailor. The circumstance begat a suspicion among the hunters that the hare which had so bothered them was none other than Richard the Tailor himself, and that his purpose in taking that form had been to lead them a dance and bring them to the door of his inn at an hour too late for them to return home, thus compelling them to spend their money there. They stayed, however, being very tired. But they growled very hard at their landlord and were perfectly free with their comments on his base conduct. One of their party, having occasion to go out-doors during the evening, did not come back ; his name was Walter Jones, and he was well known in that part of the country. The company became uneasy at his absence, and began to abuse the landlord roundly, threatening to burn the house if Walter Jones did not return. Notwithstanding their threats, Walter Jones came not back all night. Late the next morning he made his appearance, looking like one who had been drawn through thorns and briars, with his hair in disorder, and his whole aspect terribly demoralised. His story was soon told. He had no sooner got out-doors than invisible hands had whisked him up, and whirled him along rough ways until daybreak, when he found himself near by the town of Newport, helping a man from Risca to raise a load of coal upon his horse. Suddenly he became insensible, and was whisked back again to the inn where they now saw him. The distance he traversed in going to and fro was about forty miles. And Walter Jones, who had hitherto been an ungodly man, mended his ways from that time forth.

IX.

There are many points in all these traditional stories which are suggestive of interesting comparisons, and constantly remind us of the significance of details which, at first sight, seem trivial. The supposed adoption of the hare form by the tailor recalls a host of mythological details. The hare has been identified with the sun-god Michabo of the American Indians, who sleeps through the winter months, and symbolises the sleep of nature precisely as in the fairy myth of the Sleeping Maiden, and the Welsh legends of Sleeping Heroes. Among the Hottentots, the hare figures as the servant of the moon. In China, the hare is viewed as a telluric genius in one province, and everywhere as a divine animal. In Wales, one of the most charming of the local legends relates how a hare flying from the hounds took refuge under a fair saint's robes, so that hares were ever after called Monacella's Lambs in that parish. Up to a comparatively recent time, no person in the parish would kill a hare. When a hare was pursued by dogs, it was firmly believed that if any one cried, ' God and St. Monacella be with thee,' it was sure to escape. The legend is related by Pennant, in his tour through Montgomeryshire : ' At about two miles distant from Llangynog, I turned up a small valley to the right, to pay my devotions to the shrine of St. Monacella, or, as the Welsh style her, Melangell. . . . She was the daughter of an Irish monarch, who had determined to marry her to a nobleman of his court. The princess had vowed celibacy. She fled from her father's dominions, and took refuge in this place, where she lived fifteen years without seeing the face of man. Brochwel Yscythrog, prince of Powys, being one day a hare-hunting, pursued his game till he came to a great thicket; when he was amazed to find a virgin of surprising beauty engaged in deep devotion, with the hare he had been pursuing under her robe, boldly facing the dogs, who retired to a distance, howling, notwithstanding all the efforts of the sportsmen to make them seize their prey. When the huntsman blew his horn, it stuck to his lips. Brochwel heard her story, and gave to God and her a parcel of lands to be a sanctuary to all who fled there. He desired her to found an abbey on the spot. She did so, and died abbess of it, in a good old age. She was buried in the neighbouring church. . . . Her hard bed is shown in the cleft of a neighbouring rock. Her tomb was in a little chapel, or oratory, adjoining to the church and now used as a vestry-room. This room is still called cell y bedd, (cell of the grave). . . . The legend is perpetuated by some rude wooden carvings of the saint, with numbers of hares scuttling to her for protection.'

X.

It is interesting to observe, in connection with the subject of transportation through the air, with what vitality this superstition lingers in modern spiritualism. The accounts of such transportation are familiar to every reader of newspapers. That Mr. Home was seen, by a learned English nobleman, sailing through the moonlight seventy feet from the ground, is on record; that Mrs. Guppy was transported from Highbury Park to Lamb's Conduit Street, in London, in a trance and a state of partial *déshabille*, is also on record; and that a well-known American spiritualist was borne by invisible hands from Chicago to Milwaukee and back, between mid-

M

night and 4 A.M., I have been assured by a number of persons in Illinois who thoroughly believed it, or said they did. But it certainly is not too much to demand, that people who give credence to these instances of aerial transportation should equally believe in the good old ghost stories of the Welsh. The same consistency calls for credulity as to the demoniacal elevation of Simon Magus, and the broomstick riding of the witches whose supernatural levitation was credited by Lord Bacon and Sir Matthew Hale, not to speak of Addison and Wesley.

There is something peculiarly fascinating to the gross denizens of earth in this notion of skimming like a bird over house-tops. No dreams, save those of love and dalliance, are so charming to the dreamer as visions of flying; to find oneself floating along over the tops of trees, over the streets where less favoured mortals walk, to look down on them as they stroll, is to feel an exquisite pleasure. The mind of childhood and that of ignorance, alike unable to discriminate between reality and illusion, would naturally retain the impression of such a dream with peculiar vividness. The superstition has no doubt been fostered by this fact, although it, like most superstitions, began its career in pre-historic days. The same class of belief attaches to the magical lore of widely separated lands, in all ages. The magic carpet of the Arabian Nights finds its parallel to-day in the enchanted mat of the Chinese conjuror, which carries him from place to place, at a height of twenty or thirty feet in the air. The levitation involved is in Welsh story embodied in the person of Sgilti Yscawndroed; when he was sent on a message through the wood he went along the tops of the trees; in his whole life, a blade of reed grass never bent beneath his feet, so light was his tread.[1]

XI.

It remains but to add, in connection with our household ghosts, that the method of exorcising such goblins in Wales is explicit. The objectionable spectre must be conjured, in the name of Heaven, to depart, and return no more. Not always is this exorcism effective; the ghost may have a specific purpose in hand, or it may be obstinate. The strength of the exorcism is doubled by employing the Latin language to deliver it; it receives its utmost power, however, through the clergy; three clergymen, it is thought, will exorcise any ghost that walks. The exorcism is usually for a stated period; seven years is the favourite time; one hundred years the limit. There are many instances where a ghost which had been laid a hundred years returned at the end of the time to its old haunts. In all cases it is necessary the ghost should agree to be exorcised; no power can lay it if it be possessed of an evil demon—a spirit within a spirit, as it were—which stubbornly refuses to listen to argument. In such cases the terrors of Heaven must be rigorously invoked; but the result is only temporary. Properly constituted family ghosts, however, will lend a reasonable ear to entreaty, backed by prayer. There are even cases on record where the ghost has been the entreater, as in the story of Haunted Margaret.

Haunted Margaret, or Marget yr Yspryd, was a servant-girl who lived in the parish of Panteg. She had been seduced by a man who promised to marry her, and a day was set for their wedding; but when the day came, the man was not on hand, and Margaret thereupon fell on her knees in the church and

[1] Lady Charlotte Guest's 'Mabinogion,' 225.

prayed Heaven that her seducer might have no rest either in this world or in the world to come. In due course the man died, and immediately his ghost came to haunt Margaret Richard. People heard her in the night saying to the ghost, 'What dost thou want?' or 'Be quiet, let me alone;' and hence it was that she came to be known in that parish by the nickname of Marget yr Yspryd. One evening when the haunted woman was at the house of Mrs. Hercules Jenkins, at Trosdra, she began to be uneasy, and as it grew late said, 'I must go now, or else I shall be sure to meet him on the way home.' Mrs. Jenkins advised Margaret to speak to him; 'and tell him thou dost forgive him,' said the good dame. Margaret went her way, and as she drew near a stile at the end of a foot-bridge, she saw the ghost at the stile waiting for her. When she came up to it the ghost said, 'Do thou forgive me, and God will forgive thee. Forgive me and I shall be at rest, and never trouble thee any more.' Margaret then forgave him, and he shook hands with her in a friendly way, and vanished.

CHAPTER III.

Spectral Animals—The Chained Spirit—The Gwyllgi, or Dog of Dark-
ness—The Legend of Lisworney-Crossways—The Gwyllgi of the
Devil's Nags—The Dog of Pant y Madog—Terrors of the Brute
Creation at Phantoms—Apparitions of Natural Objects—Phantom
Ships and Phantom Islands.

I.

Of spectral animals there is no great diversity in
Cambria, unless one should class under this head
sundry poetic creatures which more properly belong
to the domain of magic, or to fairyland. The spirits
of favourite animals which have died return occasionally to visit their masters. Sometimes it is a horse,
which is seen on a dark night looking in at the
window, its eyes preternaturally large. More often
it is the ghost of a dog which revisits the glimpses
of the moon. Men sometimes become as fondly
attached to a dog as they could to any human being,
and, where the creed of piety is not too severe, the
possibility of a dog's surviving after death in a better
world is admitted. 'It is hard to look in that dog's
eyes and believe,' said a Welshman to me, 'that he
has not a bit of a soul to be saved.' The almost
human companionship of the dog for man is a
familiar fact. It is not strange, therefore, that the
dog should be the animal whose spirit, in popular
belief, shares the nature of man's after death.

II.

Sometimes the spirit in animal form is the spirit
of a mortal, doomed to wear this shape for some

offence. This again trenches on the ground of magic ; but the ascription to the spirit-world is distinct in modern instances. There was a Rev. Mr. Hughes, a clergyman of the Church of England, in the isle and county of Anglesea, who was esteemed the most popular preacher thereabout in the last century, and upon this account was envied by the rest of the clergy, 'which occasioned his becoming a field preacher for a time, though he was received into the Church again.'[1] As he was going one night to preach, he came upon an artificial circle in the ground, between Amlwch village and St. Elian Church, where a spirit in the shape of a large grey-hound jumped against him and threw him from his horse. This experience was repeated on a second night. The third night he went on foot, and warily ; and now he saw that the spirit was chained. He drew near, but keeping beyond the reach of the chain, and questioned the spirit : 'Why troublest thou those that pass by?' The spirit replied that its unrest was due to a silver groat it had hidden under a stone when in the flesh, and which belonged to the church of St. Elian. The clergyman being told where the groat was, found it and paid it over to the church, and the chained spirit was released.

III.

In the Gwyllgi, or Dog of Darkness, is seen a spirit of terrible form, well known to students of folk-lore. This is a frightful apparition of a mastiff, with a baleful breath and blazing red eyes which shine like fire in the night. It is huge in size, and reminds us of the 'shaggy mastiff larger than a steed nine winters old,' which guarded the sheep before the castle of Yspaddaden Pencawr. 'All

[1] Jones, 'Apparitions.'

the dead trees and bushes in the plain he burnt with his breath down to the very ground.'[1] The lane leading from Mousiad to Lisworney-Crossways, is reported to have been haunted by a Gwyllgi of the most terrible aspect. Mr. Jenkin, a worthy farmer living near there, was one night returning home from market on a young mare, when suddenly the animal shied, reared, tumbled the farmer off, and bolted for home. Old Anthony the farm-servant, found her standing trembling by the barn-door, and well knowing the lane she had come through suspected she had seen the Gwyllgi. He and the other servants of the farm all went down the road, and there in the haunted lane they found the farmer, on his back in the mud. Being questioned, the farmer protested it was the Gwyllgi and nothing less, that had made all this trouble, and his nerves were so shaken by the shock that he had to be supported on either side to get him home, slipping and staggering in the mud in truly dreadful fashion all the way. It is the usual experience of people who meet the Gwyllgi that they are so overcome with terror by its unearthly howl, or by the glare of its fiery eyes, that they fall senseless. Old Anthony, however, used to say that he had met the Gwyllgi without this result. As he was coming home from courting a young woman of his acquaintance (name delicately withheld, as he did not marry her) late one Sunday night—or it may have been Monday morning—he encountered in the haunted lane two large shining eyes, which drew nearer and nearer to him. He was dimly able to discern, in connection with the gleaming eyes, what seemed a form of human shape above, but with the body and limbs of a large spotted dog. He threw his hat

[1] 'Mabinogion,' 230.

at the terrible eyes, and the hat went whisking right through them, falling in the road beyond. However, the spectre disappeared, and the brave Anthony hurried home as fast as his shaking legs would carry him.

As Mr. David Walter, of Pembrokeshire, 'a religious man, and far from fear and superstition,' was travelling by himself through a field called the Cot Moor, where there are two stones set up called the Devil's Nags, which are said to be haunted, he was suddenly seized and thrown over a hedge. He went there another day, taking with him for protection a strong fighting mastiff dog. When he had come near the Devil's Nags there appeared in his path the apparition of a dog more terrible than any he had ever seen. In vain he tried to set his mastiff on; the huge beast crouched frightened by his master's feet and refused to attack the spectre. Whereupon his master boldly stooped to pick up a stone, thinking that would frighten the evil dog; but suddenly a circle of fire surrounded it, which lighting up the gloom, showed the white snip down the dog's nose, and his grinning teeth, and white tail. 'He then knew it was one of the infernal dogs of hell.'[1]

Rebecca Adams was 'a woman who appeared to be a true living experimental Christian, beyond many,' and she lived near Laugharne Castle, in Carmarthenshire. One evening when she was going to Laugharne town on some business, her mother dissuaded her from going, telling her she would be benighted, and might be terrified by some apparition at Pant y Madog. This was a pit by the side of the lane leading to Laugharne, which was never known to be dry, and which was haunted, as many

[1] Jones, 'Apparitions.'

had both seen and heard apparitions there. But the bold Rebecca was not to be frighted at such nonsense, and went her way. It was rather dark when she was returning, and she had passed by the haunted pit of Pant y Madog, and was congratulating herself on having seen no ghost. Suddenly she saw a great dog coming towards her. When within about four or five yards of her it stopped, squatted on its haunches, 'and set up such a scream, so loud, so horrible, and so strong, that she thought the earth moved under her.' Then she fell down in a swoon. When she revived it was gone; and it was past midnight when she got home, weak and exhausted.

IV.

Much stress is usually laid, in accounts of the Gwyllgi, on the terror with which it inspires domestic animals. This confidence in the ability of the brute creation to detect the presence of a spirit, is a common superstition everywhere. An American journal lately gave an account of an apparition seen in Indiana, whose ghostly character was considered by the witnesses to be proven by the terror of horses which saw it. They were drawing the carriage in which drove the persons to whom the ghost appeared, and they shied from the road at sight of it, becoming unmanageable. The spectre soon dissolved in thin air and vanished, when the horses instantly became tractable. In Wales it is thought that horses have peculiarly this 'gift' of seeing spectres. Carriage horses have been known to display every sign of the utmost terror, when the occupants of the carriage could see no cause for fright; and in such cases a funeral is expected to pass there before long, bearing to his grave some person not dead at the time of the horses' fright. These phenomena are certainly extremely interesting, and well calculated to 'bid us pause,' though not, perhaps, for the purpose of considering whether a horse's eye can receive an image which the human retina fails to accept. Much weight will not be given to the fright of the lower animals, I fear, by any thoughtful person who has witnessed the terror of a horse at sight of a flapping shirt on a clothesline, or that hideous monster a railway engine. Andrew Jackson Davis has a theory that we all bear about us an atmosphere, pleasing or repulsive, which can be detected by horses, dogs, and spiritual 'mediums;' this *aura*, being spiritual, surrounds us without our will or wish, goes where we go, but does not die when we die, and is the means by which a bloodhound tracks a slave, or a fond dog finds its master. Without denying the possibility of this theory, I must record that in my observation a dog has been found to smell his master most successfully when that master was most in need of a bath and a change of linen. Also, that when the master leaves off his coat he clearly leaves—if a dog's conduct be evidence—a part of his *aura* with it. More worthy of serious attention is August Comte's suggestion that dogs and some other animals are perhaps capable of forming fetichistic notions. That dogs accredit inanimate objects with volition, to a certain extent, I am quite convinced. The thing which constitutes knowledge, in dogs as in human beings—that is to say, thought, organised by experience—corrects this tendency in animals as they grow older, precisely as it corrects the false conclusions of children, though never to the same extent. That a dog can think, I suppose no well-informed person doubts in these days.

V.

The Gwyllgi finds its counterpart in the Mauthe Doog of the Isle of Man and the Shock of the Norfolk coast. It there comes up out of the sea and travels about in the lanes at night. To meet it is a sign of trouble and death. The Gwyllgi also is confined to sea-coast parishes mainly, and although not classed among death-omens, to look on it is deemed dangerous. The hunting dogs, Cwn Annwn, or dogs of hell, whose habitat is the sky overhead, have also other attributes which distinguish them clearly from the Gwyllgi. They are death-omens, ancient of lineage and still encountered. The Gwyllgi, while suggesting some interesting comparisons with the old mythology, appears to have lost vogue since smuggling ceased to be profitable.

VI.

Confined to the coast, too, are those stories of phantom ships and phantom islands which, too familiar to merit illustration here, have their origin in the mirage. That they also touch the ancient mythology is undoubted; but their source in the mirage is probably true of the primeval belief as well as of the medieval, and that of our time. The Chinese also have the mirage, but not its scientific explanation, and hence of course their belief in its supernatural character is undisturbed.

CHAPTER IV.

Grotesque Ghosts—The Phantom Horseman—Gigantic Spirits—The Black Ghost of Ffynon yr Yspryd—Black Men in the Mabinogion—Whirling Ghosts—Antic Spirits—The Tridoll Valley Ghost—Resemblance to Modern Spiritualistic Performances—Household Fairies.

I.

THE grotesque ghosts of Welsh folk-lore are often most diverting acquaintances. They are ghosts on horseback, or with coloured faces, or of huge and monstrous form; or they indulge in strange gymnastics, in whirling, throwing stones, or whistling. A phantom horseman, encountered by the Rev. John Jones, of Holywell, in Flintshire. as described by himself, is worthy of Heinrich Zschokke. This Mr. Jones was a preacher of extraordinary power, renowned and respected throughout Wales. He was one day travelling alone on horseback from Bala, in Merionethshire, to Machynlleth, Montgomeryshire, and as he approached a forest which lay in his way he was dogged by a murderous-looking man carrying a sharp sickle. The minister felt sure this man meditated an attack on his life, from his conduct in running crouched along behind hedges, and from his having met the man at the village inn of Llanuwchllyn, where the minister exposed his watch and purse. Presently he saw the man conceal himself at a place where the hedge was thick, and where a gate crossed the road; and feeling sure that here he should be attacked, he stopped his horse to reflect on the situation. No house was in sight, and the road was hidden by high hedges on either side. Should he turn back? 'In despair, rather than in a spirit of humble trust and confidence,' says the good man, 'I bowed my head, and offered up a silent prayer. At this juncture my horse, growing impatient of the delay, started off. I clutched the reins, which I had let fall on his neck, when, happening to turn my eyes, I saw, to my utter astonishment, that I was no longer alone : there, by my side, I beheld a horseman in a dark dress, mounted on a white steed. In intense amazement I gazed upon him. Where could he have come from ? He appeared as suddenly as if he had sprung from the earth ; he must have been riding behind and have overtaken me, and yet I had not heard the slightest sound. It was mysterious, inexplicable ; but joy overcame my feelings of wonder, and I began at once to address my companion. I asked him if he had seen any one, and then described to him what had taken place, and how relieved I felt by his sudden appearance. He made no reply, and on looking at his face he seemed paying but slight attention to my words, but continued intently gazing in the direction of the gate, now about a quarter of a mile ahead. I followed his gaze, and saw the reaper emerge from his concealment and run across a field to our left, resheathing his sickle as he hurried along. He had evidently seen that I was no longer alone, and had relinquished his intended attempt.' Seeking to converse with the mysterious horseman, the minister found the phantom was speechless. In vain he addressed it in both Welsh and English ; not a word did it utter, save that once the minister thought it said 'Amen,' to a pious remark. Suddenly it was gone. 'The mysterious horseman was gone ; he was not to be seen ; he had disappeared as mysteriously as he had come. ·What could have become of him ? He could not have gone through the gate, nor have made his horse leap the high hedges, which on both sides shut in the road. Where was he ? had I been dreaming ? was it an apparition—a spectre, which had been riding by my side for the last ten minutes ? was it but a creature of my imagination ? I tried hard to convince myself that this was the case ; but why had the reaper resheathed his murderous-looking sickle and fled ? And then a feeling of profound awe began to creep over my soul. I remembered the singular way of his first appearance, his long silence, and the single word to which he had given utterance after I had mentioned the name of the Lord ; the single occasion on which I had done so. What could I then believe but that . . . in the mysterious horseman I had a special interference of Providence, by which I was delivered from a position of extreme danger ? '

II.

Of gigantic ghosts there are many examples which are very grotesque indeed. Such was the apparition which met Edward Frank, a young man who lived in the parish of Lantarnam. As he was coming home one night he heard something walking towards him, but at first could see nothing. Suddenly his way was barred by a tall dismal object which stood in the path before him. It was the ghost of a marvellous thin man, whose head was so high above the observer's line of vision that he nearly fell over backward in his efforts to gaze at it. His knees knocked together and his heart sank. With great difficulty he gasped forth, ' In the name of God what is here ? Turn out of my way or I will strike thee ! ' The giant ghost then disappeared, and the frightened Edward, seeing a cow not far off, went towards her to lean on her, which the cow stood still and permitted him to do. The naïveté of this conclusion is convincing.

Equally prodigious was the spectre seen by Thomas Miles Harry, of the parish of Aberystruth. He was coming home by night from Abergavenny, when his horse took fright at something which it saw, but which its master could not see. Very much terrified, the latter hastened to guide the animal into an adjoining yard, and dismount; whereupon he saw the apparition of a gigantic woman. She was so prodigiously tall, according to the account of the horrified Harry, that she was fully half as high as the tall beech trees on the other side of the road ; and he hastened to hide from his eyes the awful sight, by running into the house, where they listened open-mouthed to his tale Concerning this Mr. Harry we are assured that he was of an affable disposition, innocent and harmless, and the grandfather of that eminent and famous preacher of the Gospel, Thomas Lewis, of Llanharan, in Glamorganshire.[1] The same narrator relates that Anne, the daughter of Herbert Jenkins, of the parish of Trefethin, 'a young woman well disposed to what is good,' was going one evening to milk the cows by Rhiw-newith, when as she passed through a wood she saw a horrible black man standing by a holly tree. She had with her a dog, which saw it also, and ran towards it to bark at it, upon which it stretched out a long black tongue, and the dog ran affrighted back to the young woman, crawling and cringing about her feet for fear. She was in great terror at all this, but had the courage still to go on after the cows, which had strayed into another field. She drove them

---

[1] Jones, ' Apparitions.'

back to their own field, and in passing the holly-tree avoided looking that way for fear of seeing the black man again. However, after she had got safely by she looked back, and saw the monster once more, 'very big in the middle and narrow at both ends,' and as it walked away the ground seemed to tremble under its heavy tread. It went towards a spring in that field called Ffynon yr Yspryd, (the Fountain of the Spirit,) where ghosts had been seen before, and crossing over the stile into the common way, it whistled so loud and strong that the narrow valley echoed and re-echoed with the prodigious sound. Then it vanished, much to the young woman's relief.

III.

That giants should appear in the Welsh spirit-land will surprise no one, but the apparition of black men is more unique. The Mabinogion, however, are full of black men, usually giants, always terrible to encounter. The black man whom Pere-dur slew had but one eye, having lost the other in fighting with the black serpent of the Carn. 'There is a mound, which is called the Mound of Mourning; and on the mound there is a carn, and in the carn there is a serpent, and on the tail of the serpent there is a stone, and the virtues of the stone are such, that whosoever should hold it in one hand, in the other he will have as much gold as he may desire. And in fighting with this serpent was it that I lost my eye.'[1] In the 'Lady of the Fountain' mabinogi the same character appears : 'a black man . . . not smaller in size than two of the men of this world,' and with 'one eye in the middle of his forehead.'[2] And there are other black men in

---

[1] 'Mabinogion,' 106.   [2] Ibid., 6.

other Mabinogion, indicating the extremely ancient lineage of the spectre seen by Anne Jenkins at the Fountain of the Spirit. Whatever Anglo-Saxon scoffers may say of Welsh pedigrees of mere flesh and blood, the antiquity of its spectral hordes may not be disputed. The black giant of Sindbad the Sailor and the monster woodward of Cynan alike descend from the Polyphemus blinded by Odysseus.

IV.

Another grotesque Welsh goblin goes whirling through the world. Three examples are given by the Prophet Jones. *First:* Lewis Thomas, the father of the Rev. Thomas Lewis, was on his return from a journey, and in passing through a field near Bedwellty, saw this dreadful apparition, to wit, the spectre of a man walking or whirling along on its hands and feet; at sight of which Lewis Thomas felt his hair to move on his head; his heart panted and beat violently, ' his body trembled, and he felt not his clothes about him.' *Second:* John Jenkins, a poor man, who lived near Abertillery, hanged himself in a hay-loft. His sister soon after came upon his dead body there hanging, and screamed loudly. Jeremiah James, who lived in Abertillery House, hearing the scream, looked in that direction and saw the 'resemblance of a man' coming from the hay-loft 'and violently turning upwards and downwards topsy turvy,' towards the river, 'which was a dreadful sight to a serious godly man.' *Third:* Thomas Andrew, living at a place called The Farm, in the parish of Lanhiddel, coming home late at night saw a whirling goblin on all fours by the side of a wall, which fell to scraping the ground and wagging its head, 'looking aside one way and the other,' making at the

N

same time a horrible mowing noise; at which Thomas Andrew 'was terribly frightened.'

V.

The antics of these and similar inhabitants of the Cambrian spirit-world at times outdo the most absurd capers of modern spiritualism. At the house of a certain farmer in the parish of Llanllechid, in Carnarvonshire, there was great disturbance by a spirit which threw stones into the house, and from one room to another, which hit and hurt the people who lived there. The stones were of various sizes, the largest weighing twenty-seven pounds. Most of them were river stones, from the stream which runs hard by. Some clergymen came from Bangor and read prayers in the house, to drive the spirit away, but their faith was not strong enough, and stones were thrown at them, so that they retired from the contest. The family finally had to abandon the house.

On the farm of Edward Roberts, in the parish of Llangunllo, in Radnorshire, there was a spirit whose antics were somewhat remarkable. As the servant-man was threshing, the threshel was taken out of his hand and thrown upon the hay-loft. At first he did not mind this so much, but when the trick had been repeated three or four times he became concerned about it, and went into the house to tell of it. The master of the house was away, but the wife and the maid-servant laughed at the man, and merrily said they would go to the barn to protect him. So they went out there and sat, the one to knit and the other to wind yarn. They were not there long before their things were taken from their hands and tumbled about the barn. On returning to the house, they perceived the dishes on the shelves move to and fro, and some were thrown on to the stone floor and broken. That night there was a terrible clattering among the dishes, and next morning they could scarcely tread without stepping on the wrecks of crockery which lay about. This pleasant experience was often repeated. Neighbours came to see. People even came from far to satisfy their curiosity—some from so far as Knighton; and one who came from Knighton to read prayers for the exorcising of the spirit, had the book taken out of his hand and thrown upstairs. Stones were often cast at the people, and once iron was projected from the chimney at them. At last the spirit set the house on fire, and nothing could quench it; the house was burnt down: nothing but the walls and the two chimneys stood, long after, to greet the eyes of people who passed to and from Knighton market.

VI.

A spirit which haunted the house of William Thomas, in Tridoll Valley, Glamorganshire, used to hit the maid-servant on the side of her head, as it were with a cushion, when she was coming down the stairs. 'One time she brought a marment of water into the house,' and the water was thrown over her person. Another time there came so great an abundance of pilchards in the sea, that the people could scarcely devour them, and the maid asked leave of her master to go and fetch some of them. 'No,' said he, being a very just man, 'the pilchards are sent for the use of poor people; we do not want them.' But the maid was very fond of pilchards, and so she went without leave, and brought some to the house. After giving a turn about the house, she went to look for her fish, and found them thrown out upon the dunghill. 'Well,' said her master, 'did not I tell thee not to go?' Once a pot of meat was on the fire, and when they took it off they found both meat and broth gone, none knew where, and the pot as empty as their own bellies. Sometimes the clasped Bible would be thrown whisking by their heads; and 'so it would do with the gads of the steller, and once it struck one of them against the screen where a person then sat, and the mark of it still to be seen in the hard board.' Once the china dishes were thrown off the shelf, and not one broke. 'It was a great business with this light-hating spirit to throw an old lanthorn about the house without breaking it.' When the maid went a-milking to the barn, the barn-door would be suddenly shut upon her as she was milking the cow; then when she rose up the spirit began to turn the door backwards and forwards with an idle ringing noise. Once it tried to make trouble between the mistress and the maid by strewing charcoal ashes on the milk. When William Evans, a neighbour, went there to pray, as he knelt by the bedside, it struck the bed such a bang with a trencher that it made a report like a gun, so that both the bed and the room shook perceptibly. On another occasion it made a sudden loud noise, which made the master think his house was falling down, and he was prodigiously terrified; it never after that made so loud a noise.

The Rev. R. Tibbet, a dissenting minister from Montgomeryshire, was one night sleeping in the house, with another person in the bed with him; and they had a tussle with the Tridoll spirit for possession of the bed-clothes. By praying and pulling with equal energy, the parson beat the spirit, and kept the bed-clothes. But the spirit, apparently angered by this failure, struck the bed with the cawnen (a vessel to hold grain) such a blow that

the bed was knocked out of its place. Then they
lit a light and the spirit left them alone. It was a
favourite diversion with this goblin to hover about
William Thomas when he was shaving, and occasionally cuff him on the side of his head—the consequence being that the persecuted farmer shaved
himself by fits and starts, in a very unsatisfactory
manner, and in a most uncomfortable state of mind.
For about two years it troubled the whole of that
family, during which period it had intervals of quiet
lasting for a fortnight or three weeks. Once it
endeavoured to hinder them from going to church,
by hiding the bunch of keys, on the Lord's day, so
that for all their searching they could not find them.
The good man of the house bade them not to yield
to the devil, and as they were loth to appear in their
old clothes at meeting, they were about to break
the locks; but first concluded to kneel in prayer,
and so did. After their prayers they found the
keys where they used to be, but where they could
not find them before. One night the spirit divided
the books among the members of the family, after
they had gone to bed. To the man of the house it
gave the Bible, to the woman of the house 'Allen's
Sure Guide,' and upon the bed of the maid-servant
(whom it was specially fond of plaguing) it piled a lot
of English books, which language she did not understand. The maid was heartily afraid of the spirit,
and used to fall on her knees and go to praying
with chattering teeth, at all hours of the day or
night; and prayer this spirit could not abide.
When the maid would go about in the night with a
candle, the light thereof would diminish, grow feeble
as if in dampness, and finally go out. The result
was the maid was generally excused from making
journeys into cellar or garret after dark, very much
to her satisfaction.

Particularly did this frisky Tridoll spirit trouble
the maid-servant after she had gone to bed—in
winter hauling the bed-clothes off her; in summer
piling more on her. Now there was a young man,
a first cousin to William Thomas, who could not be
got to believe there was a spirit at his kinsman's
house, and said the family were only making tricks
with one another, 'and very strong he was, a hero
of an unbeliever, like many of his brethren in
infidelity.' One night William Thomas and his wife
went to a neighbour's wake, and left the house in
charge of the doubting cousin, who searched the
place all over, and then went to bed there; and no
spirit came to disturb him. This made him stronger
than ever in his unbelief. But soon after he slept
there again, when they were all there, and before
going to bed he said aloud to the maid, 'If anything
comes to disturb thee, Ally, call upon me, as I lie
in the next room to you.' During the night the
maid cried out that the spirit was pulling the clothes
off her bed, and the doubting cousin awoke, jumped
out of bed, and ran to catch the person he believed
to be playing tricks with the maid. But there was
no creature visible, although there rained upon his
doubting head a series of cuffs, and about his person
a fusillade of kicks, which thrust the unbelief quite
out of him, so that he doubted no more. The
departure of this spirit came about thus: William
Thomas being in bed with his wife, heard a voice
calling him. He awaked his wife, and rising on
his elbow said to the invisible spirit, 'In the name
of God what seekest thou in my house? Hast
thou anything to say to me?' The spirit answered,
'I have,' and desired him to remove certain things
out of a place where they had been mislaid.
'Satan,' answered William Thomas, in a candid
manner, 'I'll do nothing thou biddest me; I

command thee, in the name of God, to depart from my house.' And it obeyed.

VII.

This long and circumstantial account, which I have gathered from different sources, but mainly from the two books of the Prophet Jones, will impress the general reader with its resemblance, in many respects, to modern newspaper ghost stories. The throwing about of dishes, books, keys, etc.; its raps and touches of the person; its making of loud noises by banging down metal objects; all these antics are the tricks of contemporaneous spiritualism. But this spectre is of a date when our spiritualism was quite unknown. The same is true of the spirit which threw stones, another modern spiritualistic accomplishment.[1] The spiritualists will argue from all this that their belief is substantiated, not by any means that it is shaken. The doubter will conclude that there were clever tricksters in humble Welsh communities some time before the American city of Rochester had produced its 'mediums.'

[1] For the sake of comparison, I give the latest American case which comes under my notice. The scene is Akron, a bustling town in the State of Ohio; the time October, 1878. 'Mr. and Mrs. Michael Metzler, middle-aged Germans, with their little daughter, ten years of age, and Mrs. Knoss, Metzler's mother-in-law, recently moved to a brick house in the suburbs known as Hell's Half Acre. The house is a good, substantial building, situated in a somewhat open space, and surrounded by a lonesome deserted air. A few days after they had moved, they were disturbed by sharp rappings all over the house, produced by small stones or pebbles thrown against the window panes. Different members of the family were hit by these stones coming to and going from the house. Other persons were hit by them, the stones varying in size from a pea to a hen's egg. Mrs. Metzler said that when she went after the cow in the evening, she could hear these stones whistling around her head. Mr. and Mrs. Metzler, who are devout Catholics, had Father Brown come to the house to exorcise the spirits which were tormenting them. The reverend father, in the midst of his exercises, was struck by a stone, and so dismayed thereby that he went home in despair.' (Newspaper account.)

The student of comparative folk-lore, in reading these accounts, will be equally impressed with their resemblance to phenomena noted in many other lands. The conclusion is irresistible that we here encounter but another form of the fairy which goes in Wales by the name of the Bwbach, and in England is called the Hobgoblin, in Denmark the Nis, in Scotland the Brownie. Also, the resemblance is strong in all stories of this class to certain of the German Kobolds. In several of these accounts of spirits in Wales appear the leading particulars of the Kobold Hinzelmann, as condensed by Grimm from Feldman's long narrative.[1] There is also a close correspondence to certain ghost stories found in China. In the story of Woo, from the 'Che-wan-luk,'[2] appear details much like those in Hinzelmann, and equally resembling Welsh particulars, either in the stories given above, or those which follow. But we are now drawn so near to the division of Familiar Spirits that we may as well enter it at once.

[1] ' Deutsche Sagen,' i. 103.
[2] Dennys, ' Folk-Lore of China,' 86.

CHAPTER V.

Familiar Spirits—The Famous Sprite of Trwyn Farm—Was it a Fairy ?—The Familiar Spirits of Magicians—Sir David Llwyd's Demon—Familiar Spirits in Female Form—The Legend of the Lady of the Wood—The Devil as a Familiar Spirit—His Disguises in this Character—Summoning and Exorcising Familiars—Jenkin the Pembrokeshire Schoolmaster—The Terrible Tailor of Glanbran.

I.

INNUMERABLE are the Welsh stories of familiar spirits. Sometimes these are spectres of the sort whose antics we have just been observing. More often they are confessedly demons, things of evil. In numberless cases it is no less a personage than the diawl himself who makes his appearance in the guise of a familiar spirit. The familiar spirit which takes up its abode in the household is, as we have seen, a pranksome goblin. Its personal appearance —or rather its invisibility—is the saving circumstance which prevents it from being deemed a fairy. The familiar spirit which haunted the house of Job John Harry, at the Trwyn Farm, in the parish of Mynyddyslwyn, was a stone-thrower, a stroker of persons, etc., but could not be seen. It is famous in Wales under the cognomen of Pwca 'r Trwyn, and is referred to in my account of the Ellylldan.[1] The tenants at present residing on the Trwyn Farm are strangers who have recently invaded the home of this ancestral spook, but I was able to glean abundant information concerning it from people thereabout. It made a home of Mr. Harry's

[1] Supra, p. 21.

house some time in the last century, for a period beginning some days before Christmas, and ending with Easter Wednesday, on which day it departed. During this time it spoke, and did many remarkable things, but was always invisible. It began at first to make its presence known by knocking at the outer door in the night; but when persons went to open the door there was no one there. This continued for some time, much to the perplexity of the door-openers. At last one night it spoke to the one who opened the door, and the family were in consequence much terrified. Some of the neighbours, hearing these tales, came to watch with the family; and Thomas Evans foolishly brought a gun with him, 'to shoot the spirit,' as he said. But as Job John Harry was coming home that night from a journey, the familiar spirit met him in the lane and said, 'There is a man come to your house to shoot me, but thou shalt see how I will beat him.' So Job went on to the house, and immediately stones were thrown at the unbelieving Thomas who had brought the gun, stones from which he received severe blows. The company tried to defend him from the stones, which did strike and hurt him, and no other person; but their efforts were in vain. The result was, that Thomas Evans took his gun and ran home as fast as his legs would carry him, and never again engaged in an enterprise of that sort.

As this familiar spirit got better acquainted with its quarters, it became more talkative, and used often to speak from out of an oven by the hearth's side. It also took to making music o' nights with Job's fiddle. One night as Job was going to bed, the familiar spirit gave him a gentle stroke on the toe. 'Thou art curious in smiting,' said Job. 'I can smite thee where I please,' replied the spirit. As time passed on the family became accustomed to their ghostly visitor, and seeing it never did them any harm, but on the contrary was a source of recreation to them, they used to boldly speak to it, and indulge in entertaining conversation. One old man, a neighbour, more bold than wise, hearing the spirit just by his side, but being unable to see it, threatened to stick it with his knife. ' Thou fool,' quoth the spirit, ' how canst thou stick what thou canst not see with thine eyes?' When questioned about its antecedents, the spirit said, ' I came from Pwll y Gasseg' (Mare's Pit, a place in the adjacent mountain), ' and I knew ye all before I came hither.' The wife of Morris Roberts desired one of the family to ask the spirit who it was that killed William Reilly the Scotchman; which being done, the spirit said, ' It was Blanch y Byd who bade thee ask that question;' and Blanch y Byd (Worldly Blanche) was Morris Roberts' wife ever after called. On Easter Wednesday the spirit departed, saying, ' Dos yn iach, Job,' (fare thee well, Job,) and Job asked the spirit, ' Where goest thou?' The reply was, ' Where God pleases.'[1]

There are other accounts of this Trwyn sprite which credit it to a time long anterior to last century; but all are consistent in this, that the goblin is always invisible. The sole exception to this rule is the legend about its having once shown a white hand to some girls in the kitchen, thrusting it

---

[1] Let me recommend the scene of this story to tourists. It is a most romantic spot, on the top of a mountain, a glorious tramp from Crumlyn, returning by another road to Abercarne. Wheels cannot go there, though a sure-footed horse might bear one safely up. The ancient farmhouse is one of the quaintest in Wales, and must be hundreds of years old; and its front porch looks out over a ravine hardly less grand and lonely than a Californian gulch.

through the floor of its room overhead for that purpose. Now invisibility is a violation of fairy traditions, while ghosts are very often invisible—these rapping and stone-throwing ghosts, always. It might be urged that this spirit was a Bwbach, if a fairy at all, seeing that it kept pretty closely to the house; but on the whole I choose to class it among the inhabitants of the spirit-world; and really, the student of folk-lore must classify his materials distinctly in some understandable fashion, or go daft.

II.

The sort of familiar spirit employed by magicians in the eighteenth and preceding centuries was distinctly a demon. The spirit of this class which was controlled by Sir David Llwyd is celebrated in Wales. This Sir David was a famous dealer in the black art, who lived in Cardiganshire. He was a physician, and at one time a curate; but being known to deal in the magic art, he was turned out of the curacy, and obliged to live by practising physic. It was thought he learned the magic art in Oxford. 'It was this man's great wickedness,' says the Prophet Jones, 'to make use of a familiar spirit. . . . The bishop did well in turning him out of the sacred office, though he was no ill-tempered man, for how unfit was such a man to read the sacred Scripture! With what conscience could he ask the sponsors in baptism to undertake for the child to renounce the world, the flesh and the devil, who himself was familiar with one of the spirits of darkness? . . . Of this Sir David I have heard much, but chiefly depend upon what was told to me by the Rev. Mr. Thomas Lewis, the curate of Landdw and Tolachdy, an excellent preacher of the gospel; and not sufficiently esteemed by his

people, (which likely will bring a judgment on them
in time to come.) Mr. Lewis knew the young
woman who had been Sir David's maid servant,
and the house where he lived.' His familiar spirit
he kept locked up in a book. Once while he was
in Radnorshire, in going from one house to another
he accidentally left this book behind him, and sent
his boy back to fetch it. The boy, being of an
inquisitive turn of mind, opened the book—a thing
his master had expressly charged him not to do—
and the familiar spirit immediately demanded to be
set at work. The boy, though very much alarmed,
had the wit to answer, 'Tafl gerrig o'r afon,'
(throw stones out of the river,) which the spirit
immediately did, so that the air was for a time full
of flying stones, and the boy was fain to skip about
in a surprisingly active manner in order to dodge
the same. After a while, having thrown up a great
quantity of stones out of the river, (the Wye,) the
spirit again, with the pertinacity of its kind, asked
for something to do; whereupon the boy bade it
throw the stones back again, which it did. Sir
David having waited a long time for the boy to
return, began to suspect that things had gone
wrong, and so hastened back after him, and commanded the familiar spirit again into his book.

III.

Familiar spirits of this class are not always invisible; and they can assume such forms as may
be necessary to serve their purposes. A favourite
shape with them is that of a young and lovely
woman. Comparisons are here suggested with the
water-maidens, and other like forms of this fancy;
but they need not be pursued. It is necessary for
the student of phantoms to constantly remind him-

self of the omnipresent danger of being enticed too far afield, unless he keep somewhat sternly to the path he has marked out. How ancient is the notion of a familiar spirit in female form, may be seen from accounts which are given by Giraldus and other old writers. Near Caerleon, (Monmouthshire,) in the twelfth century, Giraldus tells us [1] there lived 'a Welshman named Melerius, who by the following means acquired the knowledge of future events and the occult sciences: Having on a certain night met a damsel whom he loved, in a pleasant and convenient place, while he was indulging in her embraces, instead of a beautiful girl he found in his arms a hairy, rough and hideous creature, the sight of which deprived him of his senses; and after remaining many years in this condition he was restored to health in the church of St. David's, through the merits of its saints. But having always had an extraordinary familiarity with unclean spirits, by seeing them, knowing them, talking with them, and calling each by his proper name, he was enabled through their assistance to foretell future events; he was indeed often deceived (as they are) with respect to circumstances at a great distance; but was less mistaken in affairs which were likely to happen soon, or within the space of a year. They appeared to him on foot, equipped as hunters, with horns suspended from their necks, and truly as hunters not of animals but of souls; he particularly met them near monasteries and religious places; for where rebellion exists there is the greatest need of armies and strength. He knew when any one spoke falsely in his presence, for he saw the devil as it were leaping and exulting upon the tongue of the liar; and if he looked into a book faultily or falsely written, although wholly

[1] Sir R. C. Hoare's Trans., i. 105.

illiterate he would point out the place with his finger. Being questioned how he could gain such knowledge, he said he was directed by the demon's finger to the place.' In the same connection Giraldus mentions a familiar spirit which haunted Lower Gwent, 'a demon incubus, who from his love for a certain young woman, and frequenting the place where she lived, often conversed with men, and frequently discovered hidden things and future events.'

IV.

The legend of the Lady of the Wood is contained in the Iolo MSS., and is of considerable antiquity. It is a most fascinating tale: Einion, the son of Gwalchmai, 'was one fine summer morning walking in the woods of Treveilir,' when 'he beheld a graceful slender lady of elegant growth, and delicate feature, and her complexion surpassing every white and red in the morning dawn and the mountain snow, and every beautiful colour in the blossoms of wood, field, and hill. And then he felt in his heart an inconceivable commotion of affection, and he approached her in a courteous manner, and she also approached him in the same manner; and he saluted her, and she returned his salutation; and by these mutual salutations he perceived that his society was not disagreeable to her. He then chanced to cast his eye upon her foot, and he saw that she had hoofs instead of feet, and he became exceedingly dissatisfied,' as well he might. But the lady gave him to understand that he must pay no attention to this trifling freak of nature. 'Thou must,' she said, 'follow me wheresoever I go, as long as I continue in my beauty.' The son of Gwalchmai thereupon asked permission to go and say good-bye to his wife, at least. This the lady agreed to; 'but,' said she,

' I shall be with thee, invisible to all but thyself.' ' So he went, and the goblin went with him; and when he saw Angharad, his wife, he saw her a hag like one grown old, but he retained the recollection of days past, and still felt extreme affection for her, but he was not able to loose himself from the bond in which he was. " It is necessary for me," said he, " to part for a time, I know not how long, from thee, Angharad, and from thee, my son, Einion," and they wept together, and broke a gold ring between them; he kept one half and Angharad the other, and they took their leave of each other, and he went with the Lady of the Wood, and knew not where; for a powerful illusion was upon him, and he saw not any place, or person, or object under its true and proper appearance, excepting the half of the ring alone. And after being a long time, he knew not how long, with the goblin, the Lady of the Wood, he looked one morning as the sun was rising upon the half of the ring, and he bethought him to place it in the most precious place he could, and he resolved to put it under his eyelid; and as he was endeavouring to do so, he could see a man in white apparel, and mounted on a snow-white horse, coming towards him, and that person asked him what he did there; and he told him that he was cherishing an afflicting remembrance of his wife Angharad. " Dost thou desire to see her?" said the man in white. " I do," said Einion, " above all things, and all happiness of the world." " If so," said the man in white, " get upon this horse, behind me;" and that Einion did, and looking around he could not see any appearance of the Lady of the Wood, the goblin, excepting the track of hoofs of marvellous and monstrous size, as if journeying towards the north. " What delusion art thou under?" said the man in white. Then

Einion answered him and told everything how it
occurred 'twixt him and the goblin. " Take this
white staff in thy hand," said the man in white, and
Einion took it. And the man in white told him to
desire whatever he wished for. The first thing he
desired was to see the Lady of the Wood, for he
was not yet completely delivered from the illusion.
And then she appeared to him in size a hideous and
monstrous witch, a thousand times more repulsive of
aspect than the most frightful things seen upon
earth. And Einion uttered a cry of terror ; and the
man in white cast his cloak over Einion, and in less
than a twinkling Einion alighted as he wished on
the hill of Treveilir, by his own house, where he
knew scarcely any one, nor did any one know him.'
The goblin meantime had gone to Einion's wife, in
the disguise of a richly apparelled knight, and made
love to her, pretending that her husband was dead.
' And the illusion fell upon her ; and seeing that she
should become a noble lady, higher than any in
Wales, she named a day for her marriage with him.
And there was a great preparation of every elegant
and sumptuous apparel, and of meats and drinks,
and of every honourable guest, and every excellence
of song and string, and every preparation of banquet
and festive entertainment.' Now there was a beautiful harp in Angharad's room, which the goblin
knight desired should be played on ; ' and the harp-
ers present, the best in Wales, tried to put it in tune,
and were not able.' But Einion presented himself
at the house, and offered to play on it. Angharad,
being under an illusion, ' saw him as an old, decrepit, withered, grey-haired man, stooping with age,
and dressed in rags.' Einion tuned the harp, ' and
played on it the air which Angharad loved. And
she marvelled exceedingly, and asked him who he

o

was. And he answered in song : . . . " Einion the golden-hearted." . . .

" Where hast thou been ! "
" In Kent, in Gwent, in the wood, in Monmouth,
    In Maenol, Gorwenydd ;
    And in the valley of Gwyn, the son of Nudd ;
    See, the bright gold is the token."

And he gave her the ring.

" Look not on the whitened hue of my hair,
    Where once my aspect was spirited and bold ;
    Now gray, without disguise, where once it was yellow.
    Never was Angharad out of my remembrance,
    But Einion was by thee forgotten."

But Angharad 'could not bring him to her recollection. Then said he to the guests :

" If I have lost her whom I loved, the fair one of polished mind,
    The daughter of Ednyved Vychan,
    I have not lost (so get you out !)
    Either my bed, or my house, or my fire."

'And upon that he placed the white staff in Angharad's hand, and instantly the goblin which she had hitherto seen as a handsome and honourable nobleman, appeared to her as a monster, inconceivably hideous ; and she fainted from fear, and Einion supported her until she revived. And when she opened her eyes, she saw there neither the goblin, nor any of the guests, nor of the minstrels, nor anything whatever except Einion, and her son, and the harp, and the house in its domestic arrangement, and the dinner on the table, casting its savoury odour around. And they sat down to eat . . . and exceeding great was their enjoyment. And they saw the illusion which the demoniacal goblin had cast over them. . . . And thus it ends.'[1]

[1] Iolo MSS. 587, et seq.

V.

There is hardly a goblin in the world more widely known than this spectre of the forest. Her story appears in the legends of very many lands, including China. Its ancient Grecian prototype is found in the Odyssey.[1]

When it is the Diawl himself who appears in the role of the familiar spirit, his majesty is usually in some other form than that of a man, with hoofs, horns, and tail. The orthodox form of Satan has indeed been seen in many parts of Wales, but not when doing duty as a familiar spirit. A Welsh poet of the thirteenth century mentions this form :

> And the horned devil,
> With sharp hoofs
> On his heels.[2]

He is variously called cythraul, dera, diafol, all euphemisms for devil, equivalent to our destroyer, evil one, adversary—as well as plain diawl, devil. In his character of a familiar spirit he assumes the shape of a fiery ball, a donkey, a black calf, a round bowl, a dog, a roaring flame, a bull, a goose, and numberless others, including the imp that goes into a book. In all this he bears out the character given him in old mythology, where he grows big or little at pleasure, and roars in a gale as Hermes, the wind-god, howls as a dog, enters a walnut as in the Norse Tale, or is confined in a bottle as the genie of the 'Arabian Nights.'

---

[1] In his fascinating essay on the 'Folk-Lore of France,' in the 'Folk-Lore Record' for 1878 (published by the Folk-Lore Society) Mr. A. Lang says : 'So widespread is this superstition, that a friend of mine declares he has met with it among the savages of New Caledonia, and has known a native who actually died, as he himself said he would, after meeting one of the fairy women of the wild wood.'

[2] Gruffydd ab yr Ynad Coch.

To that eminent nonconformist preacher, Vavasor Powell, the devil once appeared in shape like a house. 'Satan . . . appeared several times, and in several wayes, to me : as once like a house, stood directly in my way, with which sight I fell on my face as dead. . . . Another time, being alone in my chamber . . . I perceived a strong cold wind to blow . . . it made the hair of my flesh to stand up, and caused all my bones to shake ; and on the suddain, I heard one walk about me, tramping upon the chamber floor, as if it had been some heavie big man . . . but it proved in the end to be no other than . . . Satan.'[1]

A black calf, which haunted a Pembrokeshire brook early in the present century, was believed to be the devil in familiar guise. It appeared at a certain spot near the village of Narberth—a village which has figured actively in mythic story since the earliest ages of which there is any record. One night two peasants caught the terrible calf and took it home, locking it up safely in a stable with some other cattle, but it had vanished when morning came.

Henry Llewelyn, of Ystrad Defoc parish, Glamorganshire, was beset by the devil in the shape of a round bowl. He had been sent by his minister (Methodist) to fetch from another parish a load of religious books—Bibles, Testaments, Watts' 'Psalms, Hymns and Songs for Children'—and was coming home with the same, on horseback, by night, when he saw a living thing, round like a bowl, moving to and fro across the lane. The bold Llewelyn

---

[1] 'The Life and Death of Mr. Vavasor Powell,' p. 8. (A curious seventeenth century book, no two existing copies of which appear to be alike. I here cite from that in the library of the Marquis of Bute, than which a more perfect copy is rarely met with.)

having concluded it was the devil, resolved to speak to it. 'What seekest thou, thou foul thing?' he demanded, adding, 'In the name of the Lord Jesus go away!' And to prove that it was the adversary, at these words it vanished into the ground, leaving a sulphurous smell behind.

To William Jones, a sabbath-breaker, of Risca village, the devil appeared as an enormous mastiff dog, which transformed itself into a great fire and made a roaring noise like burning gorse. And to two men at Merthyr Tydfil, in Glamorganshire, the fiend appeared in the shape of a gosling. These men were one night drinking together at the Black Lion Inn, when one dared the other to go to conjure. The challenge was accepted, and they went, but conducted their emprise with such drunken recklessness, that the devil put out the eyes of one of them, so that he was blind the rest of his days.

VI.

The mode of summoning and of exorcising familiar spirits—in other words, of laying and raising the devil—varies little the world over. Even in China, the magic circle is entered and incantations are muttered when the fiend is summoned; and for the exorcism of devils there are laws like our own—though since modern Christianity has been introduced in China the most popular exorcist is the Christian missionary.[1] In Wales, the popular belief is compounded of about equal parts of foul magic and fair Biblical text; magic chiefly for summoning, the Book for exorcising.

John Jenkin, a schoolmaster in Pembrokeshire, was a conjuror of renown in that part of Wales. One of his scholars who had a curiosity to see the

[1] Dennys, 'Folk-Lore of China,' 89.

devil made bold to ask the master to assist him to that entertainment. 'May see him.' said the master, 'if thou hast the courage for it. Still,' he added, 'I do not choose to call him till I have employment for him.' So the boy waited; and not long after a man came to the master saying he had lost some money, and wished to be told who had stolen it. 'Now,' the master said to the scholar, 'I have some business for him.' At night they went into the wood together and drew a circle, which they entered, and the schoolmaster called one of the spirits of evil by its name. Presently they saw a light in the sky, which shot like lightning down to the circle, and turned round about it. The conjuror asked it who had stolen the man's money; the spirit did not know, and it disappeared. Then the schoolmaster called another evil spirit by its name; and presently they saw the resemblance of a bull flying through the air towards them, so swiftly and fiercely as if it would go through them; and it also turned about the circle. But the conjuror asked it in vain who had the stolen money. 'I must call still another,' said he. The schoolboy was now almost dead with fear, and the conjuror considerately waited till he was somewhat revived before calling the third spirit. But when he did call, there came out of the wood a spirit dressed in white, and went about the circle. 'Ah,' said the schoolmaster, 'we shall now hear something from this.' And sure enough 'this' told the conjuror (in a language the boy could not understand) where the money was, and all about it. Then it vanished in red fire; and that boy 'has never been well since, the effect of the great fright still cleaving to him.'

Not far from Glanbran, in Carmarthenshire, lived

a tailor, who added to his trade as a breeches-mender the loftier, if wickeder, employments of a worker in magic. A certain Mr. Gwynne, living at Glanbran, took it upon himself to ridicule this terrible tailor, for the tailor was a little man, and Mr. Gwynne was a burly six-footer, who feared nobody. 'Thou have the courage to look upon the devil!' sneered Gwynne; 'canst thou show him to me?' 'That I can,' said the tailor, his eyes flashing angrily; 'but you are not able to look at him.' 'What!' roared Gwynne, 'thou able to look at him, and not I?' 'Very well,' quoth the tailor; if you are able to look at him I will show him to you.' It was in the day time, but the tailor went immediately into a little grove of wood in a field hard by, and made a circle in the usual manner. In a short time he returned to fetch the incredulous Mr. Gwynne, saying, 'Come with me and you shall see him.' The two then crossed the field until they came to the stile by the wood, when suddenly the tailor cried, 'Look yonder! there it is!' And looking, Mr. Gwynne saw, in the circle the tailor had drawn, 'one of the fallen angels, now become a devil.' It was so horrible a sight that the terrified Mr. Gwynne was never after able to describe it; but from that time forth he had a proper respect for the tailor.

CHAPTER VI.

The Evil Spirit in his customary Form—The stupid Medieval Devil in Wales—Sion Cent—The Devil outwitted—Pacts with the Fiend and their Avoidance — Sion Dafydd's Foul Pipe — The Devil's Bridge and its Legends—Similar Legends in other Lands—The Devil's Pulpit near Tintern—Angelic Spirits—Welsh Superstitions as to pronouncing the Name of the Evil Spirit—The Bardic Tradition of the Creation — The Struggle between Light and Darkness and its Symbolization.

I.

THE devil has often appeared in Wales in his customary form, or with his distinctive marks covered up by such clothing as mortals wear. There was even a tailor in Cardiganshire who had the honour of making a suit of clothes for his sulphuric majesty. The medieval view of this malignant spirit—which makes the devil out as dull and stupid as he is mendacious and spiteful—still lingers in some parts. Those formal pacts with the devil, the first traces of which are found in the twelfth and thirteenth centuries, have been made in great numbers in Wales; and tales in which the devil is outwitted by a mortal are still preserved with much distinctness in various localities. That the myth of Polyphemus reappears in all accounts of this sort, is pretty well agreed among students of folk-lore. Hercules and Cacus, Polyphemus and Odysseus, Peredur and the one-eyed monster of the Mabinogion, Gambrinus and der Teufel, Jack the Giant-Killer, Norse Jötuns and Arabian genii tricked and bottled; all these are deemed outgrowths of the same primeval idea, to wit, the victory of the sun-god over the night-fiend;

and the story of Sion Cent's compact with the diawl
is doubtless from the same root. Certain it is that
were not the devil at times gullible, he never would
have been so useful as a familiar spirit, never could
have been made so completely a slave to his mortal
masters. The Pope (Benedict IX.) who had seven
evil spirits in a sugar-bottle, merely subdivided the
arch-fiend in the same way the genii of the old
tales are subdivided—now existing as a dense and
visible form, again expanding to blot out the sky,
and again entering the narrow compass of a bottle
or a nut-shell; co-existing in a million places at the
same instant, yet having a single individuality.

II.

Tradition relates that Sion Cent was a famous
necromancer in Monmouthshire, who outwitted the
devil, not once but many times. He lives in popular
legend simply as a worker in magic, but in reality
he was a worthy minister, the Rev. John Kent, who
flourished from 1420 to 1470, and wrote several
theological works in Latin. In his native Welsh he
confined himself to poetry, and Sion Cent was his
Cymric pseudonym. Like many learned men in
those days, he was accredited with magical powers
by the ignorant peasantry, and of his transactions
with the devil many stories were then invented
which still survive. One relates that he once served
as a farmer's boy, and was set to keep the crows
from the corn, but preferring to go to Grosmont
fair, he confined the crows in an old roofless barn
by a magic spell till the next day, when he returned.
His compact with the devil enabled him to build the
bridge over the Monnow, near Grosmont, which still
bears his name. The compact gave the devil the
man's soul, as all such compacts do—the stipulation

being that if his body were buried either in or out of the church, his soul should be forfeit to the diawl. But the shrewd Welshman gave orders that he should be buried exactly under the chancel wall, so that he should lie neither in the church nor out of it; and the devil was made a fool of by this device. A precisely similar tradition exists concerning an old gentleman in Carmarthenshire.

III.

A popular legend giving the origin of the jack-o'-lantern in Wales deals with the idea of a stupid devil: A long time ago there lived on the hills of Arfon an old man of the name of Sion Dafydd, who used to converse much with one of the children of the bottomless pit. One morning Sion was on his way to Llanfair-Fechan, carrying a flail on his shoulder, for he had corn there, when whom should he meet but his old friend from the pit, with a bag on his back, and in it two little devils like himself. After conversing for some time they began to quarrel, and presently were in the midst of a terrible fight. Sion fell to basting the devils with his flail, until the bag containing the two little ones went all to pieces, and the two tumbling out, fled for their lives to Rhiwgyfylchi, which village is considered to this day a very wicked place from this fact. Sion then went his way rejoicing, and did not for a long time encounter his adversary. Eventually, however, they met, and this time Sion had his gun on his shoulder. 'What's that long thing you're carrying?' inquired the devil. 'That's my pipe,' said Sion. Then the devil asked, 'Shall I have a whiff out of it?' 'You shall,' was Sion's reply, and he placed the mouth of his gun in the devil's throat and drew the trigger. Well; that was the loudest report from a gun that was ever heard on this earth. 'Ach!—tw!—tw!' exclaimed the smoker, 'your pipe is very foul,' and he disappeared in a flame. After a lapse of time, Sion met him again in the guise of a gentleman, but the Welshman knew it was the tempter. This time he made a bargain for which he was ever afterwards sorry, i.e., he sold himself to the devil for a sum down, but with the understanding that whenever he could cling to something the devil should not then control him. One day when Sion was busily gardening, the evil one snatched him away into the air without warning, and Sion was about giving up all hopes of again returning to earth, when he thought to himself, 'I'll ask the devil one last favour.' The stupid devil listened. 'All I want is an apple,' said Sion, 'to moisten my lips a bit down below; let me go to the top of my apple-tree, and I'll pick one.' 'Is that all?' quoth the diawl, and consented. Of course Sion laid hold of the apple-tree, and hung on. The devil had to leave him there. But the old reprobate was too wicked for heaven, and the devil having failed to take him to the other place, he was turned into a fairy, and is now the jack-o'-lantern.[1]

IV.

Best known among the natural objects in various parts of Wales which are connected with the devil in popular lore, is the Devil's Bridge, in Cardiganshire. Associated with this bridge are several legends, which derive their greatest interest from their intrinsic evidences of an antiquity in common with the same legends in other lands. The guide-books of the region, like guide-books everywhere, in their effort to avoid being led into unwarranted

[1] 'Cymru Fu,' 355 et seq.

statement, usually indulge in playfully sarcastic references to these ancient tales. They are much older,
however, than the bridge itself can possibly be. The
devil's activity in bridge-building is a myth more
ancient than the medieval devil of our acquaintance.
The building story of the Devil's Bridge in Cardiganshire runs briefly thus: An old woman who had lost
her cow spied it on the other side of the ravine, and
was in great trouble about it, not knowing how to
get over where the animal was. The devil, taking
advantage of her distress, offered to throw a bridge
over the ravine, so that she might cross and get her
cow; but he stipulated that the first living creature
to cross the bridge should be his. The old woman
agreed; the bridge was built; and the devil waited
to see her cross. She drew a crust of bread from
her pocket, threw it over, and her little black dog
flew after it. 'The dog's yours, sir,' said the dame;
and Satan was discomfited. In the story told of the
old bridge over the Main at Frankfort, a bridge-
contractor and his troubles are substituted for the
old woman and her cow; instead of a black dog
a live rooster appears, driven in front of him by
the contractor. The Welsh Satan seems to have
received his discomfiture good-naturedly enough; in
the German tale he tears the fowl to pieces in his
rage. In Switzerland, every reader knows the story
told of the devil's bridge in the St. Gothard pass.
A new bridge has taken the place, for public use, of
the old bridge on the road to Andermatt, and to the
dangers of the crumbling masonry are added superstitious terrors concerning the devil's power to catch
any one crossing after dark. The old Welsh bridge
has been in like manner superseded by a modern
structure; but I think no superstition like the last
noted is found at Hafod.

V.

The English have a saying that the devil lives in the middle of Wales. There is in every part of Wales that I have seen a custom of whitening the doorsteps with chalk, and it is said to have originated in the belief that his Satanic majesty could not enter a door thus protected. The devil of slovenliness certainly would find difficulty in entering a Welsh cottage if the tidiness of its doorstep is borne out in the interior. But out-of-doors everywhere there are signs of the devil's active habits. His flowers grow on the river-banks; his toes are imprinted on the rocks. Near Tintern Abbey there is a jutting crag overhung by gloomy branches of the yew, called the Devil's Pulpit. His eminence used in other and wickeder days to preach atrocious morals, or immorals, to the white-robed Cistercian monks of the abbey, from this rocky pulpit. One day the devil grew bold, and taking his tail under his arm in an easy and *dégagée* manner, hobnobbed familiarly with the monks, and finally proposed, just for a lark, that he should preach them a nice red-hot sermon from the rood-loft of the abbey. To this the monks agreed, and the devil came to church in high glee. But fancy his profane perturbation (I had nearly written holy horror) when the treacherous Cistercians proceeded to shower him with holy water. The devil clapped his tail between his legs and scampered off howling, and never stopped till he got to Llandogo, where he leaped across the river into England, leaving the prints of his talons on a stone.

VI.

Where accounts of the devil's appearance are so numerous, it is perhaps somewhat surprising so little is heard of apparitions of angels.   There are reasons for this, however, which might be enlarged upon. Tradition says that 'in former times' there were frequent visits of angels to Wales; and their rare appearance in our days is ascribed to the completion of revelation.   One or two modern instances of angelic visitation are given by the Prophet Jones. There was David Thomas, who lived at a place called the Pantau, between the towns of Carmarthen and Laugharne; he was 'a gifted brother, who sometimes preached,' in the dissenting way.   One night, when he was at prayer alone in a room which stood apart from his house, there was suddenly a great light present, which made the light of the candle no longer visible.   And in that light appeared a band of angels, like children, very beautiful in bright clothing, singing in Welsh these words :

> Pa hyd?   Pa hyd?   Dychwelwch feibion Adda !
> Pa hyd?   Pa hyd yr erlidiwch y Cristnogion duwiol?
>
> How long?   How long?   Return ye sons of Adam !
> How long?   How long will ye persecute the godly Christians?

After a time they departed; reappeared; departed again; the great light faded; and the light of Mr. Thomas's candle was once more visible on his table. There was also Rees David, a man of more than common piety, who lived in Carmarthenshire, near Whitlands.   At the time of his death, it was testified by 'several religious persons who were in the room,' that there was heard, by them and by the dying man, the singing of angels.   It drew nearer and nearer as his death-struggle grew imminent, and after his death they 'heard the pleasant incomparable singing gradually depart, until it was out of hearing.'

That the dying do see something more, in the last moment of expiring nature, than it is given to living eyes to see, is a cherished belief by numberless Christian men and women, whom to suspect of superstitious credulity were to grossly offend. This belief is based on exclamations uttered by the dying, while with fixed and staring eyes they appeared to gaze intently at some object not visible to the by-standers. But that the bystanders also saw, or heard, voice or vision from the Unknown, is not often pretended.

VII.

Reference has been made to the euphemisms in use among all peoples to avoid pronouncing the name of the devil. That many good folk still consider the word devil, lightly spoken, a profane utterance only second to a similar utterance of God's name, is a curious survival of old superstitions. No prohibition of this sort attaches to the words demon, fiend, etc., nor to such euphemisms, common in both Welsh and English, as the adversary, the evil one, etc. It is an old custom in North Wales to spit at the name of the devil, even when so innocently used as in pronouncing the name of the Devil's Bridge. The peasantry prefer to call the bridge ' Pont y Gwr Drwg,' the Bridge of the Wicked One ; and spitting and wiping off the tongue are deemed a necessary precaution after saying devil, diafol, or diawl. The phrase ' I hope to goodness,' so common in Wales and elsewhere, is clearly but another euphemism for God ; the goodness meant is the Divine beneficence. ' Goodness' sake ' is but a contraction of ' For God's sake !' The Hebrew tetragrammaton which was invested with such terror, as representing the great ' I am,' finds an explanation, according to the ideas of Welsh scholars, in the Bardic traditions. These relate that, by the utterance of His Name, God created this world ; the Name being represented by the symbol /|\, three lines which typify the focusing of the rising sun's rays at the equinoxes and solstices. The first ray is the Creator, the second the Preserver, and the third the Destroyer; the whole are God's Name. This name cannot be uttered by a mortal; he has not the power; therefore it remains for ever unuttered on earth. At the creation the universe uttered it in joy at the new-born world; 'the morning stars sang together.' At the last day it will be uttered again. Till then it is kept a secret, lest it be degraded, as it has been by the Hindus, who, from the three rays created their three false gods, Brahma, Vishnu, and Siva. Tradition relates that Einigan Gawr saw the Divine Name appear, and inscribed it on three rods of mountain ash. The people mistook the three rods thus inscribed for God himself, and Einigan died from grief at their error.[1]

VIII.

The devil with which we are acquainted is a character unknown to Greek or Roman mythology; this devil was a later invention; but his identity with the genii, or jinns of the 'Arabian Nights,' the Dïvs of Persian history, is clear enough. Ahriman, the evil spirit, king of the realms of darkness and of fire, was apparently the progenitor of Satan, as Vritra was of Ahriman. Both these ancient arch-fiends appeared as serpents in form, and were myths representing the darkness, slain by the light, or the sun-god, in the one case called Indra, in the other Ormuzd. The medieval devil with horns and hoofs does not appear in the records of Judaism. He is an outgrowth of the moral principle of the Christian era; and traced to his origins he is simply a

[1] 'Dosparth Edeyrn Dafod Aur,' 3.

personification of the adversary in the never-ending struggle on earth between light and darkness. That struggle is not, in nature, a moral one ; but it remains to-day, as it was in the beginning, the best type we have of the battle between right and wrong, and between truth and error. When God said, ' Let there be light,' the utterance became the symbol and guide of virtue, of brave endeavour, and of scientific research, until the end.

CHAPTER VII.

Cambrian Death-Portents—The Corpse-Bird—The Tan-Wedd—List-
ening at the Church-Door—The Lledrith—The Gwrach y Rhibyn—
The Llandaff Gwrach—Ugliness of this Female Apparition—The
Black Maiden—The Cyhyraeth, or Crying Spirit—Its Moans on
Land and Sea—The St. Mellons Cyhyraeth—The Groaning Spirit
of Bedwellty.

I.

THERE are death portents in every country, and in
endless variety; in Wales these portents assume
distinct and striking individualities, in great number
and with clearly defined attributes. The banshee,
according to Mr. Baring-Gould, has no corresponding feature in Scandinavian, Teutonic, or classic
mythology, and belongs entirely to the Celts. The
Welsh have the banshee in its most blood-curdling
form under the name of the Gwrach y Rhibyn;
they have also the Cyhyraeth, which is never seen,
but is heard, moaning dolefully and dreadfully in
the night; the Tolaeth, also only heard, not groaning
but imitating some earthly sound, such as sawing,
singing, or the tramping of feet; the Cwn Annwn
and Cwn y Wybr, Dogs of Hell and Dogs of the
Sky; the Canwyll Corph, or Corpse Candle; the
Teulu, or Goblin Funeral, and many others—all of
them death-portents. These, as the more important
and striking, I will describe further; but there are
several others which must first be mentioned.

The Aderyn y Corph is a bird which chirps at the
door of the person who is about to die, and makes
a noise that sounds like the Welsh word for

'Come! come!' the summons to death.[1] In ancient tradition, it had no feathers nor wings, soaring without support high in the heavens, and, when not engaged upon some earthly message, dwelling in the land of illusion and phantasy.[2] This corpse-bird may properly be associated with the superstition regarding the screech-owl, whose cry near a sick-bed inevitably portends death. The untimely crowing of a cock also foretells the sudden demise of some member of the family. In North Wales the cry of the golden plover is a death-omen; these birds are called, in this connection, the whistlers.[3] The same superstition prevails in Warwickshire, and the sound is called the seven whistlers.

Thunder and lightning in mid-winter announce the death of the great man of the parish. This superstition is thought to be peculiar to Wales, or to the wilder and more secluded parts of North Wales.[4] Also deemed peculiar to Wales is the Tan-wedd, a fiery apparition which falls on the lands of a freeholder who is about to die. It is described as appearing somewhat similar to falling stars, but slower of motion. 'It lighteneth all the air and ground where it passeth,' says 'the honest Welshman, Mr. Davis, in a letter to Mr. Baxter,' adding, 'lasteth three or four miles or more, for aught is known, because no man seeth the rising or beginning of it; and when it falls to the ground it sparkleth and lighteth all about.'[5] It also comes as a duty-performing goblin, after a death, haunting the graveyard, and calling attention to some special grave by its conduct, as in the following account: Walter Watkins, of the Neuadd, in a parish of

---

[1] 'Dewch! dewch!' [2] 'Cymru Fu,' 299.
[3] 'Camb. Quarterly,' iv., 487. [4] 'Arch. Camb.' 4th Se., iii., 333.
[5] Brand, 'Pop. Ant.' iii., 127.

Brecknockshire, was going one dark night towards Taf Fechan Chapel, not far from his house, when he saw a light near the chapel. It increased till it was as big as a church tower, and decreased again till it was as small as a star; then enlarged again and decreased as before; and this it did several times. He went to his house and fetched his father and mother to see it, and they all saw it plainly, much to their astonishment and wonder. Some time after, as a neighbour was ploughing in a field near the chapel, about where the mysterious light had been seen, the plough struck against a large flat stone. This the ploughman raised up, after a deal of difficulty, and under it he found a stone chest, in which was the jawbone of a man, and nought else except an earthen jug. The bone was supposed to be the remains of a man who had disappeared long before, and whose wife had since married; and on her being told of it, she fell ill and died. The light, which had often been seen before by various persons, was after this seen no more. It was believed to be the spirit of the murdered man, appearing as a light.

Listening at the church-door in the dark, to hear shouted by a ghostly voice in the deserted edifice the names of those who are shortly to be buried in the adjoining churchyard, is a Hallow E'en custom in some parts of Wales. In other parts, the window serves the same purpose. There are said to be still extant, outside some village churches, steps which were constructed in order to enable the superstitious peasantry to climb to the window to listen. The principle of 'expectant attention,' so well known to physiological science, would be likely in this case to act with special force as a ghost-raiser. In an ancient MS. by Llywelyn Sion, of Llangewydd, there is mention of a frightful monster called the Fad Felen, which was seen through the key-hole of Rhos church by Maelgwn Gwynedd, who 'died in consequence.' This monster was predicted in a poem by Taliesin, as a 'strange creature' which should come from the sea marsh, with hair and teeth and eyes like gold. The yellow fever plague, which raged in Wales during some five years in the sixth century, is the monster referred to in this legend.

The Scotch wraith and Irish fetch have their parallel in Wales in the Lledrith, or spectre of a person seen before his death; it never speaks, and vanishes if spoken to. It has been seen by miners previous to a fatal accident in the mine. The story is told of a miner who saw himself lying dead and horribly maimed in a phantom tram-car, led by a phantom horse, and surrounded by phantom miners. As he watched this dreadful group of spectres they passed on, looking neither to the right nor the left, and faded away. The miner's dog was as frightened as its master at the sight, and ran howling into the darkness. Though deeming himself doomed, the miner continued to work in the pit; and as the days passed on, and no harm came to him, he grew more cheerful, and was so bold as to laugh at the superstition. The day he did this, a stone fell from the roof and broke his arm. As soon as he recovered he resumed work in the pit; his death followed instantly. A stone crushed him, and he was borne maimed and dead in the tram along the road where his lledrith had appeared, 'a mile below the play of sunshine and wave of trees.'[1]

The Mallt y Nos, or night-fiend, is a death-omen

[1] 'Tales and Sketches of Wales,' in 'Weekly Mail.'

mentioned by Rev. D. R. Thomas in the 'Archæo-logia Cambrensis'; and Croker[1] gives as the Welsh parallel of the Irish death-coach a spectre called ceffyl heb un pen, or the headless horse. The marw coel, or 'yellow spot before death,' is another death-omen which I have been able to trace no further than the pages where I find it.[2]

II.

A frightful figure among Welsh apparitions is the Gwrach y Rhibyn, whose crowning distinction is its prodigious ugliness. The feminine pronoun is generally used in speaking of this goblin, which unlike the majority of its kind, is supposed to be a female. A Welsh saying, regarding one of her sex who is the reverse of lovely, is, ' Y mae mor salw a Gwrach y Rhibyn,' (She is as ugly as the Gwrach y Rhibyn.) The spectre is a hideous being with dishevelled hair, long black teeth, long, lank, withered arms, leathern wings, and a cadaverous appearance. In the stillness of night it comes and flaps its wings against the window, uttering at the same time a blood-curdling howl, and calling by name on the person who is to die, in a lengthened dying tone, as thus : ' Da-a-a-vy !' ' De-i-i-o-o-o ba-a-a-ch !' The effect of its shriek or howl is in-describably terrific, and its sight blasting to the eyes of the beholder. It is always an omen of death, though its warning cry is heard under vary-ing circumstances ; sometimes it appears in the mist on the mountain side, or at cross-roads, or by a piece of water which it splashes with its hands. The gender of apparitions is no doubt as a rule the neuter, but the Gwrach y Rhibyn defies all rules

---

[1] 'Fairy Legends of the South of Ireland,' 341.
[2] 'The Vale of Glamorgan.'

by being a female which at times sees fit to be a male. In its female character it has a trick of crying at intervals, in a most doleful tone, 'Oh! oh! fy ngwr, fy ngwr!' (my husband! my husband!) But when it chooses to be a male, this cry is changed to 'Fy ngwraig! fy ngwraig!' (my wife! my wife!) or 'Fy mlentyn, fy mlentyn bach!' (my child, my little child!) There is a frightful story of a dissipated peasant who met this goblin on the road one night, and thought it was a living woman; he therefore made wicked and improper overtures to it, with the result of having his soul nearly frightened out of his body in the horror of discovering his mistake. As he emphatically exclaimed, 'Och, Dduw! it was the Gwrach y Rhibyn, and not a woman at all.'

III.

The Gwrach y Rhibyn recently appeared, according to an account given me by a person who claimed to have seen it, at Llandaff. Surely, no more probable site for the appearance of a spectre so ancient of lineage could be found, than that ancient cathedral city where some say was the earliest Christian fane in Great Britain, and which was certainly the seat of the earliest Christian bishopric. My narrator was a respectable-looking man of the peasant-farmer class, whom I met in one of my walks near Cardiff, in the summer of 1878. 'It was at Llandaff,' he said to me, 'on the fourteenth of last November, when I was on a visit to an old friend, that I saw and heard the Gwrach y Rhibyn. I was sleeping in my bed, and was woke at midnight by a frightful screeching and a shaking of my window. It was a loud and clear screech, and the shaking of the window was very plain, but it seemed to go by like the wind. I was not so much frightened, sir, as you may think; excited I was—that's the word—excited; and I jumped out of bed and rushed to the window and flung it open. Then I saw the Gwrach y Rhibyn, saw her plainly, sir, a horrible old woman with long red hair and a face like chalk, and great teeth like tusks, looking back over her shoulder at me as she went through the air with a long black gown trailing along the ground below her arms, for body I could make out none. She gave another unearthly screech while I looked at her; then I heard her flapping her wings against the window of a house just below the one I was in, and she vanished from my sight. But I kept on staring into the darkness, and as I am a living man, sir, I saw her go in at the door of the Cow and Snuffers Inn, and return no more. I watched the door of the inn a long time, but she did not come out. The next day, it's the honest truth I'm telling you, they told me the man who kept the Cow and Snuffers Inn was dead—had died in the night. His name was Llewellyn, sir—you can ask any one about him, at Llandaff—he had kept the inn there for seventy years, and his family before him for three hundred years, just at that very spot. It's not these new families that the Gwrach y Rhibyn ever troubles, sir, it's the old stock.'

IV.

The close resemblance of this goblin to the Irish banshee (or benshi) will be at once perceived. The same superstition is found among other peoples of Celtic origin. Sir Walter Scott mentions it among the highlands of Scotland.[1] It is not traced among other than Celtic peoples distinctly, but its associa-

[1] 'Demonology and Witchcraft,' 351.

tion with the primeval mythology is doubtless to be found in the same direction with many other death-omens, to wit, the path of the wind-god Hermes.

The frightful ugliness of the Gwrach y Rhibyn is a consistent feature of the superstition, in both its forms; it recalls the Black Maiden who came to Caerleon and liberated Peredur:[1] 'Blacker were her face and her two hands than the blackest' iron covered with pitch; and her hue was not more frightful than her form. High cheeks had she, and a face lengthened downwards, and a short nose with distended nostrils. And one eye was of a piercing mottled gray,· and the other was as black as jet, deep-sunk in her head. And her teeth were long and yellow, more yellow were they than the flower of the broom. And her stomach rose from the breast-bone, higher than her chin. And her back was in the shape of a crook, and her legs were large and bony. And her figure was very thin and spare, except her feet and legs, which were of huge size.' The Welsh word 'gwrach' means a hag or witch, and it has been fancied that there is a connection between this word and the mythical Avagddu,[2] whose wife the gwrach was.

The Gwrach y Rhibyn appears also as a river-spectre, in Glamorganshire.

V.

A death-portent which is often confused with the Gwrach y Rhibyn, yet which is rendered quite distinct by its special attributes, is the 'Cyhyraeth. This is a groaning spirit. It is never seen, but the noise it makes is no less terrible to the ear than the

---

[1] 'Mabinogion,' 114.
[2] Avagddu means both hell and the devil, as our word Heaven means both the Deity and his abode.

appearance of its visible sister is to the eye. Among groaning spirits it is considered to be the chief. The Prophet Jones succinctly characterises it as 'a doleful, dreadful noise in the night, before a burying.' David Prosser, of Llanybyther parish, 'a sober, sensible man and careful to tell the truth,' once heard the Cyhyraeth in the early part of the night, his wife and maid-servant being together in the house, and also hearing it; and when it came opposite the window, it 'pronounced these strange words, of no signification that we know of,' viz. '*Woolach! Woolach!*' Some time afterward a funeral passed that way. The judicious Joshua Coslet, who lived by the river Towy in Carmarthenshire, testified that the Cyhyraeth is often heard there, and that it is 'a doleful, disagreeable sound heard before the deaths of many, and most apt to be heard before foul weather. The voice resembles the groaning of sick persons who are to die; heard at first at a distance, then comes nearer, and the last near at hand; so that it is a threefold warning of death. It begins strong, and louder than a sick man can make; the second cry is lower, but not less doleful, but rather more so; the third yet lower, and soft, like the groaning of a sick man almost spent and dying.' A person 'well remembering the voice' and coming to the sick man's bed, 'shall hear his groans exactly like' those which he had before heard from the Cyhyraeth. This crying spirit especially affected the twelve parishes in the hundred of Inis Cenin, which lie on the south-east side of the river Towy, 'where some time past it groaned before the death of every person who lived that side of the country.' It also sounded before the death of persons 'who were born in these parishes, but died elsewhere.' Sometimes the voice is heard long before death, but not longer than three quarters of a year. So common was it in the district named, that among the people there a familiar form of reproach to any one making a disagreeable noise, or 'children crying or groaning unreasonable,' was to ejaculate, 'Oh 'r Cyhyraeth!' A reason why the Cyhyraeth was more often heard in the hundred of Inis Cenin was thought to be that Non, the mother of St. David, lived in those parts, where a village is called after her name, Llan-non, the church of Non.

On the southern sea-coast, in Glamorganshire, the Cyhyraeth is sometimes heard by the people in the villages on shore passing down the channel with loud moans, while those dismal lights which forebode a wreck are seen playing along the waves. Watchers by the sea-shore have also heard its moan far out on the ocean, gradually drawing nearer and nearer, and then dying away; and when they thought it gone it has suddenly shrieked close to their startled ears, chilling their very marrows. Then, long after, they would hear it, now faint, now loud, going along the sands into the distant darkness. One or more corpses were usually washed ashore soon after. In the villages the Cyhyraeth is heard passing through the empty streets and lanes by night, groaning dismally, sometimes rattling the window-shutters, or flinging open the door as it flits by. When going along the country lanes it will thus horrify the inmates of every house it passes. Some old people say it is only heard before the death of such as are of strayed mind, or who have long been ill; but it always comes when an epidemic is about to visit the neighbourhood.

A tradition of the Cyhyraeth is connected with the parish churchyard at St. Mellons, a quaint old-

fashioned village within easy tramping distance of
Cardiff, but in Monmouthshire.   It is of a boy who
was sent on an errand, and who heard the Cyhyraeth
crying in the churchyard, first in one place, then in
another, and finally in a third place, where it rested.
Some time after, a corpse was brought to that
churchyard to be buried, but some person came and
claimed the grave.   They went to another place,
but that also was claimed.   Then they went to
a third place, and there they were allowed to bury
their dead in peace.   And this going about with the
corpse was 'just the same as the boy declared it.'
Of course the boy could not know what was to
come to pass, 'but this crying spirit knew exactly
what would come to pass.'   I was also told by a
person at St. Mellons that a ghost had been seen
sitting upon the old stone cross which stands on the
hillside near the church.

VI.

Other groaning spirits are sometimes heard.   A
girl named Mary Morgan, living near Crumlyn
Bridge, while standing on the bridge one evening
was seized with mortal terror on hearing a groaning
voice going up the river, uttering the words, 'O
Dduw, beth a wnaf fi?' (O God, what shall I do?)
many times repeated, amid direful groans.   The
conclusion of this narration is a hopeless mystery,
as Mary fainted away with her fright.

Much more satisfactory, as a ghost-story with a
moral, is the tale of the groaning spirit of Bedwellty.[1]
There was one night a wake at the house of
Meredith Thomas, over the body of his four-year-
old child, at which two profane men (named Thomas
Edward Morgan and Anthony Aaron) began playing

[1] Jones, 'Apparitions,' 24.

at cards, and swearing most horribly. In the parish of Bedwellty, the wakes—or watch-nights, as they are more commonly called in Wales—were at that time very profanely kept. 'Few besides the dissenters,' says Jones (who was himself a dissenter, it must be remembered), 'had the sense and courage to forbid' this wickedness, but 'suffered it as a custom, because the pretence was to divert the relations of the dead, and lessen their sorrows.' While the aforementioned profane men were playing cards and swearing, suddenly a dismal groaning noise was heard at the window. At this the company was much frightened, excepting the card-players, who said 'Pw!' and went on playing. But to pacify the rest of the company they finally desisted, and at once the groaning ceased. Soon after they began playing again, when at once the groaning set up in most lamentable tones, so that people shuddered; but the profane men again said, 'Pw! it is some fellow playing tricks to frighten us.' 'No,' said William Harry Rees, a good man of the Baptist persuasion, 'it is no human being there groaning, but a spirit,' and again he desired them to give over. But though they were so bold with their card-playing, these wicked men had not the hardihood to venture out and see who it was 'playing tricks,' as they called it. However, one of the company said, 'I will go, and take the dogs with me, and see if there be any human being there.' The groaning still continued. This bold person then 'took the prime staff, and began to call the dogs to go with him;' but the dogs could not be induced to go out, being in great terror at the groaning noise, and sought to hide themselves under the stools, and about the people's feet. In vain they beat the dogs, and kicked and scolded them, outdoor they would not go. This at last convinced the profane men, and they left off playing, for fear the devil should come among them. For it was told in other places that people had played cards till his sulphurous majesty appeared in person.

CHAPTER VIII.

I.

THE Tolaeth is an ominous sound, imitating some
earthly sound of one sort or another, and always
heard before either a funeral or some dreadful
catastrophe. Carpenters of a superstitious turn of
mind will tell you that they invariably hear the
Tolaeth when they are going to receive an order to
make a coffin ; in this case the sound is that of the
sawing of wood, the hammering of nails, and the
turning of screws, such as are heard in the usual
process of making a coffin. This is called the
' Tolaeth before the Coffin.' The ' Tolaeth before
Death ' is a supernatural noise heard about the
house, such as a knocking, or the sound of footsteps
in the dead of night. Sometimes it is the sound of
a tolling bell, where no bell is ; and the direction
in which the ear is held at the time points out the
place of the coming death. Formerly the veritable
church-bell in its steeple would foretell death, by
tolling thrice at the hour of midnight, unrung by
human hands. The bell of Blaenporth, Cardiganshire, was noted for thus warning the neighbours.
The ' Tolaeth before the Burying ' is the sound of
the funeral procession passing by, unseen, but heard.

The voices are heard singing the 'Old Hundredth,' which is the psalm tune usually sung by funeral bands; the slow regular tramp of the feet is heard, and the sobbing and groaning of the mourners. The Tolaeth touches but one sense at a time. When this funeral procession is heard it cannot be seen. But it is a peculiarity of the Tolaeth that after it has been heard by the ear, it sometimes makes itself known to the eye also—but in silence. The funeral procession will at first be heard, and then if the hearer stoop forward and look along the ground, it may perhaps be seen; the psalm-singers, two abreast, with their hats off and their mouths open, as in the act of singing; the coffin, borne on the shoulders of four men who hold their hats by the side of their heads; the mourners, the men with long black hatbands streaming behind, the women pale and sorrowful, with upheld handkerchiefs; and the rest of the procession stretching away dimly into shadow. Not a sound is heard, either of foot or voice, although the singers' mouths are open. After the procession has passed, and the observer has risen from his stooping posture, the Tolaeth again breaks on the ear, the music, the tread of feet, and the sobbing, as before. A real funeral is sure to pass that way not long afterwards.

This form of the Tolaeth should not be confused with the Teulu, or Goblin Funeral proper, which is a death-warning occupying its own place.

II.

John Clode, an honest labouring man living on the coast of Glamorganshire, near the Sker Rocks, had just gone to bed one night, when he and his wife heard the door open, the tread of shuffling feet, the moving about of chairs, and the grunting of men as if setting down a load. This was all in the room where they lay, it being the only room their cottage afforded, except the one upstairs. 'John, John!' cried his wife in alarm, 'what is this?' In vain John rubbed his eyes and stared into the darkness. Nothing could he see. Two days afterward their only son was brought home drowned; and his corpse being borne into the house upon a ladder, there were the same noises of opening the door, the shuffling of feet, the moving of chairs, the setting down of the burden, that the Tolaeth had touched their ears with. 'John, John!' murmured poor Mrs. Clode; 'this is exactly what I heard in the night.' 'Yes, wife,' quoth John, 'it was the Tolaeth before Death.'

Before Ewythr Jenkin of Nash died, his daughter Gwenllian heard the Tolaeth. She had taken her old father's breeches from under his pillow to mend them (for he was very careful always to fold and put his breeches under his pillow, especially if there was a sixpence in the pocket), and just as she was about sitting down at the table on which she had thrown them, there came a loud rap on the table, which startled her very much. 'Oh, Jenny, what was that?' she asked of the servant girl; but Jenny could only stare at her mistress, more frightened than herself. Again did Gwenllian essay to sit and take the breeches in hand, when there came upon the table a double rap, much louder than the first, a rap, in fact, that made all the chairs and kettles ring. So then Gwenllian fainted away.

At a place called by its owner Llynwent, in Radnorshire, at a certain time the man of the house and his wife were gone from home. The rest of the family were sitting at supper, when three of the servants heard the sound of horses coming toward the house, and cried out, 'There, they are coming!' thinking it was their master and mistress returning home. But on going out to meet them, there was nobody near. They re-entered the house, somewhat uneasy in their minds at this strange thing, and clustered about the fire, with many expressions of wonderment. While they were so seated, 'Hark!' said one, and all listening intently, heard footsteps passing by them and going up stairs, and voices of people talking among themselves. Not long afterward three of the family fell sick and died.

III.

An instance of recent occurrence is given by a local newspaper correspondent writing from the scene of a Welsh railway accident in October, 1878. It was at Pontypridd, famous the world over for its graceful bridge, (now old and superannuated,) and renowned in Druidic story as a seat of learning. A victim of the railway accident was, a few days before the collision, 'sitting with his wife at the fireside, when he had an omen. The house was still, and they were alone, only a little servant girl being with them. Then, while so sitting and talking, they both heard a heavy footstep ascending the stairs, step by step, step by step, as that of one carrying a burden. They looked at one another, and the husband called, "Run, Mary, upstairs; some one has gone up." Mary did run, but there was no one. She was told to look in every room, and she did so, and it was put down as fancy. When the news was borne to the poor wife on Saturday night, she started up and said, "There now, that was the omen!"'[1] That his readers may not by any perversity fail to understand him as

[1] 'Western Mail,' Oct. 23, 1878.

alluding to the Tolaeth before Death, our newspaper correspondent states his creed : ' I believe in omens. I knew a lady who heard distinctly three raps at her door. Another lady was sitting with her near it too. The door was an inner door. No servant was in the house. The two ladies heard it, and yet no human hand touched that door, and at the time when the knock was heard a dear brother was dying. I know of strange things of this sort. Of voices crying the names of half-sleeping relatives when the waves were washing some one dear away to the mighty deep ; but then the world laughs at all this and the world goes on.' The correspondent is severe ; there is nothing here to laugh at.

IV.

The Tolaeth has one other form—that of a Voice which speaks, in a simple and natural manner, but very significant words. Thus Edward Lloyd, in the parish of Llangurig, was lying very ill, when the people that were with him in his chamber heard a voice near them, but could see no one ; nor could they find any one anywhere about the house, to whom the voice might belong. Soon afterwards they heard it utter, so distinctly that it seemed to be in the room where they were, these words, ' Y mae nenbren y tŷ yn craccio,' (the upper beam of the house cracketh.) Soon the Voice spoke again, saying, ' Fe dor yn y man,' (it will presently break.) And once more it spoke : ' Dyna fe yn tori,' (there it breaks.) That moment the sick man gave up the ghost.

John, the son of Watkin Elias Jones, of the parish of Mynyddyslwyn, was one day ploughing in the field, when the oxen rested, and he sent the lad who drove the oxen, to fetch something which he wanted ; and while thus alone in the field, he saw a cloud coming across the field to him. When the cloud had come to that part of the field where he was, it stopped, and shadowed the sun from him ; and out of the cloud came a Voice, which asked him which of these three diseases he would choose to die of—fever, dropsy, or consumption. Being a man who could give a plain answer to a plain question, he replied that he would rather die of consumption. The lad now returning, he sent him home with the oxen, and then, feeling inclined to sleep, lay down and slept. When he awoke he was ill, and fell by degrees into a consumption, of which he died one year from the day of this warning. He did not tell of this apparition, however, until within six weeks of his death.

V.

One of the most beautiful legends in the Iolo MSS, gives an ancient tale of the Tolaeth which may be thus condensed : A great and wealthy lord, rich in land, houses and gold, enjoying all the luxuries of life, heard a voice proclaim thrice distinctly : 'The greatest and richest man of this parish shall die to-night.' At this he was sadly troubled, for he knew that the greatest and richest man of that parish could be no other than he ; so he sent for the physician, but made ready for death. Great, however, was his joy when the night passed, the day broke, and he was yet alive. At sunrise the church bell was heard tolling, and the lord sent in haste to know who was dead. Answer came that it was an old blind beggar man, who had asked, and been refused, alms at the great man's gate. Then the lord knew the meaning of the warning voice he had heard : that very great and very rich man had been the poor beggar — his treasures and wealth in the kingdom of heaven. He took the warning wisely to heart, endowed religious houses, relieved all who were in poverty, and when at last he was dying, the voices of angels were heard to sing a hymn of welcome; and he was buried, according to his desire, in the old beggar's grave.[1]

VI.

Of the Teulu, or Goblin Funeral, a death-portent of wide prevalence in Wales, numberless stories are told. This omen is sometimes a form of the Tolaeth, but in itself constitutes an omen which is simple and explicit. A funeral procession is seen passing down the road, and at the same time it is heard. It has no shadowy goblin aspect, but appears to be a real funeral. Examination shows its shadowy nature. Subsequently a real funeral passes the same way, and is recognised as the fulfilment of the omen. The goblin funeral precedes the other sometimes by days, sometimes by weeks. Rees Thomas, a carpenter of Carmarthenshire, passing by night through Rhiw Edwst, near Capel Ywen, heard a stir as of a procession of people coming towards him, walking and speaking; and when they were close to him he felt the touch of an unseen hand upon his shoulder, and a voice saying to him, 'Rhys bach, pa fodd yr y'ch chwi?' (my dear Rees, how are you?) A month after, passing that way again, he met a funeral in that very place, and a woman of the company put her hand upon his shoulder and spoke exactly the same Welsh words to him that the invisible spirit had spoken. Rev. Howel Prosser, many years ago curate of Aberystruth, late one evening saw a

[1] Iolo MSS., 592.

funeral procession going down the church lane. Supposing it to be the funeral of a man who had recently died in the upper part of his parish, yet wondering he had not been notified of the burial, he put on his band in order to perform his office over the dead, and hastened to meet the procession. But when he came to it he saw that it was composed of strangers, whom he had never seen before. Nevertheless, he laid his hand on the bier, to help carry the corpse, when instantly the whole vanished, and he was alone; but in his hand he found the skull of a dead horse. 'Mr. Prosser was my schoolmaster, and a right honest man,' says Edmund Jones,[1] who is responsible for this story, as well as for the ensuing: Isaac William Thomas, who lived not far from Hafodafel, once met a Goblin Funeral coming down the mountain toward Llanhiddel church. He stood in a field adjoining the highway, and leaned against the stone wall. The funeral came close to the other side of the wall, and as the bier passed him he reached forth his hand and took off the black veil which was over the bier. This he carried to his home, where many people saw it. 'It was made of some exceeding fine stuff, so that when folded it was a very little substance, and very light.' That he escaped being hurt for this bold act was long the marvel of the parish; but it was believed, by their going aside to come so near him, that the goblins were willing he should do as he did.

An old man who resided near Llanllwch church, in Carmarthenshire, used to assert in the most solemn manner that he had seen the Teulu going to church again and again. On a certain evening hearing one approaching, he peeped over a wall to look at it. The persons composing the procession

[1] 'Account of the Parish of Aberystruth,' 17.

were all acquaintances of his, with the exception of one who stood apart from the rest, gazing mournfully at them, and who appeared to be a stranger. Soon afterwards there was a real burying, and the old man, determined to see if there would be in the scene any resemblance to his last Teulu, went to the churchyard and waited. When the procession arrived, all were there as he had seen them, except the stranger. Looking about him curiously, the old man was startled by the discovery that he was himself the stranger! He was standing on the identical spot where had stood the man he did not recognise when he saw the Teulu. It was his own ghost.

VII.

The death portent called Cwn Annwn, or Dogs of Hell, is a pack of hounds which howl through the air with a voice frightfully disproportionate to their size, full of a wild sort of lamentation. There is a tradition that one of them once fell on a tombstone, but no one was able to secure it. A peculiarity of these creatures is that the nearer they are to a man the less loud their voice sounds, resembling then the voice of small beagles, and the farther off they are the louder is their cry. Sometimes a voice like that of a great hound is heard sounding among them—a deep hollow voice, as if it were the voice of a monstrous bloodhound. Although terrible to hear, and certain portents of death, they are in themselves harmless. 'They have never been known,' says a most respectable authority,[1] 'to commit any mischief on the persons of either man or woman, goat, sheep, or cow.' Sometimes they are called Cwn y Wybr, or Dogs of the Sky, but the mo sulphreurous name is the favourite one. They

[1] 'Cambro-Briton,' i., 350.

are also sometimes called Dogs of the Fairies.
Their origin in fairyland is traced to the famous
mabinogi of Pwyll, Prince of Dyfed; but in that
fascinating tale of enchantment their right to be
called Cwn Annwn is clearly set forth, for they are
there the hounds of a King of Annwn. There are
several translations of this mabinogi in existence,
and its popularity in South Wales is great, for the
villages, vales, and streams mentioned in it are
familiar to residents in Pembroke, Carmarthen, and
Cardigan shires. Pwyll, the Prince, was at Narberth, where was his chief palace, when he went
one day to a wood in Glyn Cych. Here 'he
sounded his horn and began to enter upon the
chase, following his dogs and separating from his
companions. And as he was listening to the cry
of his pack, he could distinctly hear the cry of
another pack, different from that of his own, and
which was coming in an opposite direction. He
could also discern an opening in the woods towards
a level plain; and as his pack was entering the
skirt of the opening he perceived a stag before the
other pack, and about the middle of the glade the
pack in the rear coming up and throwing the stag
on the ground. Upon this he fixed his attention
on the colour of the pack, without recollecting to
look at the stag: and of all the hounds in the
world he had ever seen he never saw any like them
in colour. Their colour was a shining clear white,
with red ears; and the whiteness of the dogs and
the redness of their ears were equally conspicuous.'[1]
They were the hounds of Arawn, a crowned king
in the land of Annwn, the shadow-land of Hades.

The Cwn Annwn are sometimes held to be the
hell-hounds which hunt through the air the soul of

[1] Dr. W. Owen Pughe's Trans., 'Camb.-Briton,' ii., 271.

the wicked man, the instant it quits the body—a truly terrific idea to the vulgar mind. The Prophet Jones has several accounts of them: Thomas Phillips, of Trelech parish, heard them with the voice of the great dog sounding among them, and noticed that they followed a course that was never followed by funerals, which surprised him very much, as he had always heard that the Dogs of the Sky invariably went the same way that the corpse was to follow. Not long after a woman from an adjoining parish died at Trelech, and being carried to her own parish church to be buried, her corpse did actually pass the same way in which the spirit dogs had been heard to hunt. Thomas Andrew, of the parish of Llanhiddel, heard them one night as he was coming home. 'He heard them coming towards him, though he saw them not.' Their cry grew fainter as they drew near him, passed him, and louder again as they went from him. They went down the steeps towards the river Ebwy. And Thomas Andrew was 'a religious man, who would not have told an untruth for fear or for favour.'

VIII.

No form of superstition has had a wider popularity than this of spiritual hunting dogs, with which was usually connected in olden time the wild huntsman, a personage who has dropped quite out of modern belief, at least in Wales. In France this goblin was called Le Grand Veneur, and hunted with his dogs in the forests of Fontainebleau; in Germany it was Hackelberg, who sold himself to the devil for permission to hunt till doomsday. In Britain it was King Arthur who served as the goblin huntsman. Peasants would hear the cry of the hounds and the sounding of the horns, but the huntsman was invisible. When they called out after him, however, the answer came back : 'We are King Arthur and his kindred.' Mr. Baring-Gould,[1] in giving an account of the myth of Odin, the Wild Huntsman, who rides over the forests by night on a white horse, with his legion of hell-hounds, seems to ascribe the superstition to the imagination of a belated woodcutter frightened by the wind in the tree-tops. William Henderson[2] presumes the belief in the Wild Huntsman's pack, which prevails in the North of England, to come from the strange unearthly cries uttered by wild fowl on their passage southward, and which sound like the yelping of dogs. These natural phenomena have not served, however, to keep the old belief alive in Wales.

That the Cwn Annwn are descendants of the wish-hound of Hermes, hardly admits of doubt. The same superstition prevails among all Aryan peoples, with details differing but little. The souls of the dying are carried away by the howling winds, the dogs of Hermes, in the ancient mythology as in surviving beliefs ; on this follows the custom of opening the windows at death, so that the released soul may escape. In Devonshire they say no soul can escape from the house in which its body dies, unless all the locks and bolts are opened. In China a hole is made in the roof for a like purpose. The early Aryan conception of the wind as a howling dog or wolf speeding over the house-tops caused the inmates to tremble with fear, lest their souls should be called to follow them. It must be constantly borne in mind that all these creatures of fancy were more or less interchangeable, and the god Hermes was at times his own dog, which

[1] 'Iceland, its Scenes and Sagas,' 199–203.
[2] 'Notes on Folk-Lore,' 97.

escorted the soul to the river Styx. The winds were now the maruts, or spirits of the breeze, serving Indra, the sky-god; again they were the great psychopomp himself. The peasant who to-day tells you that dogs can see death enter the house where a person is about to die, merely repeats the idea of a primeval man whose ignorance of physical science was complete.

CHAPTER IX.

The Corpse Candle—Its Peculiarities—The Woman of Caerau—
Grasping a Corpse Candle—The Crwys Candle—Lights issuing
from the Mouth—Jesting with the Canwyll Corph—The Candle at
Pontfaen—The Three Candles at Golden Grove—Origin of Death-
Portents in Wales—Degree of Belief prevalent at the Present Day
—Origin of Spirits in General—The Supernatural—The Question of
a Future Life.

I.

PERHAPS the most picturesque of the several death-
omens popular in Wales is the Canwyll Corph, or
Corpse Candle. It is also, according to my observation, the most extensively believed in at the present day. Its details are varied and extremely
interesting. The idea of a goblin in the form of a
lighted tallow candle is ludicrous enough, at first
sight; and indeed I know several learned Welsh
gentlemen who venture to laugh at it; but the
superstition grows more and more grim and less
risible the better one becomes acquainted with it.
It is worth noting here that the canwyll, or candle,
is a more poetic thing among the Welsh—has a
higher literary place, so to speak—than among
English-speaking peoples. In the works of their
ancient poets the candle is mentioned in passages
where we should use the word light or lamp—as in
this verse, which is attributed to Aneurin (sixth
century):

> The best candle for man is prudence.

The candle is the favourite figure for mental
guidance among the Welsh;[1] there is no book in

[1] Stephens, 'Lit. of the Kymry,' 287. (New Ed., 1876.)

the Welsh language so popular as a certain work of religious counsel by a former Vicar of Llandovery, called 'The Candle of the Cymry.' The Corpse Candle is always and invariably a death-warning. It sometimes appears as a stately flambeau, stalking along unsupported, burning with a ghastly blue flame. Sometimes it is a plain tallow 'dip' in the hand of a ghost, and when the ghost is seen distinctly it is recognised as the ghost of some person yet living, who will now soon die. This, it will be noticed, is a variation upon the wraith, or Lledrith. Sometimes the goblin is a light which issues from a person's mouth or nostrils. According to the belief of some sections, the size of the candle indicates the age of the person who is about to die, being large when it is a full-grown person whose death is foretold, small when it is a child, still smaller when an infant. Where two candles together are seen, one of which is large and the other small, it is a mother and child who are to die. When the flame is white, the doomed person is a woman ; when red, a man.

II.

Among the accounts of the Corpse Candle which have come under my notice none are more interesting than those given me by a good dame whom I encountered at Caerau, near Cardiff. Caerau is a little village of perhaps one hundred souls, crouched at the foot of a steep hill on whose summit are the ancient earthworks of a Roman camp. On this summit also stands the parish church, distinctly visible from Cardiff streets, so ponderous is its square tower against the sky. To walk there is a pleasant stroll from the late Marquis of Bute's statue in the centre of the seaport town. I am thus particular merely for emphasis of the fact that this superstition is not confined to remote and out-of-the-way districts. Caerau is rural, and its people are all poor people, perhaps; but its church is barely three miles from the heart of a busy seaport. In this church I met the voluble Welshwoman who gave me the accounts referred to. One was to this effect: One night her sister was lying very ill at the narrator's house, and she was alone with her children, her husband being in the lunatic asylum at Cardiff. She had just put the children to bed, and had set her candle on the floor preparatory to going to bed herself, when there came a 'swish' along the floor, like the rustling of grave-clothes, and the candle was blown out. The room, however, to her surprise, remained glowing with a feeble light as from a very small taper, and looking behind her she beheld 'old John Richards,' who had been dead ten years. He held a Corpse Candle in his hand, and he looked at her in a chill and steadfast manner which caused the blood to run cold in her veins. She turned and woke her eldest boy, and said to him, 'Don't you see old John Richards?' The boy asked 'Where?' rubbing his eyes. She pointed out the ghost, and the boy was so frightened at sight of it that he cried out 'O wi! O Dduw! I wish I may die!' The ghost then disappeared, the Corpse Candle in its hand; the candle on the floor burned again with a clear light, and the next day the sick sister died.

Another account ran somewhat thus: The narrator's mother-in-law was ill with a cancer of the breast. 'Jenny fach,' she said to the narrator one night, 'sleep by me—I feel afraid.' 'Hach!' said Jenny, thinking the old woman was foolishly nervous; but she stayed. As she was lying in bed by the side of her mother-in-law, she saw at the foot of the bed the faint flame of a Corpse Candle, which shed no

light at all about the room ; the place remained as
dark as it was before. She looked at it in a sort of
stupor for a short time, and then raised herself
slowly up in bed and reached out to see if she
could grasp the candle. Her fingers touched it,
but it immediately went out in a little shower of
pale sparkles that fell downward. At that moment
her mother-in-law uttered a groan, and expired.

'Do you know Thomas Mathews, sir?' she asked
me ; 'he lives at Crwys now, but he used to live
here at Caerau.' 'Crwys?' I repeated, not at
once comprehending. 'Oh, you must know Crwys,
sir ; it's just the other side of Cardiff, towards Newport.' 'Can you spell it for me?'[1] The woman
blushed. ''Deed, sir,' said she, 'I ought to be a
scholar, but I've had so much trouble with my old
man that I've quite forgot my spellin'.' However,
the story of Thomas Mathews was to the effect
that he saw a Corpse Candle come out of his father's
mouth and go to his feet, and away a bit, then back
again to the mouth, which it did not exactly enter,
but blended as it were with the sick man's body.
I asked if the candle was tallow at any point
in its excursion, to which I was gravely answered
that it was the spirit of tallow. The man died
not long after, in the presence of my informant,
who described the incident with a dramatic force
and fervour peculiarly Celtic, concluding with the
remark : 'Well, well, there's only one way to come
into the world, but there's a many ways to go out
of it.'

The light issuing from the mouth is a fancy frequently encountered. In the 'Liber Landavenis'
it is mentioned that one day as St. Samson was
celebrating the holy mysteries, St. Dubricius with

---

[1] It is pronounced Croo-iss.

two monks saw a stream of fire to proceed glittering from his mouth.[1]   In old woodcuts, the souls of the dying are represented as issuing from the mouth in the form of small human figures ; and the Tyrolese peasants still fancy the soul is seen coming out of the mouth of a dying man like a little white cloud.[2] From the mouth of a patient in a London hospital some time since the nurses observed issuing a pale bluish flame, and soon after the man died.   The frightened nurses—not being acquainted with the corpse-candle theory of such things—imagined the torments of hell had already begun in the still living body.   A scientific explanation of the pheno-menon ascribed it to phosphuretted hydrogen, a result of incipient decomposition.[3]

III.

It is ill jesting with the Corpse Candle.   Persons who have endeavoured to stop it on its way have come severely to grief thereby.   Many have been struck down where they stood, in punishment of their audacity, as in the case of William John, a blacksmith of Lanboydi.   He was one night going home on horseback, when he saw a Corpse Candle, and his natural caution being at the moment some-what overcome by potables, he resolved to go out of his way to obstruct its passage.   As the candle drew near he saw a corpse upon a bier, the corpse of a woman he knew, and she held the candle between her forefingers, and dreadfully grinned at him.   Then he was struck from his horse, and lay in the road a long time insensible, and was ill for weeks thereafter.   Meantime, the woman whose

---

[1] 'Liber Landavensis,' 299.
[2] Tylor, ' Primitive Culture,' 391.
[3] 'Transactions Cardiff Nat. Soc.,' iv. 5.

spectral corpse he had seen, died and was buried, her funeral passing by that road.

A clergyman's son in Carmarthenshire, (subsequently himself a preacher,) who in his younger days was somewhat vicious, came home one night late from a debauch, and found the doors locked. Fearing to disturb the folk, and fearing also their reproaches and chidings for his staying out so late, (as many a young fellow has felt before and since,) he went to the man-servant, who slept in an out-room, as is sometimes the custom in Welsh rural districts. He could not awake the man-servant, but while standing over him, he saw a small light issue from the servant's nostrils, which soon became a Corpse Candle. He followed it out. It came to a foot-bridge which crossed a rivulet. Here the young man became inspired with the idea of trying an experiment with the Corpse Candle. He raised the end of the foot-bridge off the bank, and watched to see what the ghostly light would do. When it came to the rivulet it seemed to offer to go over, but hesitated, as if loth to cross except upon the bridge. So the young man put the bridge back in its place, and stayed to see how the candle would act. It came on the bridge, and as it passed the young man it struck him, as with a handkerchief. But though the blow was thus light and phantom-like, it doubled the young man up and left him a senseless heap on the ground, where he lay till morning, when he recovered and went home. It is needless to add that the servant died.

IV.

Morris Griffith was once schoolmaster in the parish of Pontfaen, in Pembrokeshire, but subsequently became a Baptist preacher of the Gospel.

He tells this story: 'As I was coming from a place called Tre-Davydd, and was come to the top of the hill, I saw a great light down in the valley, which I wondered at; for I could not imagine what it meant. But it came to my mind that it was a light before a burying, though I never could believe before that there was such a thing. The light which I saw then was a very red light, and it stood still for about a quarter of an hour in the way which went towards Llanferch-Llawddog church. I made haste to the other side of the hill, that I might see it farther; and from thence I saw it go along to the churchyard, where it stood still for a little time and entered into the church. I remained waiting to see it come out, and it was not long before it came out, and went to a certain part of the churchyard, where it stood a little time, and then vanished out of my sight. A few days afterwards, being in school with the children about noon, I heard a great noise overhead, as if the top of the house was coming down. I ran out to see the garret, and there was nothing amiss. A few days afterwards, Mr. Higgon of Pontfaen's son died. When the carpenter came to fetch the boards to make the coffin, (which were in the garret,) he made exactly such a stir, in handling the boards in the garret, as was made before by some spirit, who foreknew the death that was soon to come to pass. In carrying the body to the grave, the burying stood where the light had stood for about a quarter of an hour, because there was some water crossing the way, and the people could not go over it without wetting their feet, therefore they were obliged to wait till those that had boots helped them over. The child was buried in that very spot of ground in the churchyard, where I saw the light stop after it came out of the church. This is what I can boldly testify, having seen and heard what I relate—a thing which before I could not believe.'

Joshua Coslet, before mentioned in these pages, suddenly met a Corpse Candle as he was going through Heol Bwlch y Gwynt, (Windgap Lane) in Llandilo Fawr parish. It was a small light when near him, but increased as it went farther from him. He could easily see that there was some dark shadow passing along with the candle, and the shadow of a man carried it, holding it ' between his three forefingers over against his face.' He might perhaps have seen more, but he was afraid to look too earnestly upon it. Not long after, a burying passed through Heol Bwlch y Gwynt. Another time he saw the likeness of a candle carried in a skull. ' There is nothing unlikely or unreasonable in either of these representations,' says the Prophet Jones, their historian.

A Carmarthenshire tradition relates that one day, when the coach which runs between Llandilo and Carmarthen was passing by Golden Grove, the property of the Earl of Cawdor, three Corpse Candles were observed on the surface of the water gliding down the stream which runs near the road. All the passengers saw them. A few days after, some men were about crossing the river near there in a coracle, when one of them expressed his fear at venturing, as the river was flooded, and he remained behind. Thus the fatal number crossed the river— three—three Corpse Candles having foretold their fate ; and all were drowned.

V.

Tradition ascribes the origin of all these death-portents to the efforts of St. David. This saint appears to have been a great and good man, and a zealous Catholic, who, as a contemporary of the historical Arthur, is far enough back in the dim past to meet the views of romantic minds. And a prelate who by his prayers and presence could enable King Arthur to overthrow the Saxons in battle, or who by his pious learning could single-handed put down the Pelagian heresy in the Cardiganshire synod, was surely strong enough to invoke the Gwrach y Rhibyn, the Cyhyraeth, the Corpse Candle, and all the dreadful brood. This the legend relates he did by a special appeal to Heaven. Observing that the people in general were careless of the life to come, and could not be brought to mind it, and make preparation for it, St. David prayed that Heaven would give a sign of the immortality of the soul, and of a life to come, by a presage of death. Since that day, Wales, and particularly that part of Wales included in the bishopric of St. David, has had these phantoms. More materialistic minds consider these portents to be a remainder of those practices by which the persecuted Druids performed their rites and long kept up their religion in the land which Christianity had claimed : a similar origin, in fact, is here found for goblin omens as for fairies.

That these various portents are extensively believed in at the present day there cannot be a doubt ; with regard to the most important of them, I am able to testify with the fullest freedom ; I have heard regarding them story after story, from the lips of narrators whose sincerity was expressed vividly in face, tones, and behaviour. The excited eye, the paling cheek, the bated breath, the sinking voice, the intense and absorbed manner—familiar phenomena in every circle where ghost stories are told

—evidenced the perfect sincerity, at least, of the speakers.

It is unnecessary here to repeat, what I for my own part never forget, nor, I trust, does the reader, that Wales is no exception to the rest of the world in its credulity. That it is more picturesque is true, and it is also true that there is here an unusual amount of legend which has not hitherto found its way into books. Death-omens are common to all lands ; even in America, there are tales of the banshee, imported from Ireland along with the sons of that soil. In one recent case which came under my notice the banshee belonged to a Cambridgeshire Englishman. This was at Evansville, Indiana, and the banshee had appeared before the deaths of five members of a family, the last of whom was the father. His name was Feast, and the circumstances attending the banshee's visits were gravely described in a local journal as a matter of news. Less distinguished death-portents are common enough in the United States. That the Cambrian portents are so picturesque and clearly defined must be considered strong testimony to the vivid imagination of the Welsh. Figures born of the fancy, as distinguished from creatures born of the flesh, prove their parentage by the vagueness of their outlines. The outlines of the Cyhyraeth and the Gwrach y Rhibyn sometimes run into and mingle with each other, and so do those of the Tolaeth and the Goblin Funeral ; but the wonder is they are such distinct entities as they are.

VI.

To say that all the visible inhabitants of the mundane spirit-world are creatures of the disordered human liver, is perhaps a needless harshness of statement. The question of a future life

is not involved in this subject, nor raised by the
best writers who are studying it; but, religious
belief quite apart, it remains to be proved that
spirits of a supernatural world have any share in
the affairs of a world governed by natural law.
A goblin which manifests itself to the human eye,
it seems to me, becomes natural, by bowing before
the natural laws which rule in optics. Yet believers in ghosts find no difficulty in this direction;
the word 'supernatural' covers a multitude of sins.
'What is the supernatural?' asks Disraeli, in
'Lothair.' 'Can there be anything more miraculous than the existence of man and the world?
anything more literally supernatural than the origin
of things?'

Surely, in this life, nothing! The student who
endeavours to govern his faith by the methods
of science asks no more of any ghost that ever
walked the earth, than that it will prove itself a
reality. Man loves the marvellous. The marvels
of science, however, do not melt away into thin
air on close examination. They thrive under the
severest tests, and grow more and more extraordinary the more they are tried. The spectro-
scope and the radiometer are more wonderful than
any 'supernatural' thing yet heard of. Transportation through the air in the arms of a spirit
is a clear impossibility; but it is less wonderful
than the every-day feats of electricity in our time,
the bare conception of which would have filled
Plato and Aristotle with awe.

The actual origin of the phantoms of the spirit-
world is to be found in the lawless and luxuriant
fancy of primeval man. The creatures of this
fancy have been perpetuated throughout all time,
unto our own day, by that passionate yearning in

men for continued life and love, which is ineradicable in our nature. Men will not, they can not, accept the doubt which plunges an eternal future into eternal darkness, and separates them for ever from the creatures of their love. Hence, when the remorseless fact of Death removes those creatures, they look, with a longing which is indescribably pathetic, into the Unknown where their beloved have gone, and strive to see them in their spirit-life.

On this verge the finite mind must pause; to question that life is to add a terrible burden to all human woe; it need not be questioned. But to question the power of anything in that life to manifest itself to man through natural law, is to do what science has a right to do. 'The living know that they shall die: but the dead know not any thing . . . neither have they any more a portion for ever in any thing that is done under the sun.'[1]

[1] 'Eccles.' ix., 5, 6.

BOOK III.

QUAINT OLD CUSTOMS.

Where in an agede cell with moss and iveye growne,
In which nor to this daye the sunn had ever showne,
Their reverend British saint, in zealous ages paste,
To contemplation lived, and did so truly faste,
As he did onlie drink what chrystal [rivers] yields,
And fed upon the leakes he gather'd in the fields :
In memory of whom, in the revolving year,
The Welchman on that daye that sacred herb doth wear.

MS. in Bodleian Library.

—◆—

CHAPTER I.

Serious Significance of seemingly Trivial Customs—Their Origins—Common Superstitions—The Age we Live in—Days and Seasons—New Year's Day—The Apple Gift—Lucky Acts on New Year's Morning—The First Foot—Showmen's Superstitions—Levy Dew Song—Happy New Year Carol—Twelfth Night—The Mari Lwyd—The Penglog—The Cutty Wren—Tooling and Sowling—St. Valentine's Day—St. Dewi's Day—The Wearing of the Leek—The Traditional St. David—St. Patrick's Day—St. Patrick a Welshman—Shrove Tuesday.

I.

NUMBERLESS customs in Wales which appear to be meaningless, to people of average culture, are in truth replete with meaning. However trivial they may seem, they are very seldom the offspring of mere fooling. The student of comparative folklore is often able to trace their origin with surprising distinctness, and to evolve from them a significance before unsuspected. In many cases these quaint

old customs are traced to the primeval mythology. Others are clearly seen to be of Druidical
origin. Many spring from the rites and observances of the Roman Catholic Church in the early
days of Christianity on Welsh soil—where, as is
now generally conceded, the Gospel was first
preached in Great Britain. Some embody historical traditions ; and some are the outgrowth of
peculiar states of society in medieval times.
Directly or indirectly, they are all associated with
superstition, though in many instances they have
quite lost any superstitious character in our
day.

Modern society is agreed, with respect to many
curious old customs, to view them as the peculiar
possession of ignorance. It is very instructive to
note, in this connection, how blandly we accept
some of the most superstitious of these usages,
with tacit approval, and permit them to govern our
conduct. In every civilised community, in every
enlightened land on earth, there are many men and
women to whom this remark applies, who would
deem themselves shamefully insulted should you
doubt their intelligence and culture. Men and
women who 'smile superior' at the idea of Luther
hurling inkstands at the devil, or at the Welsh
peasant who thinks a pig can see the wind, will
themselves avoid beginning a journey on a Friday,
view as ominous a rainy wedding-day, throw an old
slipper after a bride for luck, observe with interest
the portents of their nightly dreams, shun seeing
the new moon over the left shoulder, throw a pinch
of salt over the same member when the salt-cellar
is upset, tie a red string about the neck to cure
nose-bleed, and believe in the antics of the modern
spiritualistic 'control.' Superstition, however, they

leave to the ignorant! The examples of every-day fetichism here cited are familiar to us, not specially among the Welsh, but among the English also, and the people of the United States—who, I may again observe, are no doubt as a people uncommonly free from superstition, in comparison with the older nations of the earth; but modesty is a very becoming wear for us all, in examining into other people's superstitions.

Aside from their scientific interest, there is a charm about many of the quaint customs of the Welsh, which speaks eloquently to most hearts. They are the offspring of ignorance, true, but they touch the 'good old times' of the poet and the romancer, when the conditions of life were less harsh than now. So we love to think. As a matter of scientific truth, this idea is itself, alas! but a superstition. This world has probably never been so fair a place to live in, life never so free from harsh conditions, as now; and as time goes on, there can be no doubt the improving process will continue. The true halcyon days of man are to be looked for in the future—not in the past; but with that future we shall have no mortal part.

II.

In treating of customs, no other classification is needful than their arrangement in orderly sequence in two divisions : first, those which pertain to certain days and seasons ; second, those relating to the most conspicuous events in common human life, courtship, marriage, and death.

Beginning with the year : there is in Glamorganshire a New Year's Day custom of great antiquity and large present observance, called the apple gift, or New Year's gift. In every town and village you will encounter children, on and about New Year's Day, going from door to door of shops and houses, bearing an apple or an orange curiously tricked out. Three sticks in the form of a tripod are thrust into it to serve as a rest; its sides are smeared with flour or meal, and stuck over with oats or wheat,

THE NEW YEAR'S APPLE.

or bits of broken lucifer matches to represent oats; its top is covered with thyme or other sweet evergreen, and a skewer is inserted in one side as a handle to hold it by. In its perfection, this piece of work is elaborate; but it is now often a decrepit affair, in the larger towns, where the New Year is welcomed (as at Cardiff) by a midnight chorus of steam-whistles.

The Christian symbolism of this custom is supposed to relate to the offering, by the Wise Men, of gold, frankincense, and myrrh to the infant Jesus. The older interpretation, however, takes the custom back to the Druidic days, and makes it a form of the solar myth. In the three supporting sticks of the apple are seen the three rays of the sun, /|\, the mystic Name of the Creator; the apple is the round sun itself; the evergreens represent its perennial life; and the grains of wheat, or oats, Avagddu's spears. Avagddu is the evil principle of darkness—hell, or the devil—with which the sun fights throughout the winter for the world's life.

Thousands of children in Wales seek to win from their elders a New Year's copper by exhibiting the apple gift, or by singing in chorus their good wishes. A popular verse on this occasion hopes the hearer will be blessed with an abundance of money in his pocket and of beer in his cellar, and draws attention to the singers' thin shoes and the bad character of the walking. In many cases the juvenile population parades the street all night, sometimes with noisy fife bands, which follow the death knell, as it sounds from the old church tower, with shrill peals of a merrier if not more musical sort.

In Pembrokeshire, to rise early on New Year's morning is considered luck-bringing. On that morning also it is deemed wise to bring a fresh loaf into the house, with the superstition that the succession of loaves throughout the year will be influenced by that incident. A rigid quarantine is also set up, to see that no female visitor cross the threshold first on New Year's morning; that a male visitor shall be the first to do so is a lucky thing, and the

reverse unlucky. A superstition resembling this
prevails to this day in America among showmen.
'There's no showman on the road,' said an
American manager of my acquaintance, 'who would
think of letting a lady be first to pass through the
doors when opening them for a performance.
There's a sort of feeling that it brings ill-luck.
Then there are cross-eyed people ; many a veteran
ticket-seller loses all heart when one presents himself at the ticket-window. A cross-eyed patron and
a bad house generally go together. A cross-eyed
performer would be a regular Jonah. With circuses
there is a superstition that a man with a yellow
clarionet brings bad luck.' Another well-known
New York manager in a recent conversation
assured me that to open an umbrella in a new play
is deemed certain failure for the piece. An umbrella
may be carried closed with impunity, but it must
not be opened unless the author desire to court
failure. The Chinese have the Pembrokeshire
superstition exactly, as regards the first foot on
New Year's Day. They consider a woman peculiarly unlucky as a first foot after the New Year
has begun, but a Buddhist priest is even more
unlucky than a woman, in this light.[1]

Another Pembrokeshire custom on New Year's
morning is quaint and interesting. As soon as it is
light, children of the peasantry hasten to provide a
small cup of pure spring water, just from the well,
and go about sprinkling the faces of those they
meet, with the aid of a sprig of evergreen. At the
same time they sing the following verses :

> Here we bring new water from the well so clear,
> For to worship God with, this happy new year ;

---

[1] Dennys, 'Folk-Lore of China,' 31.

Sing levy dew, sing levy dew, the water and the wine,
With seven bright gold wires, and bugles that do shine ;
Sing reign of fair maid, with gold upon her toe ;
Open you the west door and turn the old year go ;
Sing reign of fair maid, with gold upon her chin ;
Open you the east door and let the new year in !

This custom also is still observed extensively. The words 'levy dew' are deemed an English version of Llef i Dduw, (a cry to God).

A Welsh song sung on New Year's Day, in Glamorganshire, by boys in chorus, somewhat after the Christmas carol fashion, is this :

Blwyddyn newydd dda i chwi,
Gwyliau llawen i chwi,
Meistr a meistres bob un trwy'r ty,
Gwyliau llawen i chwi,
Codwch yn foreu, a rheswch y tan,
A cherddwch i'r ffynon i ymofyn dwr glan.

A happy new year to you,
Merry be your holidays,
Master and mistress—every one in the house ;
Arise in the morning; bestir the fire,
And go to the well to fetch fresh water.

III.

Among Twelfth Night customs, none is more celebrated than that called Mary Lwyd. It prevails in various parts of Wales, notably in lower Glamorganshire. The skeleton of a horse's head is procured by the young men or boys of a village, and adorned with 'favours' of pink, blue, yellow, etc. These are generally borrowed from the girls, as it is not considered necessary the silken fillets and rosettes should be new, and such finery costs money. The bottoms of two black bottles are inserted in the sockets of the skeleton head to serve as eyes, and a substitute for ears is also contrived. On Twelfth Night they carry this object about from house to house, with shouts and songs, and a general cultivation of noise and racket. Sometimes a duet is sung in Welsh, outside a door, the singers begging to be invited in ; if the door be not opened they tap on it, and there is frequently quite a series of *awen* sung, the parties within denying the outsiders admission, and the outsiders urging the same. At last the door is opened, when in bounces the merry crowd, among them the Mary Lwyd, borne by one personating a horse, who is led by another personating the groom. The horse chases the girls around the room, capering and neighing, while the groom cries, 'So ho, my boy—gently, poor fellow ! ' and the girls, of course, scream with merriment. A dance follows—a reel, performed by three young men, tricked out with ribbons. The company is then regaled with cakes and ale, and the revellers depart, pausing outside the door to sing a parting song of thanks and good wishes to their entertainers.

The penglog (a skull, a noddle) is a similar custom peculiar to Aberconwy (Conway) in Carnarvonshire. In this case the horse's skull is an attention particularly bestowed upon prudes.

Mary Lwyd may mean Pale Mary, or Wan Mary, or Hoary Mary, but the presumption is that it means in this case Blessed Mary, and that the custom is of papal origin. There is, however, a tradition which links the custom with enchantment, in connection with a warlike princess, reputed to have flourished in Gwent and Morganwg in the early ages, and who is to be seen to this day, mounted on her steed, on a rock in Rhymney Dingle.[1]

The cutty wren is a Pembrokeshire Twelfth Night custom prevailing commonly during the last century, but now nearly extinct. A wren was placed in a little house of paper, with glass windows, and this

---

[1] Vide W. Roberts's ' Crefydd yr Oesoedd Tywyll,' i.

was hoisted on four poles, one at each corner. Four men bore it about, singing a very long ballad, of which one stanza will be enough :

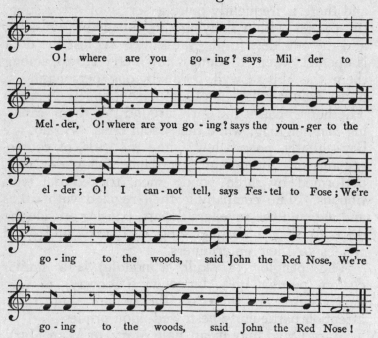

O! where are you go-ing? says Mil-der to Mel-der, O! where are you go-ing? says the youn-ger to the el-der; O! I can-not tell, says Fes-tel to Fose; We're go-ing to the woods, said John the Red Nose, We're go-ing to the woods, said John the Red Nose!

The immediate purpose of this rite was to levy contributions. Another such custom was called 'tooling,' and its purpose was beer. It consisted in calling at the farm-houses and pretending to look for one's tools behind the beer cask. 'I've left my saw behind your beer cask,' a carpenter would say; 'my whip,' a carter; and received the tool by proxy, in the shape of a cup of ale. The female portion of the poorer sort, on the other hand, practised what was called sowling, viz., asking for 'sowl,' and receiving, accordingly, any food eaten with bread, such as cheese, fish, or meat. This custom is still maintained, and 'sowling day' fills many a poor woman's bag. The phrase is supposed to be from the French *soûl*, signifying one's fill.

IV.

Connected with St. Valentine's Day, there is no Welsh custom which demands notice here; but it is perhaps worthy of mention that nowhere in the world is the day more abundantly productive of its orthodox crop—love-letters. The post-offices in the Principality are simply deluged with these missives on the eve and morning of St. Valentine's. In Cardiff the postmaster thinks himself lucky if he gets off with fifteen thousand letters in excess of the ordinary mail. Nineteen extra sorters and carriers were employed for this work on February 14th, 1878, and the regular force also was heavily worked beyond its usual hours. The custom is more Norman than Cambrian, I suppose; the word Valentine comes from the Norman word for a lover, and the saint is a mere accident in this connection.

V.

St. Dewi is to the Welsh what St. George is to the English, St. Andrew to the Scotch, and St. Patrick to the Irish. His day is celebrated on the 1st of March throughout Wales, and indeed throughout the world where Welshmen are. In some American ports (perhaps all) the British consulate displays its flag in honour of the day. In Wales there are processions, grand dinners; places of business are closed; the poor are banqueted; speeches are made and songs are sung. The most characteristic feature of the day is the wearing of the leek. This feature is least conspicuous, it may be noted, in those parts of Wales where the English residents are fewest, and least of all in the ultra-

Welsh shires of Cardigan and Carmarthen, where St. David is peculiarly honoured. The significance of this fact no doubt lies in the absence of any necessity for asserting a Cambrianism which there are none to dispute. In the border towns, every Welshman who desires to assert his national right wears the leek in his hat or elsewhere on his person; but in the shadow of St. David's College at Lampeter, not a leek is seen on St. Dewi's Day. In Glamorganshire may be found the order of Knights of the Leek, who hold high festival on the 1st of every March, gathering in the Welsh bards and men of letters.

Why is the leek worn? Practically, because the wearer is a Welshman who honours tradition. But the precise origin of the custom is involved in an obscurity from which emerge several curious and interesting traditions. The verses cited at the opening of this Part refer to one of these; they are quoted by Manby[1] without other credit than 'a very antient manuscript.' Another tradition is thus given in a pamphlet of 1642:[2] 'S. David when hee always went into the field in Martiall exercise he carried a Leek with him, and once being almost faint to death, he immediately remembred himself of the Leek, and by that means not only preserved his life but also became victorious: hence is the Mythologie of the Leek derived.' The practice is traced by another writer[3] to 'the custom of Cymhortha, or the neighbourly.

---

[1] 'Hist. and Ant. of the Parish of St. David,' 54.

[2] 'The Welchmen's Ivbilee to the honour of St. David, shewing the manner of that solemn celebration which the Welchmen annually hold in honour of St. David, describing likewise the trve and reall cause why they wear that day a *Leek* on their Hats, with an excellent merry Sonnet annexed unto it, composed by T. Morgan Gent. London. Printed for I. Harrison.'

[3] Owen, 'Camb. Biog.' 86.

aid practised among farmers, which is of various kinds. In some districts of South Wales all the neighbours of a small farmer without means appoint a day when they all attend to plough his land, and the like; and at such a time it is a custom for each individual to bring his portion of leeks, to be used in making pottage for the whole company; and they bring nothing else but the leeks in particular for the occasion.' Some find the true origin of the custom in Druidical days, but their warrant is not clear, nor how it came to be associated with the 1st of March in that case. The military origin bears down the scale of testimony, and gives the leek the glory of a Cambrian victory as its consecrator to ornamental purposes. Whether this victory was over the Saxon or the Gaul does not exactly appear; some traditions say one, some the other. The battle of Poietiers has been named; also that of Cressy, where the Welsh archers did good service with the English against a common enemy; but an older tradition is to the effect that the Saxon was the foe. The invaders had assumed the dress of the Britons, that they might steal upon them unsuspected; but St. David ordered the Welshmen to stick leeks in their caps as a badge of distinction. This he did merely because there was a large field of leeks growing near the British camp. The precaution gave the day to the favoured of St. Dewi.

It cannot be denied that there have been found Englishmen rude enough to ridicule this honourable and ancient custom of the Welsh, though why they should do so there is no good reason. The leek is not fragrant, perhaps; but if an old custom must smell sweet or be laughed at, there is work enough for our risibles in every English parish. The following is one of the foolish legends of the English respecting the leek : ' The Welsh in olden days were so infested by ourang outangs that they could obtain no peace day or night, and not being themselves able to extirpate them they invited the English to assist, who came ; but through mistake killed several of the Welsh, so that in order to distinguish them from the monkeys they desired them to stick a leek in their hats.' The author of this ridiculous tale deserves the fate of Pistol, whom Fluellen compelled to eat his leek, skin and all.

Flu. I peseech you heartily, scurvy lowsy knave, at my desires, and my requests, and my petitions, to eat, look you, this leek ; because look you, you do not love it, nor your affections, and your appetites and your digestions, does not agree with it, I would desire you to eat it.

Pist. Not for Cadwallader, and all his goats.

Flu. There is one goat for you. [*Strikes him.*] Will you be so good, scald knave, as eat it ?

Pist. Base Trojan, thou shalt die.

Flu. You say very true, scald knave, when Got's will is : I will desire you to live in the meantime, and eat your victuals. . . . If you can mock a leek you can eat a leek. . . .

Pist. Quiet thy cudgel ; thou dost see, I eat.

Flu. Much goot do you, scald knave, heartily. Nay, 'pray you, throw none away ; the skin is goot for your proken coxcomb. When you take occasions to see leeks hereafter, I pray you, mock at them ! that is all.[1]

VI.

The traditional St. David is a brilliant figure in Welsh story ; with the historical character this work has not to deal. The legendary account of him represents a man of gigantic stature and fabulous beauty, whose age at his death was 147 years. He was a direct descendant of the sister of the Virgin Mary, and his first miracles were performed while he was yet unborn. In this condition he regulated the diet of his virgin mother, and struck dumb a

[1] Shaks., K. Henry V., Act V., Sc. 1.

preacher who presumed to preach in her presence. At the hour of his birth St. Dewi performed a miracle; another when he was baptized; and he was taught his lessons (at a place called The Old Bush, in South Wales) by a pigeon with a golden beak, which played about his lips. As he grew up, his miraculous powers waxed stronger; and magicians who opposed him were destroyed by fire which he called from heaven to consume them. Thirsty, a fountain rose in Glyn Hodnant at his call, and from this fountain ran not water but good wine. When he went about the country he was always accompanied by an angel. On the banks of the river Teify, a miserable woman wept over her son who lay dead; she appealed to Dewi, who laid hold of the boy's right hand and he arose from the dead as if from a sleep. At Llandewi Brefi, in Cardiganshire, as he was preaching on the surface of the flat ground, the ground rose as a high mount under his feet, so that the people all about could see him as well as hear him. A labourer lifted his pickaxe to strike a friend of Dewi's, which the saint seeing from afar off, raised his hand and willed that the labourer's hand should become stiff—which it did. Another friend, going away to Ireland, forgot and left behind him a little bell that Dewi had given him; but Dewi sent the bell across the sea by an angel, so that it arrived there next day without the aid of human hands. And finally, having made up his mind that he would die and go to heaven, he did so—but quite of his own will—at his own request, so to speak. Having asked that his soul might be taken, an angel informed him it would be taken on the first of March proximo. So David bade his friends good-bye on the 28th of February, greatly to their distress. 'Alas!' they cried, 'the earth

will not swallow us! Alas! fire will not consume
us! Alas! the sea will not come over the land!
Alas! the mountains will not fall to cover us!' On
Tuesday night, as the cocks were crowing, a host
of angels thronged the streets of the city, and filled
it with joy and mirth; and Dewi died. 'The angels
took his soul to the place where there is light
without end, and rest without labour, and joy without
sorrow, and plenty of all good things, and victory,
and brightness, and beauty.' There Abel is with
the martyrs, Noah is with the sailors, Thomas is
with the Indians, Peter is with the apostles, Paul is
with the Greeks, other saints are with other suitable
persons, and David is with the kings.[1]

On the summit which rose under St. Dewi while
he stood on it and preached, now stands St. David's
church, at Llandewi Brefi. In the days of its glory
—i.e. during nearly the whole period of Roman
Catholic rule—it was renowned beyond all others in
Britain. To go twice to St. David's was deemed
equal to going once to Rome, and a superstitious
belief prevailed that every man must go to St.
David's once, either alive or dead. William the
Conqueror marched through Wales in hostile array
in 1080, but arriving at St. David's shrine laid aside
the warrior for the votary.

VII.

St. Patrick's Day is celebrated in Wales with
much enthusiasm. The Welsh believe that St.
Patrick was a Welshman. Born at Llandeilo Taly-
bont, in Glamorganshire, and educated at the famous
college of Llantwit Major, he held St. David's place
till the coming of Dewi was announced to him;
then he went into Ireland, to do missionary work,

[1] Cambro-British Saints,' 402, etc.

as it were. This is the monastic tale. Patrick was comfortably settled in the valley of Rosina, and intended to pass his life there, but an angel came to him and said, 'Thou must leave this place to one who is not yet born.' Patrick was annoyed, even angered, but obedient, and went off to Ireland, where he became a great man.[1] The story of the Iolo MSS., however, presents the matter in a different light: 'About A.D. 420 the Island of Britain seemed to have neither ruler nor proprietor.' The Irish took advantage of this state of things to invade and oppress Britain, robbing her of corn, cattle, 'and every other moveable property that they could lay their hands on.' Among other things, they stole away St. Patrick from the college at Llantwit Major, 'whence that college became destitute of a principal and teacher for more than forty years, and fell into dilapidation'—a condition it remains in at present, by the way. 'Patrick never returned to Wales, choosing rather to reside in Ireland; having ascertained that the Irish were better people than the Welsh, in those times.'[2] Still, it is not the native Welsh who are as a rule the celebrators of St. Patrick's Day in Wales.

VIII.

Shrove Tuesday was once characterised by a custom called throwing at cocks, now obsolete. Hens which had laid no eggs before that day were threshed with a flail, as being good for nothing. The person who hit the hen with the flail and killed her got her for his reward.

The more reputable custom of cramming with crammwythau (pancakes) still survives, and is undoubtedly of extreme antiquity.

[1] 'Cambro-British Saints,' 403.   [2] Iolo MSS., 455.

CHAPTER II.

I.

WEARING mourning throughout Lent was formerly common in Wales. In Monmouthshire, Mothering Sunday—the visiting of parents on Mid-Lent Sunday —was observed in the last century, but is nowhere popular in Wales at present. Palm Sunday takes precedence among the Welsh, and is very extensively and enthusiastically observed. The day is called Flowering Sunday, and its peculiar feature is strewing the graves of the dead with flowers. The custom reaches all classes, and all parts of the Principality. In the large towns, as Cardiff, many thousands of people gather at the graves. The custom is associated with the strewing of palms before Christ on his entry into Jerusalem, but was observed by the British Druids in celebration of the awakening life of the earth at this season.

II.

In Pembrokeshire, it was customary up to the close of the last century, to walk barefoot to church on Good Friday, as had been done since times prior to the Reformation. The old people and the young joined in this custom, which they said was done so as not to 'disturb the earth.' All business was suspended, and no horse nor cart was to be seen in the town.

Hot-cross buns also figured in a peculiar manner at this time. They were eaten in Tenby after the return from church. After having tied up a certain number in a bag, the folk hung them in the kitchen, where they remained till the next Good Friday, for use as medicine. It was believed that persons labouring under any disease had only to eat a portion of a bun to be cured. The buns so preserved were used also as a panacea for all the diseases of domestic animals. They were further believed to be serviceable in frightening away goblins of an evil sort.

That these buns are of Christian invention is the popular belief, and indeed this notion is not altogether exploded among the more intelligent classes. Their connection with the cross of the Saviour is possible by adoption—as the early Christians adopted many pagan rites and customs—but that they date back to pre-historic times there is abundant testimony.

Innumerable are the superstitious customs and beliefs associated with Good Friday. In Pembrokeshire there was a custom called 'making Christ's bed.' A quantity of long reeds were gathered from the river and woven into the shape of a man. This effigy was then stretched on a wooden cross, and laid in some retired field or garden, and left there.

The birth of a child on that day is very unlucky—indeed a birth on any Friday of the whole year is to be deprecated as a most unfortunate circumstance.

III.

The bad odour in which Friday is everywhere held is naturally associated, among Christians, with the crucifixion; but this will not account for the existence of a like superstition regarding Friday among the Brahmins of India, nor for the prevalence of other lucky and unlucky days among both Aryan and Mongolian peoples. In the Middle Ages Monday and Tuesday were unlucky days. A Welshman who lived some time in Russia, tells me Monday is deemed a very unlucky day there, on which no business must be begun. In some English districts Thursday is the unlucky day. In Norway it is lucky, especially for marrying. In South Wales, Friday is the fairies' day, when they have special command over the weather; and it is their whim to make the weather on Friday differ from that of the other days of the week. 'When the rest of the week is fair, Friday is apt to be rainy, or cloudy; and when the weather is foul, Friday is apt to be more fair.'

The superstitious prejudice of the quarrymen in North Wales regarding Holy Thursday has been cited. It is not a reverential feeling, but a purely superstitious one, and has pervaded the district from ancient times. It has been supposed that Thursday was a sacred day among the Druids. There is a vulgar tradition (mentioned by Giraldus), that Snowdon mountains are frequented by an eagle, which perches on a fatal stone on every Thursday and whets her beak upon it, expecting a battle to occur, upon which she may satiate her hunger with the carcases of the slain; but the battle is ever deferred, and the stone has become almost perforated with the eagle's sharpening her beak upon it. There may perhaps be a connection traced between these superstitions and the lightning-god Thor, whose day Thursday was.

IV.

Easter is marked by some striking customs. It is deemed essential for one's well-being that some new article of dress shall be donned at this time, though it be nothing more than a new ribbon. This is also a Hampshire superstition. A servant of mine, born in Hampshire, used always to say, ' If you don't have on something new Easter Sunday the dogs will spit at you.' This custom is associated with Easter baptism, when a new life was assumed by the baptized, clothed in righteousness as a garment. A ceremony called ' lifting ' is peculiar to North Wales on Easter Monday and Tuesday. On the Monday bands of men go about with a chair, and meeting a woman in the street compel her to sit, and be lifted three times in the air amidst their cheers : she is then invited to bestow a small compliment on her entertainers. This performance is kept up till twelve o'clock, when it ceases. On Easter Tuesday the women take their turn, and go about in like manner lifting the men. It has been conjectured that in this custom an allusion to the resurrection is intended.

A custom, the name of which is now lost, was that the village belle should on Easter Eve and Easter Tuesday carry on her head a piece of chinaware of curious shape, made expressly for this purpose, and useless for any other. It may be described as a circular crown of porcelain, the points whereof were cups and candles. The cups were solid details of the crown : the candles were stuck with clay upon the spaces between the cups.

The cups were filled with a native beverage called bragawd, and the candles were lighted. To drink

LIFTING. (*From an old drawing.*)

the liquor without burning yourself or the damsel at the candle was the difficulty involved in this

performance. A stanza was sung by the young woman's companions, the last line of which was,

Rhag i'r feinwen losgi ei thalcen.
(Lest the maiden burn her forehead.[1])

Stocsio is an Easter Monday custom observed from time immemorial in the town of Aberconwy, and still practised there in 1835. On Easter Sunday crowds of men and boys carrying wands of gorse went to Pen Twthil, and there proclaimed the laws and regulations of the following day. They were to this effect: all men under sixty to be up and out before 6 A.M.; all under forty, before 4 A.M.; all under twenty, to stay up all night. Penalty for disobedience: the stocks. The crier who delivered this proclamation was the man last married in the town previous to Easter Sunday. Other like rules were proclaimed, amid loud cheers. Early next morning a party, headed by a fife and drum, patrolled the town with a cart, in search of delinquents. When one was discovered, he was hauled from his bed and made to dress himself; then put in the cart and dragged to the stocks. His feet being secured therein, he was duly lectured on the sin of laziness, and of breaking an ancient law of the town by lying abed in violation thereof. His right hand was then taken, and he was asked a lot of absurd questions, such as 'Which do you like best, the mistress or the maid?' 'Which do you prefer, ale or buttermilk?' 'If the gate of a field were open, would you go through it, or over the stile?' and the like. His answers being received with derision, his hand was smeared with mud, and he was then released amid cheers. 'This sport, which would be impracticable in a larger and

[1] Arch. Camb. 4 Se., iii., 334.

less intimate community, is continued with the greatest good humour until eight ; when the rest of the day is spent in playing ball at the Castle.'[1]

V.

Ball-playing against the walls of the church between hours of service was a fashion of Easter which is within recollection. It was also common on the Sabbath day itself in many parishes, in the days when dissent was unknown and parishioners had long distances to traverse on a Sunday ; 'and that, too, with the sanction of the clergyman, and even his personal superintendence. Old people can remember such a state of things, when the clergyman gave notice that the game must cease by putting the ball into his pocket and marched his young friends into church.'[2]   Nowhere less than in a custom like this would the ordinary observer look for traditionary significance ; yet there is no doubt our Easter eggs are but another surviving form of the same ancient rite.   Before the Reformation there was a Church of England custom of playing ball *in* church at Easter, according to Dr. Fosbrooke, the dean and clergy participating.

There were other sports and pastimes common alike to Easter and to the Sabbath day, which are full of curious interest.   Some of them no doubt arose out of the social exigencies of sparsely settled neighbourhoods, which caused people to remain at the church between services, instead of returning to distant homes ; but a Druidic origin seems necessary to account for others.   That the people should between services gather near the church to talk over the gossip of the day, is natural enough, and

---

[1] 'Hist. and Ant. of Aberconwy,' 108.
[2] 'Arch. Camb.' 4 Se., iii., 333.

is a phenomenon which may still be witnessed in remote parts of the United States. In St. Dogmell's parish, Pembrokeshire, there is a tump which bears the name of 'Cnwc y Celwydd,' videlicet, the Tump of Lies. Here were men and women formerly in the habit of gathering together on the Lord's day in great crowds, and entertaining each other with the inventing and telling of the most lying and wonderful yarns they could conjure up with the aid of an imagination spurred to exercise by rivalry and applause. The custom is discontinued; but there is still hardly a neighbourhood in Wales so rich in tales of fairies and other goblins.

The custom of dancing in churchyards was common in many parts of the Principality in the early part of this century. At Aberedwy, Malkin saw a large yew tree in the churchyard under which as many as sixty couples had been seen dancing at once.[1] The dancing was not in that part of the yard consecrated to the dead, but on the north side of the church, where it was not the custom to bury. A tradition is preserved by Giraldus of a solemn festival dance which took place in the churchyard at St. Almedha's church, Breconshire, on that saint's day. The dance was 'led round the churchyard with a song,' and succeeded by the dancers falling down in a trance, followed by a sort of religious frenzy. This is believed to have been a Druidical rite, described on hearsay by Giraldus, and embellished by him with those pious inventions not uncommon in his day.

One of the customs of Easter, at a comparatively recent period in Wales, was getting the children up early in the morning to see the sun dance. This exercise the sun was said to perform at rising on

[1] Malkin's 'South Wales,' 281.

Easter Day, in honour of the rising of our Lord. The sun was sometimes aided in this performance by a bowl of clear water, into which the youth must look to see the orb dance, as it would be dangerous to look directly on the sun while thus engaged. The religious dance of the ancient Druids is believed to exist in modern times in a round dance wherein the figures imitate the motions of the sun and moon. The ball-playing in church mentioned above was also accompanied by dancing.

VI.

The first of April is in Welsh called Calan Ebrill, and an April Fool a Ffwl Ebrill ; the similarity of English and Welsh words may be said to typify the similarity of observance. The universality of this observance among Aryan peoples would certainly indicate an origin in a time preceding the dispersion of the human family over the world. The Druids, tradition says, celebrated the revival of Nature's powers in a festival which culminated on the first of April in the most hilarious foolery. The Roman Saturnalia or feast of fools perpetuated the rite, though the purpose of the Christian revelry may quite possibly have been to ridicule the Druidic ceremonies.

The festivities of May-day are in like manner associated with the powers of Nature, whose vigour and productiveness were symbolized by the Maypole round which village lads and lasses danced. The rites of love were variously celebrated at this time, and some of these customs locally have long survived the Maypole itself. The ordinance for the destruction of Maypoles in England and Wales, printed in 1644, declared them ' a heathenish vanity, generally abused to superstition and wickedness,' wherefore it was ordained that they should be destroyed, and that no Maypole should thereafter be 'set up, erected, or suffered to be within this kingdom of England or dominion of Wales.'

The Maypole in Wales was called Bedwen, because it was always made of birch, bedw, a tree still associated with the gentler emotions. To give a lover a birchen branch, is for a maiden to accept his addresses ; to give him a collen, or hazel, the reverse. Games of various sorts were played around the bedwen. The fame of a village depended on its not being stolen away, and parties were constantly on the alert to steal the bedwen, a feat which, when accomplished, was celebrated with peculiar festivities. This rivalry for the possession of the Maypole was probably typical of the ancient idea that the first of May was the boundary day dividing the confines of winter and summer, when a fight took place between the powers of the air, on the one hand striving to continue the reign of winter, on the other to establish that of summer. Here may be cited the Mabinogi of Kilhwch and Olwen, where it speaks of the daughter of Llud Llaw Ereint. 'She was the most splendid maiden in the three Islands of the Mighty, and in the three Islands adjacent,' and for her does Gwyn ap Nudd, the fairy king, fight every first of May till the day of doom.[1] She was to have been the bride of Gwythyr, the son of Greidawl, when Gwyn ap Nudd carried her off by force. The bereaved bridegroom followed, and there was a bloody struggle, in which Gwyn was victorious, and which he signalized by an act of frightful cruelty ; he slew an old warrior, took out his heart from his breast, and constrained the warrior's son to eat the heart of his father.

[1] 'Mabinogion,' 229.

T

When Arthur heard of this he summoned Gwyn ap Nudd before him, and deprived him of the fruits of his victory. But he condemned the two combatants to fight for the radiant maiden henceforth for ever on every first of May till doomsday ; the ictor on that day to possess the maiden.[1]

VIII.

In the remote and primitive parish of Defynog, in Breconshire, until a few years since, a custom survived of carrying the King of Summer and the King of Winter. Two boys were chosen to serve as the two kings, and were covered all over with a dress of brigau bedw, (birchen boughs,) only their faces remaining visible. A coin was tossed and the boy chosen was the summer king ; a crown of bright-hued ribbons was put upon his head. Upon the other boy's head was placed a crown of holly, to designate the winter king. Then a procession was formed, headed by two men with drawn swords to clear the way. Four men supported the summer king upon two poles, one under his knees and the other under his arms ; and four others bore the winter king in a similar undignified posture. The procession passed round the village and to the farm-houses near by, collecting largess of coin or beer, winding up the perambulation at the churchyard. Here the boys were set free, and received a dole for their services, the winter king getting less than the other.

Another May-day custom among the boys of that parish, was to carry about a rod, from which the bark had been partly peeled in a spiral form, and upon the top of which was set either a cock or a cross, the bearers waking the echoes of the village with ' Yo ho ! yo ho ! yo ho !'[2]

[1] 'Mabinogion,' 251.   [2] 'Arch. Camb.,' 2 Se., iv., 326.

CHAPTER III.

I.

MIDSUMMER EVE, or St. John's Eve (June 23rd), is one of the ancient Druidic festivals, still liberally honoured in Wales. The custom of lighting bonfires survives in some of the villages, and at Pontypridd there are ceremonies of a solemn sort. Midsummer Eve, in 1878, fell on a Sunday. Upon that day the 'Druids and bards' at Pontypridd held the usual feast of the summer solstice in the face of the sun. There is a breezy common on the top of a high hill overlooking the town, where stand a logan stone and a circle of upright stones constituting the 'temple of the Druids.' Here it is the custom of the present-day adherents of that ancient religion, beside which Christianity is an infant, to celebrate their rites 'within the folds of the serpent,' a circle marked with the signs of the zodiac. The venerable archdruid, Myfyr Morganwg, stands on the logan stone, with a mistletoe sprig in his button-hole, and prays to the god Kali, 'creator of sun, moon, stars, and universe.' Then the white-bearded old man delivers a discourse, and new members are initiated into the 'mysteries.' Occasionally these new members are Americans from over the sea, and they include both sexes. Large crowds gather to witness the impressive spectacle—a shadow of the ancient rites when from Belenian heights flamed high the sacrificial fires. It was a former belief that these fires protected the lands within their light from the machinations of sorcery, so that good crops would follow, and that their ashes were valuable as a medicinal charm.

The Snake-stone is another striking Welsh tradition, associated with Midsummer eve. At this time of the year there are certain convocations of snakes, which, hissing sociably together among one another, hiss forth a mystic bubble, which hardens into the semblance of a glass ring. The finder of this ring is a lucky man, for all his undertakings will prosper while he retains it. These rings are called Gleiniau Nadroedd in Welsh—snake-stones in English. They are supposed to have been used by the ancient Druids as charms. There is a Welsh saying, respecting people who lay their heads together in conversation, that the talkers are 'blowing the gem.'

II.

The traditions connected with the Beltane fires are very interesting, but the subject has received so much attention in published volumes that it need not here be dwelt upon. The lad who in the United States capers around a bonfire on the night of Independence Day has not a suspicion that he is imitating the rites of an antiquity the most remote; that in burning a heap of barrels and boxes in a public square the celebrators of the American Fourth of July imitate the priests who thus worshipped the sun-god Beal. The origins of our most familiar customs are constantly being discovered in such directions as this. On the face of the thing, nothing could be more absurd as a mode of jollification, in a little American town, with its wooden architecture, on a hot night in the midst of summer, than building a roaring fire to make the air still hotter and endanger the surrounding houses. The reason for the existence of such a custom must be sought in another land and another time; had reflection governed the matter, instead of tradition, the American anniversary would have found some more fitting means of celebration than Druidic fires and Chinese charms. (For it may be mentioned further, in this connection, that the fire-crackers of our urchins are quite as superstitious in their original purpose as the bonfire is. In China, even to this day, fire-crackers are charms pure and simple, their office to drive away evil spirits, their use as a means of jollification quite unknown to their inventors.) A far more sensible Midsummer rite, especially in a hot country, would have been to adopt the custom of St. Ulric's day, and eat fish. This saint's day falls on the fourth of July, and Barnabe Googe's translation of Naogeorgius has this couplet concerning it:

Wheresoeuer Huldryche hath his place, the people there brings in
Both carpes and pykes, and mullets fat, his fauour here to win.

III.

The Welsh saint called Cynog was one of the numberless children of that famous old patriarch Brychan Brycheiniog, and had his memory honoured, until a comparatively recent period, in the parish of Defynog. Here, on this saint's feast Monday, which fell in October, there was a custom called 'carrying Cynog.' Cynog was represented by a man who was paid for his services with money, or with a suit of clothes—sometimes a 'stranger' from an adjoining parish, but on the last recorded occasion a drunken farmer of the neighbourhood. He was clad in dilapidated garments, and borne through the village; after which he was tumbled headlong into the river amid the jeers of the crowd, to scramble out as best he might. It was not a very respectful way of commemorating a saint who had been buried a thousand years or thereabouts; but such as it was it died out early in the present century. The ducking which ended the performance has been supposed to be a puritan improvement on what was before a religious ceremony, or mystery. It is more than possibly a relic of the Druidic sacrificial rites; in cases where a river ran near, at the time of the Beltane fires, a sacrifice by water was substituted for that of flame.

The feast of St. Cynog continued for a week. On the Tuesday there was a singular marketing in the churchyard; from all about the farmers brought their tithe of cheese, and taking it to the churchyard, laid it on the tombstones, where it was sold for the parson's behoof.

IV.

All Hallows eve is by the Welsh called 'Nos Calan Gauaf,' meaning 'the first night of winter;' sometimes, 'Nos Cyn Gauaf,' the 'night before winter.' It is one of the 'Teir Nos Ysprydnos,' or 'three nights for spirits,' upon which ghosts walk, fairies are abroad, mysterious influences are in the air, strange sights are seen, and in short goblins of every sort are to be with special freedom encountered. They may be conjured to appear, by certain enchantments, and to give their visitors glimpses of the future, especially as regards the subject of marrying. On this night it is customary for the young people, gathered in many a merry circle, to seek by tricks and charms of various sort to become acquainted with their future lovers and sweethearts. Not that it is always necessary to employ such aids, for on the Teir Nos Ysprydnos the phantoms of future companions have been known to appear unsummoned. There are many such stories as that of Thomas Williams, the preacher, who slept in the hills on a Nos Ysprydnos, and although he used no charms nor tricks of any sort, he saw his future wife. As he was just about putting out his light, having jumped into bed, the door opened and the goblin mother of the young woman he subsequently married walked into the room, leading her daughter. ' Here, Thomas,' said she, ' I am going, but I leave you Mary.' And when he came down home out of the mountains he found that the old mother had died in her bed at the very moment he saw her goblin. To have done less than marry the girl, after that, would have been to insult the good old lady's ghost, and cast reflections on the reputation of All Hallows eve.

The two other spirit-nights, it may here be mentioned, are May-day eve and Midsummer eve ; which with All Hallows were three great festivals of the ancient Druids, when they commemorated the powers of Nature and love in the manner which has been alluded to. I have two accounts of this matter, however, and I know not which is the older in tradition, as I have both from the mouths of the people ; but one account calls Christmas-night the third spirit-night.

The festivities of All Hallows in Wales are in the main like those of other Christian lands, in so far as they consist of feasting and making merry. Bonfires were kindled in many places until recently and perhaps are still, in some parts, again in pursuance of the Druidic rites, which the Christian Church adopted and continued while changing their significance. In Owen's account of the Bards occurs a curious description of the autumnal fires kindled in North Wales on the eve of the first of November, and the attendant ceremonies. There was running through the fire and smoke, and casting of stones into the fire, 'all running off at the conclusion to escape from the black short-tailed sow.'[1] This custom of running through the fire is said to survive in Ireland. It is no doubt related to the ancient sacrificial rites. As testimonies to the kinship of our race, all these customs possess a deep interest, which is increased in this direction as they lose in the charm of the unique.

On the Welsh Border there prevails a Hallowe'en custom among the children of going about to the houses singing the rhymes which follow :

> Wissel wassel, bread and possel,
> Cwrw da, plas yma :
> An apple or a pear, a plum or a cherry,
> Or any good thing to make us merry.
>
> Sol cakes, sol cakes,
> Pray you, good missus, a sol cake ;
> One for Peter, and two for Paul,
> And three for the good man that made us all.
>
> The roads are very dirty,
>   My shoes are very thin,
> I've got a little pocket,
>   To put a penny in.
> Up with the kettle and down with the pan,
> Give us an answer and we'll be gan.

(A loud rap at the door.)

Spoken. Please to give us a 'apenny.

Some of these rhymes are heard in Glamorganshire and elsewhere at Christmas and New Year's.

[1] Brand, ' Pop. Ant.,' i., 191.

The puzzling jug is a vessel in use in some quarters as a means of increasing the hilarity of a Hallowe'en party. It is a stone jug, 'out of which each person is compelled to drink. From the brim, extending about an inch below the surface, it has holes fantastically arranged so as to appear like ornamental work, and which are not perceived except by the perspicacious; three projections, of the size and shape of marbles, are around the brim, having a hole of the size of a pea in each; these communicate with the bottom of the jug through the handle, which is hollow, and has a small hole at the top, which, with two of the holes being stopped by the fingers, and the mouth applied to the one nearest the handle, enables one to suck the contents with ease; but this trick is unknown to every one, and consequently a stranger generally makes some mistake, perhaps applying his mouth as he would to another jug, in which case the contents (generally ale) issue through the fissures on his person, to the no small diversion of the spectators.'[1]

Another merry custom of All Hallows was—and is—twco am 'falau, bobbing for apples. A large tub (crwc) is brought into the kitchen of a farmhouse and filled with water; a dozen apples are thrown into it, and the rustic youths bob for them with their mouths. To catch up two apples at a single mouthful is a triumphant achievement. Again the revellers will form a semicircle before the fire, while there depends above their mouths from a hook in the ceiling, a string with a stick attached. At one end of the stick is an apple, at the other end a candle. To snatch the apple with the lips, and yet avoid the candle, is the aim of the competitors. The stick is so hung that it turns easily on its axis,

[1] 'Camb. Sup.,' 174.

and the bobbers often find themselves catching the candle in their hair while aiming at the apple. This appears to be a relic of the ancient Welsh game of quintain, or gwyntyn.

V.

November the Fifth, the anniversary of the Gunpowder Plot, is much observed in Wales. 'God grant,' said Bishop Sanderson in one of his sermons, 'that we nor ours ever live to see November the Fifth forgotten, or the solemnity of it silenced.' The words are similar to those used by a great American, of the early days of the Republic, with regard to the 4th of July—God grant it might never be forgotten. But the rites by which both days are celebrated are as old as tradition, and much older than history. As the Americans have given a historical significance to bonfires and fireworks, so the English before them did to sacrificing a puppet on Guy Fawkes' Day; and so again some Catholic nations have made the rite a religious one, in the hanging of Judas. All three customs are traced to the same original—the ancient Druidic sacrifices to the sun-god Beal or Moloch. It is noteworthy that the Fifth of November and the Fourth of July —or rather the fiery features of these days—are alike voted a nuisance by respectable and steady-going people in the countries to which they respectively belong.

VI.

On St. Clement's Day (the 23rd of November) it was customary in Pembrokeshire in the last century to parade an effigy of a carpenter, which had been hung to the church steeple the night before. Cutting the effigy down from where it hung, the people carried it about the village, repeating loudly some doggerel verses which purported to be the last will and testament of St. Clement, distributing to the different carpenters in town the several articles of dress worn by the effigy. After the image was thus stripped of its garments, one by one, the padded remains were thrown down and carefully kicked to pieces by the crowd.

CHAPTER IV.

I.

WE come now to the most interesting holiday season of the year, by reason of its almost universality of observance among Christian peoples, and the variety of customs peculiar to it. In the land of Arthur and Merlin it is a season of such earnest and wide-spread cordiality, such warm enthusiasm, such hearty congratulations between man and man, that I have been nowhere equally impressed with the geniality and joyousness of the time. In some Catholic countries one sees more merriment on the day itself; indeed, the day itself is not especially merry in Wales, at least in its out-door aspects. It is the season rather than the day which is merry in Wales. The festival is usually understood, throughout Christendom, to include twelve days; the Welsh people not only make much of the twelve days, but they extend the peculiar festivities of the season far beyond those limits. Christmas has fairly begun in Wales a week or two before Christmas-day. The waits are patrolling the streets of Cardiff as early as December 5th, and Christmas festivals are held as early as December 19th, at which Christmas-trees are displayed, and their boughs denuded of the toys and lollipops in which the juvenile heart delights. After Christmas-day the festival continues I know not just how long, but apparently for weeks.

The characteristic diversions of the Christmas season are, in the main, alike in all Christian countries. In Wales many well-known old customs are retained which in some other parts of Great Britain have disappeared, such as the mummers, the waits, carols, bell-ringings, etc. Not only do the bell-ringers of the several churches throughout the principality do their handsomest on their own particular bells, but there are grand gatherings, at special points, of all the bell-ringers for leagues around, who vie with each other in showing what feats they can perform, how they can astonish you with their majors, bob-majors, and triple bob-majors, on the brazen clangers of the steeples. At Cowbridge, for instance, on Christmas will come together the ringers from Aberdare, Penarth, St. Fagan's, Llantrisant, Llanblethian, and other places, thirty or forty in number, and after they have rung till the air above the town is black with flying clefs and quavers from the steeples, they will all sit down to a jolly Christmas-dinner at the Bear. The bands of waits, or 'pipers of the watch,' who wake the echoes of the early morning with their carols, are heard in every Welsh town and village. In some towns there are several bands and much good-natured rivalry. The universal love of music among the Welsh saves the waits from degenerating into the woe-begone creatures they are in some parts, where the custom has that poor degree of life which can be kept in it by shivering clusters of bawling beggars who cannot sing. Regularly organised and trained choirs of Welshmen perambulate the Cambrian country, chanting carols at Christmas-tide, and bands of musicians play who, in many cases, would not discredit the finest military orchestras. Carols are sung in both Welsh and English; and, generally, the waits are popular. If their music be not good, they are not tolerated; irate gentlemen attack them savagely and drive them off. Not exactly that boot-jacks and empty bottles are thrown at them, but they are excoriated in 'letters to the editor,' in which strong language is hurled at them as intolerable nuisances, ambulatory disturbers of the night's quiet, and inflicters of suffering upon the innocent. But such cases are rare. The music is almost invariably good, and the effect of the soft strains of melodiously-warbled Welsh coming dreamily to one's ears through the darkness and distance on a winter morning is sweet and soothing to most ears. Sometimes small boys will pipe their carols through the key-holes. The songs vary greatly in character, but usually the religious tone prevails, as in this case:

> As I sat on a sunny bank, a sunny bank, a sunny bank,
>   All on a Christmas morning,
> Three ships came sailing by, sailing by, sailing by.
>   Who do you think was in the ships?
>   Who do you think was in the ships?
>   Christ and the Virgin Mary.

Both English and Welsh words are sung. Sometimes a group of young men and women will be seen dancing about the waits to the measure of their music, in the hours 'ayont the twal.' In one aspect the Welsh people may be spoken of as a people whose lives are passed in the indulgence of their love for music and dancing. The air of Wales seems always full of music. In the Christmas season there is an unending succession of concerts and of miscellaneous entertainments of which music forms a part, while you cannot enter an inn where a few are gathered together, without the imminent probability that one or more will break forth in song. By this is not meant a general musical howl, such as is apt to be evoked from a room full of men of any nationality when somewhat under the influence of the rosy god, but good set songs, with good Welsh or English words to them, executed with respect for their work by the vocalists, and listened to with a like respect by the rest of the company. When an Englishman is drunk he is belligerent; when a Frenchman is drunk he is amorous; when an Italian is drunk he is loquacious; when a Scotchman is drunk he is argumentative; when a German is drunk he is sleepy; when an American is drunk he brags; and when a Welshman is drunk he sings. Sometimes he dances; but he does not do himself credit as a dancer under these circumstances; for when I speak of dancing I do not refer to those wooden paces and inflections which pass for dancing in society, and which are little more than an amiable pretext for bringing in contact human elements which are slow to mix when planted in chairs about a room : I refer to the individual dancing of men who do not dance for the purpose of touching women's hands, or indulging in small talk, but for the purpose of dancing; and who apply themselves seriously and skilfully to their work—to wit, the scientific performance of a jig.

I chanced to pass one evening, in the Christmas-time, at a country inn in a little Carmarthenshire village remote from railways. Certain wanderings through green lanes (and the lanes were still green, although it was cold, mid-winter weather) had brought me to the place at dusk, and, being weary, I had resolved to rest there for the night. Some local festivity of the season had taken place during the day, which had drawn into the village an unusual number of farmer-folk from the immediate neighbourhood. After a simple dinner off a chop and a half-pint of cwrw da, I strolled into what they called the smoke-room, by way of distinguishing it from the tap-room adjoining. It was a plain little apartment, with high-backed wooden settles nearly up to the ceiling, which gave an old-fashioned air of comfort to the place. Two or three farmers were sitting there drinking their beer and smoking their pipes, and toasting their trouserless shins before the blazing fire. Presently a Welsh harper with his harp entered from out-doors, and, seating himself in a corner of the room, began to tune his instrument. The room quickly filled up with men and women, and though no drinks but beer and 'pop' were indulged in (save that some of the women drank tea), Bacchus never saw a more genial company. Some one sang an English song with words like these:

> Thrice welcome, old Christmas, we greet thee again,
> With laughter and innocent mirth in thy train;
> Let joy fill the heart, and shine on the brow,
> While we snatch a sweet kiss 'neath the mistletoe-bough—
> > The mistletoe-bough,
> > The mistletoe-bough,
> We will snatch a sweet kiss 'neath the mistletoe-bough.

The words are certainly modern, and as certainly not of a high order of literary merit, but they are extremely characteristic of life at this season in Wales, where kissing under the mistletoe is a custom still honoured by observance. There was dancing, too, in this inn company—performed with stern and determined purpose to excel, by individuals who could do a jig, and wished to do it well. The harper played a wild lilting tune; a serious individual who looked like a school-teacher took off his hat, bowed to the company, jumped into the middle of the floor, and began to dance like a madman. It was a strange sight. With a face whose grave earnestness relaxed no whit, with firmly compressed lips and knitted brow, the serious person shuffled and double-shuffled, and swung and teetered, and flailed the floor with his rattling soles, till the perspiration poured in rivulets down his solemn face. The company was greatly moved; enthusiastic ejaculations in Welsh and English were heard; shouts of approbation and encouragement arose; and still the serious person danced and danced, ending at last with a wonderful pigeon-wing, and taking his seat exhausted, amid a tremendous roar of applause.

Scenes like this are common throughout Wales at the Christmas-time; and they contrast strangely with the austerities of religious observance which are everywhere proceeding. But there is not so wide a chasm between the two as would exist in some countries. The best church-members frequently do not deem a little jollity of this sort a hanging matter, and there are ministers who can do a double-shuffle themselves if the worst comes to the worst. A worthy pastor in Glamorganshire related to me, with a suspicious degree of relish, a story about two ministers who were once riding through a certain village of Wales on horseback. One was the Rev. Evan Harris, the other a celebrated old preacher named Shenkin Harry. And, as they rode on, Harris noticed his companion's legs twitching curiously on his horse's sides. 'Why, what ails your leg?' he asked. 'Don't you hear the harp,' was the reply, 'in the public-house yonder? It makes my old toes crazy for a jig.' But the moral tone of Wales is certainly better, on the whole, than that of most countries—better even than that of Great

U

Britain generally, I should say. There is, I know, a prevailing impression quite to the contrary; but it is utterly absurd. It is an impression which has grown, I imagine, out of English injustice to Welshmen in former times, allied to English ignorance in those times concerning this people. Until within the last hundred years, English writers habitually wrote of Wales with contempt and even scurrility. But no one can live in Wales and not form the opinion that the Welsh are, in truth, an exceptionally moral people; and the nature of their public entertainments throughout the Christmas-time enforces this conclusion. Stendhal's declaration that, in true Biblical countries, religion spoils one day out of seven, destroys the seventh part of possible happiness, would find strong illustration in Wales. It is not my purpose to argue whether the illustration would prove or disprove Stendhal's assertion, though one might fairly ask whether religious people are not, perhaps, as happy in going to church on Sunday as irreligious people are in staying away.

II.

Let it not be supposed that there is any lack of amusement on Christmas-day for people who are willing to be amused in a God-fearing manner. Although you cannot go to the theatre or the circus, you can have a wide liberty of choice among oratorios, concerts, examinations, exhibitions, eisteddfodau, and other odd diversions. Concerts especially thrive. The halls in which they are held are decorated with evergreens, and the familiar custom is in Wales habitually and commonly associated with the ancient Druids, who viewed the green twigs as the symbols of perennial life. Thus a peculiar poetic grace rests with a custom beautiful in itself,

and capable in any land of being poetized by any
one poetically inclined. Many of those unique
gatherings called eisteddfodau are held in different
parts of the principality, when poetry, music, and
essays, in Welsh and in English, are put forth by
the strivers in these Olympian games of intellect and
culture, after the prizes which in Hellas would have
given them crowns of olive-leaves instead of gold-
coins of the realm. When Pindar and Sophocles
handed in poems, and Herodotus competed among
the essayists, and Phidias and Praxiteles among the
cutters of stone, there was no Christmas,—but it is
claimed there were eisteddfodau, here in Wales ; ay,
and before that ; for has not Herodotus spoken of
the British bards who held them ?

III.

In the family circle, the rules which regulate the
Sabbath in Wales—which are almost as repressive
as those of bonnie Scotland, where, by the way,
Christmas-day is scarcely observed at all—are relaxed,
and the aspect of the home is as bright as can be.
The rooms are elaborately decorated with flowers
and evergreens, holly and ivy, ferns and rare plants.
In Glamorganshire, and other of the southern
counties looking on the sea, roses and hawthorn-
sprays may be sometimes seen in full bloom out-of-
doors at Christmas. The decoration of churches
is also elaborate beyond anything I have elsewhere
seen. It is a sight to behold, the preparations for
and the work of decorating a vast pile of ecclesiastical
buildings like Llandaff Cathedral—the huge quan-
tities of evergreens and holly, flowers, cedars, etc.,
which are day by day accumulated by the ladies
who have the business in charge ; and the slow,
continual growth of forms of grace—arches, crosses,

wreaths, festoons; green coverings to font, altar, pulpit, choir-stalls, pillars, reredos, and rood-screen; panels faced with scarlet cloth bearing sacred devices worked in evergreen; the very window-sills glowing with banks of colour—until all the wide spaces in chancel, nave, and transepts, are adorned.

IV.

Of common prevalence formerly, and still observed in numerous parishes, is the custom called the Plygain, or watching for the dawn. This consists in proceeding to the church at three o'clock on Christmas morning, and uniting in a service which is held by the light of small green candles made for the purpose. Sometimes this ceremony is observed at home, the people in a farmhouse holding a jollification on the Christmas eve, and sitting up all night to greet the dawn. If the east wind blew on the Christmas eve the circumstance was deemed propitious in this connection. This wind was called 'gwynt traed y meirw,' (the wind blowing over the feet of the corpses,) because it blew towards the foot of the graves in the churchyards. It was also believed that the dumb animals paid their tribute of respect to this night; the bees would hum loudly in their hives at midnight, and the cattle in the cow-houses would bend their knees as in adoration.[1]

A Christmas-eve custom among Welsh colliers is to carry from house to house a board stuck over with lighted candles, or to wheel a handbarrow containing a bed of clay in which the candles are stuck. This is called 'the Star,' sometimes 'the Star of Bethlehem,' and when stopping before a house the men kneel about it and sing a carol. A

[1] 'Cymru Fu,' 403.

like custom exists in Belgium, among children. The
purpose is to solicit a Rhodd Nadolig, or Christmas
gift.

V.

The British Boxing-day is well known, both as
to its customs and its origin. The Christmas-box,
or thrift-box, is still to be seen in barber shops in
Wales, fastened to the wall, or standing conveniently
under the looking-glass among the pots and brushes.
At one time the custom became such a nuisance
throughout Britain that an outcry was raised about
it. It got to that pass that the butcher and baker
would send their apprentices around among their
customers to levy contributions. The English
Secretary of State for Foreign Affairs, in 1837, sent
a circular to the different embassies requesting their
excellencies and chargés d'affaires to discontinue the
customary Christmas-boxes to the 'messengers of
the Foreign Department, domestic servants of
Viscount Palmerston, foreign postmen, etc.' The
nuisance is hardly less prevalent now. The faithful
postman in Wales not only expects to be remembered at Christmas, but he expects to be given a
precise sum, and if he does not get it he is capable
of asking for it. In one case, a postman accustomed
to receive five shillings at a certain office, on asking
for his 'box,' was told the usual donor was absent
in London, whereupon he requested the clerk to
write up to him in London immediately on the subject. These things strike a stranger as very singular,
among a people usually so self-respecting. Warnings
are from time to time issued on this subject by those
in authority, but the custom is likely to survive so
long as it is not ranked outright with beggary.
Like the Christmas-tree, it is a graceful thing
among the children, or among friends or household

servants, if spontaneous; but as a tax, it is an odious perversion.[1]

VI.

The pagan origin of most of our Christmas customs is undoubted. Even the cheery Christmas-tree is a symbol of heathen rites in times long antedating Christ. The early Christian fathers, in adopting the popular usages of their predecessors, and bending them to the service of Christianity, made wondrous little change in them, beyond the substitution of new motives and names for the old festivals peculiar to several seasons of the year. The British Druids' feast of Alban, Arthur, celebrating the new birth of the sun, occurred at our Christmas time, and is still celebrated at Pontypridd, Glamorganshire, every year. It begins on the 22nd of December, and lasts three days, during which period the sun is supposed to fight with Avagddu, the spirit of darkness, the great luminary having descended into hell for that purpose. On the third day he rose, and the bards struck their harps, rejoicing that the sun had again been found. The Pontypridd ceremonies are similar to those of Midsummer-day, already mentioned. The Arch-Druid presides in the folds of the serpent circle—when he can get there, that is, for he is old, past eighty, and the Druidic hill is apt to be slippery with snow and ice at this time of the year. He prays to the pagan god, and perhaps chants a poem in Welsh.[2] The

[1] Among those who last Christmas applied at my house for 'his box sir, if you please' (as my maid put it), quite as a matter of course, were the postman, the leader of the waits, the boy who brings the daily news papers, the bookseller's boy, the chimney-sweep, the dustman, the grocer's man, etc., etc., no one of whom I had ever set eyes on. The equal of this I never encountered, except in Paris, on the *jour de l'an.*

[2] I give a free translation of this effort as delivered on Sunday December 24th, 1876 (which proved a mild day), and which I find reported in the 'Western Mail' of the 26th as follows: 'The da

Druidic fires of the winter solstice feast were continued in customs like that which survived in Herefordshire until recent years, when on old Christmaseve thirteen fires were lighted in a cornfield, twelve of them being in a circle round a central one which burned higher than the rest. The circle fires were called the Twelve Apostles, and the central one the Virgin Mary. In a shed near by was a cow with a plum-cake between or upon her horns, into whose face a pail of cider was dashed, with a rhyming address, and the cow tossing her horns from her unexpected baptism naturally threw the plum-cake down. If it fell forward, good harvests were predicted; if backward, the omen was evil. A feast among the peasants followed. In the Plygain in like manner survives the Druidic custom of going to the sacred groves before dawn on this morning, to greet the rising of the new-born sun after his struggle with the evil principle.

of the winter solstice has dawned upon us; little is the smile and the halo of Hea. The depth of winter has been reached, but the muse of Wales is budding still. Cold is the snow on the mountains; naked are the trees, and the meadows are bare; but while nature is withering the muse of Wales is budding. When the earth is decked in mourning, and the birds are silent, the muse of Wales, with its harp, is heard in the gorsedd of the holy hill. On the stone ark, within the circle of the caldron of Ceridwen, are throned the sons of Awen; though through their hair the frozen mist is wafted, their bosoms are sympathetic and they rejoice. Peace, love, and truth, encircle our throne; throne without a beginning and without ending, adorned with uchelwydd (mistletoe), symbol of perennial life. The throne of the British Bard—which remains a throne while other thrones decay into dust around it: an everlasting throne! The great wheel of ages revolves and brings around our festivities; repeating our joys it does perpetually. Muse, awake; awake, ye harps; let not any part of the year be forgotten wherein to crown usage (defod), morals (moes), and virtue. The Saviour Hea is about to be born of the winter solstice. He will rise higher still and higher shiningly, and we will have again a new year. Haste hail, haste falling snow, hasten rough storms of winter—hasten away that we may see the happy evidences of the new year.'

CHAPTER V.

Courtship and Marriage—Planting Weeds and Rue on the Graves of
Old Bachelors—Special Significance of Flowers in connection with
Virginity—The Welsh Venus—Bundling, or Courting Abed—Kissing
Schools—Rhamanta—Lovers' Superstitions—The Maid's Trick—
Dreaming on a Mutton Bone—Wheat and Shovel—Garters in a
Lovers' Knot—Egg-Shell Cake—Sowing Leeks—Twca and Sheath.

I.

WELSH courtship is a thorough-going business, early
entered upon by the boys and girls of the Principality ; and consequently most Welsh women marry
young. The ancient laws of Howell the Good (died
948) expressly provided that a woman should be
considered marriageable from fourteen upwards, and
should be entitled to maintenance from that age
until the end of her fortieth year ; 'that is to say,
from fourteen to forty she ought to be considered in
her youth.' By every sort of moral suasion it is
deemed right in Wales to encourage matrimony,
and no where are old bachelors viewed with less
forbearance. There used to be a custom—I know
not whether it be extinct now—of expressing the
popular disapprobation for celibacy by planting on
the graves of old bachelors that ill-scented plant, the
rue, and sometimes thistles, nettles, henbane, and
other unlovely weeds. The practice was even extended, most illiberally and unjustly, to the graves
of old maids, who certainly needed no such insult
added to their injury. Probably the custom was
never very general, but grew out of similar—but
other-meaning—customs which are still prevalent,

and which are very beautiful. I refer to the planting of graves with significant flowers in token of the
virtues of the dead. Thus where the red rose is
planted on a grave, its tenant is indicated as having
been in life a person of peculiar benevolence of
character. The flower specially planted on the
grave of a young virgin is the white rose. There
is also an old custom, at the funeral of a young
unmarried person, of strewing the way to the grave
with evergreens and sweet-scented flowers, and the
common saying in connection therewith is that the
dead one is going to his or her marriage-bed. Sad extremely, and touchingly beautiful, are these customs;
but wherever such exist, there are sure to be ill-con-
ditioned persons who will vent spiteful feelings by
similar means. Hence the occasional affront to the remains of antiquated single folk, who had been perhaps
of a temperament which rendered them unpopular.

The Welsh being generally of an affectionate disposition, courtship, as I have said, is a thorough-
going business. To any but a people of the strongest
moral and religious tendencies, some of their customs
would prove dangerous in the extreme; but no
people so link love and religion. More of their
courting is done while going home from church than
at any other time whatever; and the Welsh Venus
is a holy saint, and not at all a wicked Pagan character like her classic prototype. 'Holy Dwynwen,
goddess of love, daughter of Brychan,' had a church
dedicated to her in Anglesea in 590; and for ages
her shrine was resorted to by desponding swains
and lovesick maidens. Her name—*Dwyn*, to carry
off, and *wen*, white—signifies the bearer off of the
palm of fairness; and, ruling the court of love while
living, when dead

A thousand bleeding hearts her power invoked.

Throughout the poetry of the Cymric bards you constantly see the severest moral precepts, and the purest pictures of virtuous felicity, mingling in singularly perfect fusion with the most amorous strains. Among the 'Choice Things' of Geraint, the famous Blue Bard, were:

> A song of ardent love for the lip of a fair maid ;
> A softly sweet glance of the eye, and love without wantonness ;
> A secluded walking-place to caress one that is fair and slender ;
> To reside by the margin of a brook in a tranquil dell of dry soil ;
> A house small and warm, fronting the bright sunshine.

With these, versifications of all the virtues and moralities. 'In the whole range of Kymric poetry,' says the learned Thomas Stephens,[1] 'there is not, I venture to assert, a line of impiety.'

II.

The Welsh custom of Bundling, or courting abed, needs no description. The Welsh words sopen and sypio mean a bundle and to bundle, and they mean a squeezed-up mass, and to squeeze together ; but there is a further meaning, equivalent to our word baggage, as applied to a strumpet.[2] The custom of bundling is still practised in certain rural neighbourhoods of Wales. To discuss its moral character is not my province in these pages ; but I may properly record the fact that its practice is not confined to the irreligious classes. It is also pertinent here to recal the circumstance that among these people anciently courtship was guarded by the sternest laws, so that any

[1] Vide 'Lit. of the Kymry.'
[2] The Rev. Dr. Thomas, late President of Pontypool College, whose acquaintance with Welsh customs is very extensive, (and to whose erudition I have been frequently indebted during the progress of these pages through the press,) tells me he never heard the word sopen or sypio, synonymous with bundling, used for the old custom, but only 'caru yn y gwelu,' (courting abed.)

other issue to courtship than marriage was practically impossible. If a maiden forgot her duty to herself, her parents, and her training, when the evil result became known she was to be thrown over a precipice; the young man who had abused the parents' confidence was also to be destroyed. Murder itself was punished less severely. Customs of promiscuous sleeping arose in the earliest times, out of the necessities of existence in those primitive days, when a whole household lay down together on a common bed of rushes strewn on the floor of the room. In cold weather they lay close together for greater warmth, with their usual clothing on. Cæsar's misconception that the ancient Britons were polyandrous polygamists evidently had here its source.

It is only by breathing the very atmosphere of an existence whose primitive influences we may thus ourselves feel, that we can get a just conception of the underlying forces which govern a custom like this. Of course it is sternly condemned by every advanced moralist, even in the neighbourhoods where it prevails. An instance came to my knowledge but a short time ago, (in 1877,) where the vicar of a certain parish (Mydrim, Carmarthenshire) exercised himself with great zeal to secure its abolition. Unfortunately, in this instance, the good man was not content with abolishing bundling, he wanted to abolish more innocent forms of courting; and worst of all, he turned his ethical batteries chiefly upon the lads and lasses of the dissenting congregation. Of course, it was not the vicar's fault that the bundlers were among the meeting-house worshippers, and not among the established church-goers, but nevertheless it injured the impartiality of his championship in the estimation of 'the Methodys.' I am not sure the bundling might not have ceased, in deference to his opinions, notwithstanding, if he had not, in the excess of his zeal, complained of the young men for seeing the girls home after meeting, and casually stretching the walk beyond what was necessary. Such intermeddling as this taxed the patience of the courting community to its extreme limit, and it assumed a rebellious front. The vicar, quite undaunted, pursued the war with vigour; he smote the enemy hip and thigh. He returned to the charge with the assertion that these young people had 'schools for the art of kissing,' a metaphorical expression, I suppose; and that they indulged in flirtation. This was really too much. Bundling might or might not be an exclusively dissenting practice, but the most unreasonable of vicars must know that kissing and flirtation were as universal as the parish itself; and so there was scoffing and flouting of the vicar, and, as rebounds are proverbially extreme, I fear there is now more bundling in Mydrim than ever.

III.

The customs of Rhamanta, or romantic divination, by which lovers and sweethearts seek to pierce the future, are many and curious, in all parts of Wales. Besides such familiar forms of this widely popular practice as sleeping on a bit of wedding-cake, etc., several unique examples may be mentioned. One known as the Maid's Trick is thus performed; and none must attempt it but true maids, or they will get themselves into trouble with the fairies: On Christmas eve, or on one of the Three Spirit Nights, after the old folks are abed, the curious maiden puts a good stock of coal on the fire, lays a clean cloth on the table, and spreads thereon such store of eatables and drinkables as her larder will afford. Toasted cheese is considered an appropriate luxury for this occasion. Having prepared the feast, the maiden then takes off all her clothing, piece by piece, standing before the fire the while, and her last and closest garment she washes in a pail of clear spring water, on the hearth, and spreads it to dry across a chair-back turned to the fire. She then goes off to bed, and listens for her future husband, whose apparition is confidently expected to come and eat the supper. In case she hears him, she is allowed to peep into the room, should there be a convenient crack or keyhole for that purpose; and it is said there be unhappy maids who have believed themselves doomed to marry a monster, from having seen through a cranny the horrible spectacle of a black-furred creature with fiery eyes, its tail lashing its sides, its whiskers dripping gravy, gorging itself with the supper. But if her lover come, she will be his bride that same year.

In Pembrokeshire a shoulder of mutton, with nine holes bored in the blade bone, is put under the pillow to dream on. At the same time the shoes of the experimenting damsel are placed at the foot of the bed in the shape of a letter T, and an incantation is said over them, in which it is trusted by the damsel that she may see her lover in his every-day clothes.

In Glamorganshire a form of rhamanta still exists which is common in many lands. A shovel being placed against the fire, on it a boy and a girl put each a grain of wheat, side by side. Presently these edge towards each other; they bob and curtsey, or seem to, as they hop about. They swell and grow hot, and finally pop off the shovel. If both grains go off together, it is a sign the young pair will jump together into matrimony; but if they take different directions, or go off at different times, the omen is unhappy. In Glamorganshire also this is done: A man gets possession of a girl's garters, and weaves them into a true lover's knot, saying over them some words of hope and love in Welsh. This he puts under his shirt, next his heart, till he goes to bed, when he places it under the bolster. If the test be successful the vision of his future wife appears to him in the night.

IV.

A curious rhamanta among farm-women is thus described by a learned Welsh writer:[1] The maiden would get hold of a pullet's first egg, cut it through the middle, fill one half-shell with wheaten flour and the other with salt, and make a cake out of the egg, the flour, and the salt. One half of this she would eat; the other half was put in the foot of her left stocking under her pillow that night; and after offering up a suitable prayer, she would go to sleep. What with her romantic thoughts, and her thirst after eating this salty cake, it was not perhaps surprising that the future husband should be seen, in a vision of the night, to come to the bedside bearing a vessel of water or other beverage for the thirsty maid. Another custom was to go into the garden at midnight, in the season when 'black seed' was sown, and sow leeks, with two garden rakes. One rake was left on the ground while the young woman worked away with the other, humming to herself the while,

> Y sawl sydd i gydfydio,
> Doed i gydgribinio !

Or in English :

> He that would a life partner be,
> Let him also rake with me.

---

[1] Cynddelw, 'Manion Hynafiaethol,' 53.

There was a certain young Welshwoman who, about eighty years ago, performed this rhamanta, when who should come into the garden but her master! The lass ran to the house in great fright, and asked her mistress, 'Why have you sent master out into the garden to me?' 'Wel, wel,' replied the good dame, in much heaviness of heart, 'make much of my little children!' The mistress died shortly after, and the husband eventually married the servant.

The sterner sex have a form of rhamanta in which the knife plays a part. This is to enter the churchyard at midnight, carrying a twca, which is a sort of knife made out of an old razor, with a handle of sheep or goat-horn, and encircle the church edifice seven times, holding the twca at arm's length, and saying, 'Dyma'r twca, p'le mae'r wain?' (Here's the twca—where's the sheath?)

CHAPTER VI.

Wedding Customs—The Bidding—Forms of Cymmhorth—The Gwahoddwr—Horse-Weddings—Stealing a Bride—Obstructions to the Bridal Party—The Gwyntyn—Chaining—Evergreen Arches —Strewing Flowers—Throwing Rice and Shoes—Rosemary in the Garden—Names after Marriage—The Coolstrin—The Ceffyl Pren.

I.

WALES retains several ancient customs in connection with weddings, which are elsewhere extinct. No one who has ever paid any attention to Wales and its ways can have failed to hear of that most celebrated rite the Bidding, which is, however, one of several picturesque survivals less well known to the outer world. The Bidding wedding must be spoken of as an existing custom, although it be confined to rural neighbourhoods in South Wales, and to obscure and humble folk. Those who strive to prove that all such customs are obsolete everywhere—a thankless and even ungraceful task, it seems to me— will not admit that the Bidding has been known since 1870. I have evidence, however, that in Pembroke, Cardigan, and Carmarthen shires, the custom did not cease on the date named, and there is every probability that it prevails to-day. Nothing could be of smaller importance, it is true, than the precise date on which a given custom recently ceased, since any one may revive it next year who chooses to do so.

The Bidding is an invitation sent by a couple who are about to be married, soliciting the presence and donations of the neighbours on their behalf. The presents may be either sums of money or necessaries. Gifts of bread, butter, cheese, tea, sugar, and the like, are common, and sometimes articles of farming stock and household furniture. All gifts of money are recognized by a sort of promissory note, i.e., by setting down the name and residence of the donor, with the amount given ; and when a like occasion arises on the part of the giver, the debt is religiously paid. The obligation is an absolute one, and its legality has actually been recognized by the Court of Great Sessions at Cardiff. The gift is even claimable under other circumstances than the donor's getting married. Another sort of contribution is the eatables and drinkables which are set before the guests ; these are only repayable when required on a like occasion.

The method of bidding the guests was until lately through a personage called the gwahoddwr (inviter or bidder) who tramped about the country some days beforehand, proclaiming the particulars to everybody he met. He usually recited a doggerel set of rhymes before and after the special invitation—a composition of his own, or understood to be such, for rhyme-making was a part of the talent of a popular bidder. Frequently no little humour was displayed in the bidding song. But since the printing press became the cheap and ready servant of the humblest classes, the occupation of the bidder has gradually fallen to decay ; a printed circular serves in his place. At the shop of a printer in Carmarthen I procured a copy of the following bidding circular, which may be a real document, or a fictitious one :

CARMARTHENSHIRE, JULY 4TH, 1862.

As we intend to enter the Matrimonial State, on Wednesday, the 30th of July instant, we purpose to make a BIDDING on the occasion, the same day, at the Young Man's Father's House, called TY'R BWCI,

X

in the Parish of Llanfair ar y Bryn, when and where the favour of
your good and agreeable company is respectfully solicited, and whatever donation you may be pleased to confer on us then will be thank-
fully received, warmly acknowledged, and cheerfully repaid whenever
called for on a similar occasion,

By your most obedient Servants,

OWEN GWYN,
ELEN MORGAN.

The Young Man, his Father and Mother (Llewelyn and Margaret
Gwyn, of Ty'r Bwci), his Brother (Evan Gwyn, Maes y Blodau), his
Sisters (Gwladys and Hannah), and his Aunt (Mary Bowen, Llwyn y
Fedwen, Llannon), desire that all gifts of the above nature due to them
be returned to the Young Man on the above day, and will be thank-
ful for all additional favours granted.

The Young Woman, her Father (Rhys Morgan, Castell y Moch),
and her Brothers and Sister (Howel, Gruffydd, and Gwenllïan
Morgan), desire that all gifts of the above nature due to them be
returned to the Young Woman on the above day, and will be thankful
for all additional favours conferred on her.

The Young Man's company will meet in the Morning at Ty'r Bwci;
and the Young Woman's at Pant y Clacwydd, near the Village of
Llansadwrn.

The Bidding is sometimes held on the day of the
wedding, and sometimes on the day and night before
it; the custom varies in different districts, as all
these customs do. When the latter is the case, the
night is an occasion of great merry-making, with much
consumption of cwrw da, and dancing to the music
of the harp, for poor indeed would be the Welsh
community that could not muster up a harper. This
festival is called Nos Blaen, or preceding night, and
is a further source of income to the couple, from the
sale of cakes and cwrw. 'Base is the slave who
pays' is a phrase emphatically reversed at a Welsh
wedding.

The Bidding is but one form of a feature of Welsh
life which extensively prevails, known by the term
Cymmhorth. The Bidding is a Priodas Cymmhorth;
the Cyfarfod Cymmhorth, or Assistance Meeting, is
much the same thing, minus the wedding feature.

The customs of the latter festival are, however, often
of a sort distinctly tending toward matrimonial

THE OLD-TIME GWAHODDWR.

results as an eventuality. A number of farmer girls
of the humbler sort will gather at a stated time

X 2

and place to give a day's work to one needing as-sistance, and after a day spent in such toil as may be required, the festival winds up with jollity in the evening. The day is signalized on the part of those youths of the neighbourhood who are interested in the girls, by tokens of that interest in the shape of gifts. The lass who receives a gift accompanied by a twig of birch is thereby assured of her lover's constancy. To her whom the young man would inform of his change of heart, a sprig of hazel is given. An earlier feature of this ceremony was the Merry Andrew, who presented the gifts in the name of the lover. This personage was disguised fantastically, and would lead the young woman he selected into another room, where he would deliver the gift and whisper the giver's name.

The antiquity of the Bidding as a local custom is undoubted. The old-time gwahoddwr was a person of much importance, skilled in pedigrees and family traditions, and himself of good family. A chieftain would assume the character in behalf of his vassal, and hostile clans respected his person as he went about from castle to castle, from hall to hall. He bore a garlanded staff as the emblem of his office, and on entering a dwelling would strike his staff upon the floor to command the attention of the group before him, and then begin his address.

II.

The Horse-Wedding is of more ancient origin than the Bidding, and is still a living custom in some parts of Wales, especially Carmarthenshire and western Glamorganshire. It was in other days common throughout South Wales, and was scolded about by old Malkin (generally very cordial in his praise of Welsh customs) in these spicy terms : ' Ill

may it befal the traveller, who has the misfortune of
meeting a Welsh wedding on the road. He would
be inclined to suppose that he had fallen in with a
company of lunatics, escaped from their confinement.
It is the custom of the whole party who are invited,
both men and women, to ride full speed to the
church porch, and the person who arrives there first
has some privilege or distinction at the marriage
feast. To this important object all inferior consider-
ations give way; whether the safety of his majesty's
subjects, who are not going to be married, or their
own, incessantly endangered by boisterous, unskilful
and contentious jockeyship.'[1] Glamorganshire is
here spoken of. The custom varies somewhat in
different localities, but it preserves the main feature,
to force the bride away from her friends, who then
gallop after her to church, arriving *toujours trop tard*,
of course, like the carabineers in ' Les Brigands.'

There have been cases, however, when the bride
was caught by a member of the pursuing party, and
borne away—an incident which occurred in the
knowledge of an acquaintance, who related it to me.
As may readily be inferred, the bride in this case
was not unwilling to be caught; in fact she was
averse to marrying the man who was taking her to
church, and who was her parent's choice, not her own.
The lover who had her heart caught up with her by
dint of good hard riding, and whisked her on his
horse within sight of the church-door, to the intense
astonishment of the bridegroom, who gazed at them
open-mouthed as they galloped away. He thought
at first it was a joke, but as the lovers disappeared
in the distance the truth dawned upon him : a Welsh
custom had served something like its original purpose.

[1] Malkin's ' South Wales,' 67.

But usually, the whole performance is a vehicle for fun of the most good-natured and innocent sort. It begins by the arrival of the neighbours on horseback at the residence of the expectant bridegroom. An eye-witness to a certain wedding gathering in Glamorganshire a few years ago states that the horsemen exceeded one hundred in number. From among them a deputation was chosen to go (still on horseback) to the bride's residence to make formal demand for her. Her door was barred inside, and the demand was made in rhyme, and replied to in the same form from within. It often happens that a brisk contest of wits signalizes this proceeding, for if the voice of any one within is recognized by one of those outside, his personal peculiarities are made the subject of satirical verses. A voice inside being recognized as that of a man who was charged with sheep-stealing, this rhyme was promptly shouted at him :

> Gwrando, leidr hoyw'r ddafad,
> Ai ti sydd yma heddyw'n geidwad?
> Ai dyna y rheswm cloi y drysau,
> Rhag dwyn y wreigan liw dydd goleu?

(Ah, sheep-stealer, art thou a guardian of the fair one? If the doors were not locked thou wouldst steal the bride in broad daylight.)

The doors are opened in the end, of course, and after refreshments the wedding party gallops off to church. The bride is stolen away and borne off to a distance on her captor's horse, but only in sport ; her captor brings her back to the church, where she is quietly married to the proper person. Sometimes the precaution is taken of celebrating the marriage privately at an early hour, and the racing takes place afterward.

Obstructions are raised by the bride's friends, to prevent the bridegroom's party from coming to her house, and these difficulties must be overcome

ere the bride can be approached. Sometimes a mock
battle on the road is a feature of the racing to church.
The obstructions placed in the road in former days
included the Gwyntyn, a sort of game of skill which
seems to have been used by most nations in Europe,
called in English the quintain. It was an upright
post, upon which a cross-piece turned freely, at one
end of which hung a sand-bag, the other end presenting a flat side. At this the rider tilted with his
lance, his aim being to pass without being hit in the
rear by the sand-bag. Other obstructions in use are
ropes of straw and the like.

There is a Welsh custom called Chaining, which
probably arose out of the horse-wedding, and still
prevails. In the village of Sketty, Glamorganshire,
in August, 1877, I saw a chaining, on the occasion of
a marriage between an old lady of eighty and a man
of fifty. The affair had made so much talk, owing to
the age of the bride, that the whole village was in
the streets. While the wedding ceremony was in
progress, a chain was stretched across the street,
forming a barrier which the wedding party could not
pass till the chainers were 'tipped.' The driver of the
carriage containing the newly wedded pair was an
Englishman, and ignorant of the custom, at which he
was naturally indignant. His angry efforts to drive
through the barrier made great sport for the
Welshmen.

The origin of the Welsh horse-wedding may be
traced to the Romans, if no further back, and may
thus be connected with the rape of the Sabines.
That the Romans had an exactly similar custom is
attested by Apuleius, and it is said to have been
established by Romulus in memory of the Sabine
virgins. It is not improbable that the Romans may
have left the custom behind them when they quitted

this territory in the fifth century, after nearly three hundred years' rule.

IV.

Among the wealthier classes of Wales, certain joyous and genial wedding customs prevail, such as are common in most parts of the British isles, but which do not reappear in the new world across the Atlantic,—a fact by which American life is a heavy loser, in my opinion. When the Rector of Merthyr's daughter (to use the form of speech common) was married, a few months since, the tenants of the estate erected arches of evergreens over the roads, and adorned their houses with garlands, and for two or three days the estate was a scene of festivity, ending with the distribution of meat to the poor of the parish. Such festivities and such decorations are common on the estates of the country gentry not only, but in the towns as well. At Tenby, when the High Sheriff's son was married to the Rector of Tenby's daughter, in 1877, garlands of flowers were hung across the High Street, bearing pleasant mottoes, while flags and banners fluttered from house-tops in all directions. Children strewed flowers in the bride's path as she came out of church, while the bells in the steeple chimed a merry peal, and a park of miniature artillery boomed from the pier-head. This custom of children strewing flowers in the path of the new-made bride is common; so also is that of throwing showers of rice after the wedded pair, by way of expressing good wishes—a pleasanter thing to be thrown under these circumstances than the old shoes of tradition. However, since fashion has taken up the custom of rice-throwing and shoe-throwing, the shoes have become satin slippers.

As far back as the 16th century, throwing an old shoe after any one going on an important errand was deemed lucky in Wales. It is thought that in the case of a bride, the custom is derived from the old Jewish law of exchange, when a shoe was given in token that the parents for ever surrendered all dominion over their daughter. But a precisely similar custom prevails in China, where it is usual for the bride to present her husband with a pair of shoes, by way of signifying that for the future she places herself under his control. ' These are carefully preserved in the family and are never given away, like other worn-out articles, it being deemed, that to part with them portends an early separation between husband and wife.'[1] The custom of rice-throwing is also Chinese, the rice being viewed as a sign of abundance. In Sicily, as in some parts of England, wheat is thrown on the bride's head; in Russia, a handful of hops; in the north of England a plateful of shortcake;[2] in Yorkshire, bits of the bride-cake. All these customs, while popularly done ' for luck,' are apparently symbolical of the obedience and the fruitfulness of the newly-wedded wife. And as in Scandinavia the bride tries to get her husband to pick up her handkerchief as an omen of his obeying instead of compelling obedience, so in China the bride tries to sit on a part of her husband's dress. The vulgar story and adage, ' Bandbox now, bandbox always,' expresses the superstition succinctly.

There is a saying current on the Welsh border, that when rosemary flourishes in the garden of a married pair, the lady ' rules the roast,' as the phrase is—though if there is anything a woman should rule, one would think the ' roast' is that thing. ' That be rosemary, sir,' said an old gardener in Herefordshire, pointing to where the plant grew;

---

[1] Dennys, ' Folk-Lore of China,' 18.
[2] Henderson, ' Notes on Folk-Lore,' 22.

'they say it grows but where the missus is master, and it do grow here like wildfire.' The idea of feminine obedience to masculine will, merely because it is masculine, is in itself looked upon as a superstition by all cultivated people in these days, I suppose. Sex aside, if the truth were known, it would be found that the stronger is the ruler, in all lands, under all customs, be the outward show of the ruling more or less; and it is not always where the public sees it most clearly, or fancies it does, that the rule of the dame is sternest. The strength here employed is not virile strength; there is nothing necessarily masculine about it. The severest mistress of her lord I ever knew was a feeble little woman with hands like a baby's, and a face of wax, with no more will-power apparently than a week-old kitten, but whose lightest whim lay on her lord like iron, and was obeyed as faithfully as if it were backed by a cat-o'-nine-tails and a six-shooter.

To return for a moment to our Welsh wedding customs among the wealthier classes. When the couple return from their bridal tour, the fun often begins all over again. Thus at Lampeter, on the edge of Cardiganshire, last September, when Mr. and Mrs. Jones of Glandennis (Jones of Glandennis, Roberts of the Dingle, Williams of Pwlldu,--such cognomens take the place in Wales of the distinctive names which separate Englishmen one from another, and from Jones of Nevada),— when Jones of Glandennis brought home his bride, the whole neighbourhood was agog to greet them. Thousands of people gathered in a field near the station, and passed their time in athletic sports till the train arrived, when they woke the echoes with their cheers. The Joneses entered their carriage, the horses were unharnessed, and a long procession of tenantry, headed by a brass band, dragged the carriage all the way to Glandennis, two miles off, some bearing torches by the side of the carriage. Arches of evergreens were everywhere; and when they got to the house, nothing would do but Mrs. Jones must appear at a window and make a little speech of thanks to the crowd; which she did accordingly—a thing in itself shocking to superstitious ideas of chivalry, but in strictest accord with the true chivalric spirit toward woman. Then fireworks blazed up the sky, and bonfires were lighted on the tops of all the adjoining hills. Lampeter town was illuminated, and nobody went to bed till the small hours.

After marriage, Welshwomen still in some cases retain their maiden names, a custom formerly universal among them. The wife of John Thomas, though the mother of a houseful of children, may be habitually known among her neighbours as Betty Williams. In other cases, she not only assumes her husband's name, but the name of his calling as well; if he is Dick Shon the tailor, she is simply Mrs. Dick Shon the tailor.

V.

A custom called the Coolstrin is now apparently obsolete, unless in occasional rural communities remote from railroads. It resembles the old custom once known in certain parts of England, called the skimitry or skimmington, in which a man whose wife had struck him was forced to ride behind a woman, with his face to the horse's tail, while a band of pans and cow-horns made music for them. The Welsh custom is, however, more elaborate, and more comical, while it is less severe on the man. A husband who is suspected of having a termagant wife, is made the subject of espionage. If it be found that he drinks his mug of ale standing, with his eye twinkling toward the door, the circumstance is considered most suspicious. Efforts are accordingly made to induce the henpecked man to stay and be merry, and if he can be made drunk a great point is gained, as then a squad of volunteers take him inside his own door and critically observe his reception. A moral point involved appears to be that a henpecked husband is a disgrace to manhood in general; and the purpose of the coolstrin is to reform it altogether. However, although it may even be proved that a woman is in the habit of cuffing her husband, the case does not come under the jurisdiction of the coolstrin court until she has 'drawn blood on him.' Then the court is convened. It is composed, no doubt, of any rakehelly youngsters, married or single, who are ripe for sport. One of them is chosen for judge; a special point is that he must be a married man who is not afraid of his wife; and he is invested with robe and gown, that is to say, the collar-bone of a horse is set on his head, around the crown of a slouch hat, and a bed-quilt is made fast to his shoulders. He marches through the streets, with a youth behind him bearing his bed-quilt train, and mounts a chosen wall for a judge's bench. Officers with long white wands range themselves solemnly on either side of him; men are chosen as advocates; and a posse of rustics with pitchforks keeps order. The court is opened by a crier who calls on all good men who as yet wear their own clos,[1] to attend the court. The case is argued by the advocates; witnesses are examined to prove, first, that the man is henpecked, second, that his wife has struck him and drawn blood with the blow. In one case it was proved that the wife

---

[1] Breeches.

had knocked her beery lord down, and that his nose, striking a stool, had bled. The wife's advocate nearly gravelled the judge, by holding that blood drawn by a stool could not be said to have been drawn by the woman. The judge got over this by deciding that if the woman had taken the stool by one of its three legs, and hit the man, drawing blood, the blood would be clearly chargeable to her. 'And where is the difference,' asked he, triumphantly, 'between knocking the stool against him, and knocking him against the stool?' The woman was found guilty. 'For,' said the prosecuting attorney indignantly, 'if a man shan't drink a blue of beer with a neighbour or so, to what won't it come?' Her condemnation followed; to be ridden on the Ceffyl Pren. A derisive procession was formed, and two fellows were rigged up to personate the husband and wife. The male bore a broom, and the female brandished a ladle, and the two were paraded through the town. A band of 'musicians' marched before them, beating frying-pans with marrow bones, banging gridirons and kettles with pokers, tongs and shovels, and two playing on a fife and drum. These were followed by two standard bearers, one bearing a petticoat on top of a pole, the other a pair of breeches in the same manner. Other orts and ends of rabble made up the procession, which with antic and grimace marched about the village and neighbourhood. The orgie ended by the planting in front of the culprit's house of the pole and petticoat, and the pelting of it with addled eggs, stones, and mud, till it fell to the ground. The noble bifurcated emblem of manhood, the clos, was then elevated proudly aloft, and the woman's punishment was deemed complete.

This is the story of a rural village in Glamorganshire. The custom was known in other counties, and varied in its details. In Breconshire, the virago was punished through the ceffyl pren merely by the moral influence of parading it before her cottage. Quarrelsome wives were said to stand in great and constant dread of its possible appearance before their doors. In Cardiganshire, on the contrary, the custom termed the coolstrin is *vice versâ*, and it is only husbands who ill-use their wives who are amenable to its discipline.

CHAPTER VII.

I.

WITH the growth of modern refinement the people
of every land have become constantly more decorous
in their grief. The effort of the primitive and
untutored mind to utter its sorrow in loud and wild
lamentations, and of friends and neighbours to divert
the mind of the sufferer from his bereavement, gave
rise to many funeral customs of which we still find
traces in Wales. Pennant, while travelling in North
Wales, noted, with regard to one Thomas Myddleton,
a fact which he held 'to prove that the custom of the
Irish howl, or Scotch Coranich, was in use among
us (the Welsh) ; for we are told he was buried "cum
magno dolore et clamore cognatorum et propin-
quorum omnium."' No such custom now exists ; but
there is a very impressive rite, of a corresponding
character, but religious, called the Gwylnos. It is a
meeting held in the room where the corpse is lying,
on the night before the funeral. The Irish cry,
'Why did ye die ?' is replaced by pious appeals to

Heaven, in which great and strong emotion is expressed, the deceased referred to in stirring sentences, and his death made a theme for warnings on the brevity of earth-life and the importance of the future life of the soul.

On the day of the funeral, however, the customs are not always in keeping with modern notions of the praiseworthy. Indulgence in beer-drinking at funerals is still a Welsh practice, and its antiquity is indicated by a proverb : 'Claddu y marw, ac at y cwrw'—(To bury the dead, and to the beer.) [1] The collection of Welsh writings called ' Cymru Fu ' refers to the custom thus, (to translate :) ' Before the funeral procession started for the church, the nearest friends and relatives would congregate around the corpse to wail and weep their loss; while the rest of the company would be in an adjoining room drinking warm beer (cwrw brwd) and smoking their pipes ; and the women in still another room drinking tea together.' [2] The writer here speaks of the custom in the past tense, but apparently rather as a literary fashion than to indicate a fact ; at any rate, the custom is not extinct. Occasionally it leads to appearances in the police-court on the part of injudicious mourners. [3] After taking the coffin out of the house and placing it on a bier near the door, it was formerly customary for one of the relatives of the deceased to distribute bread and cheese to the poor, taking care to hand it to each one over the coffin. These poor

---

[1] So the Spanish say, ' The dead to the bier, the living to good cheer.'   [2] ' Cymru Fu,' 91.

[3] 'Two Llancaiach men named Servis and Humphrey were arrested for fighting. ' They had *been to a funeral*, had done the customary honours by the remains of the departed brother or sister who had suffered, died, and was " chested," and then, after drowning their grief in the " cwrw," finished up in the police-court with a *finale* involving the payment of 5*s.* and costs, and 8*s.* 8*d.* damage, or in default twenty-one days' hard labour.'—' Western Mail,' Jan. 31, 1877.

people were usually those who had, in expectation of this gift, been busily engaged in gathering flowers

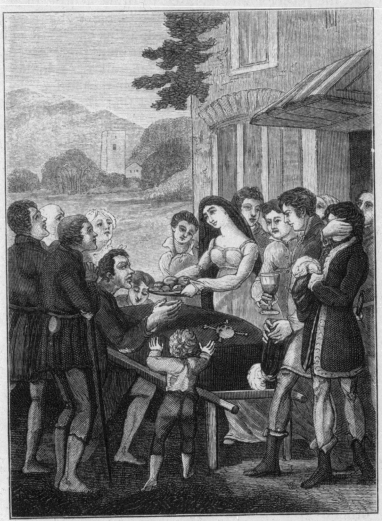

GIVING FOOD OVER THE COFFIN. (*From an old drawing.*)

and herbs with which to grace the coffin. Sometimes this dole was supplemented by the gift of a loaf

of bread or a cheese with a piece of money placed
inside it.　After that a cup of drink was presented,
and the receiver was required to drink a little of it
immediately.[1]　Alluding to this subject the Rev.
E. L. Barnwell[2] says :　'Although this custom is no
longer in fashion, yet it is to some extent represented
by the practice, especially in funerals of a higher
class, to hand to those who are invited to attend the
funeral, oblong sponge cakes sealed up in paper,
which each one puts into his or her pocket, but the
providing and distribution of these cakes are now
often part of the undertaker's duty.'

II.

What connection there may be between these
customs and the strange and striking rite of the Sin-
eater, is a question worthy of careful consideration.
It has been the habit of writers with family ties in
Wales, whether calling themselves Welshmen or
Englishmen, to associate these and like customs
with the well-known character for hospitality which
the Cymry have for ages maintained.　Thus Malkin
writes :　'The hospitality of the country is not less
remarkable on melancholy than on joyful occasions.
The invitations to a funeral are very general and
extensive ; and the refreshments are not light, and
taken standing, but substantial and prolonged.
Any deficiency in the supply of ale would be as
severely censured on this occasion, as at a festival.'[3]
Some have thought that the bread-eating and beer-
drinking are survivals of the sin-eating custom
described by Aubrey, and repeated from him by
others.　But well-informed Welshmen have denied

[1] Pennant, quoted by Roberts, 'Camb. Pop. Ant.,' 175.
[2] 'Arch. Camb.' 4th Se., iii., 332.
[3] 'South Wales,' 68.

that any such custom as that of the Sin-eater ever existed in Wales at any time, or in the border shires ; and it must not be asserted that they are wrong unless we have convincing proof to support the assertion. The existing evidence in support of the belief that there were once Sin-eaters in Wales I have carefully collated and (excluding hearsay and second-hand accounts), it is here produced. The first reference to the Sin-eater anywhere to be found is in the Lansdowne MSS. in the British Museum, in the handwriting of John Aubrey, the author. It runs thus : ' In the county of Hereford was an old custom at funerals to hire poor people, who were to take upon them the sins of the party deceased. One of them (he was a long, lean, ugly, lamentable poor rascal), I remember, lived in a cottage on Rosse highway. The manner was that when the corpse was brought out of the house, and laid on the bier, a loaf of bread was brought out, and delivered to the Sin-eater, over the corpse, as also a mazard bowl of maple, full of beer (which he was to drink up), and sixpence in money, in consideration whereof he took upon him, *ipso facto*, all the sins of the defunct, and freed him or her from walking after they were dead.' Aubrey adds, ' and this custom though rarely used in our days, yet by some people was observed in the strictest time of the Presbyterian Government; as at Dynder (*nolens volens* the parson of the parish), the kindred of a woman, deceased there, had this ceremony punctually performed, according to her will : and also, the like was done at the city of Hereford, in those times, where a woman kept many years before her death a mazard bowl for the Sin-eater ; and the like in other places in this country ; as also in Brecon, e.g., at Llangors, where Mr. Gwin, the minister, about 1640, could not hinder the performance of this custom. I believe,' says Aubrey, 'this custom was heretofore used all over Wales.' He states further, 'A.D. 1686 : This custom is used to this day in North Wales.' Upon this, Bishop White Kennet made this comment : ' It seems a remainder of this custom which lately obtained at Amersden, in the county of Oxford ; where, at the burial of every corpse, one cake and one flaggon of ale, just after the interment, were brought to the minister in the church porch.'[1]

No other writer of Aubrey's time, either English or Welsh, appears to have made any reference to the Sin-eater in Wales ; and equal silence prevails throughout the writings of all previous centuries. Since Aubrey, many references to it have been made, but never, so far as I can discover, by any writer in the Welsh language—a singular omission if there ever was such a custom, for concerning every other superstitious practice commonly ascribed to Wales the Welsh have written freely.

In August, 1852, the Cambrian Archæological Association held its sixth annual meeting at Ludlow, under the Presidency of Hon. R. H. Clive, M.P. At this meeting Mr. Matthew Moggridge, of Swansea, made some observations on the custom of the Sin-eater, when he added details not contained in Aubrey's account given above. He said : 'When a person died, his friends sent for the Sin-eater of the district, who on his arrival placed a plate of salt on the breast of the defunct, and upon the salt a piece of bread. He then muttered an incantation over the bread, which he finally ate, thereby eating up all the sins of the deceased. This done he received his fee of 2s. 6d. and vanished as quickly as possible from the general gaze ; for, as it was believed that

[1] Vide Hone's ' Year Book,' 1832, p. 858.

he really appropriated to his own use and behoof the sins of all those over whom he performed the above ceremony, he was utterly detested in the neighbourhood—regarded as a mere Pariah—as one irredeemably lost.' The speaker then mentioned the parish of Llandebie where the above practice 'was said to have prevailed to a recent period.' He spoke of the survival of the plate and salt custom near Swansea, and indeed generally, within twenty years, (i.e. since 1830) and added : 'In a parish near Chepstow it was usual to make the figure of a cross on the salt, and cutting an apple or an orange into quarters, to put one piece at each termination of the lines.' Mr. Allen, of Pembrokeshire, testified that the plate and salt were known in that county, where also a lighted candle was stuck in the salt ; the popular notion was that it kept away the evil spirit. Mr. E. A. Freeman, (the historian) asked if Sin-eater was the term used in the district where the custom prevailed, and Mr. Moggridge said it was.

Such is the testimony. I venture no opinion upon it further than may be conveyed in the remark that I cannot find any direct corroboration of it, as regards the Sin-eater, and I have searched diligently for it. The subject has engaged my attention from the first moment I set foot on Cambrian soil, and I have not only seen no reference to it in Welsh writings, but I have never met any unlettered Welshman who had ever heard of it. All this proves nothing, perhaps ; but it weighs something.[1]

[1] Mr. Eugene Schuyler's mention of a corresponding character in Turkistan is interesting : 'One poor old man, however, I noticed, who seemed constantly engaged in prayer. On calling attention to him I was told that he was an iskatchi, a person who gets his living by taking on himself the sins of the dead, and thenceforth devoting himself to prayer for their souls. He corresponds to the Sin-eater of the Welsh border.'—' Turkistan,' ii., 28.

III.

Of superstitions regarding salt, there are many in Wales. I have even encountered the special custom of placing a plate of salt on the breast of the corpse. In the case of an old woman from Cardiganshire, who was buried at Cardiff, and who was thus decked by her relatives, I was told the purpose of the plate of salt was to 'prevent swelling.' There is an Irish custom of placing a plate of snuff on the body of a corpse; hence the saying, addressed to an enemy, 'I'll get a pinch off your belly yet.' The Irish also employ the plate of salt in the same manner. In view of the universal prevalence of superstitions regarding salt, too much weight should not be placed on this detail, in connection with the accounts of the Sin-eater. Such superstitions are of extreme antiquity, and they still survive even among the most cultivated classes. Salt falling toward a person was of old considered a most unlucky omen, the evil of which could only be averted by throwing a little of the fallen salt over the shoulder. My own wife observes this heathen rite to this day, and so, I fancy, do most men's wives—jocularly, no doubt, but with a sort of feeling that 'if there *is* anything in it,' &c. Salt was the ancient symbol of friendship, being deemed incorruptible. In the Isle of Man no important business was ventured on without salt in the pocket; marrying, moving, even the receiving of alms, must be sanctified by an exchange of salt between the parties. An influential legend is noted among the Manx inhabitants, of the dissolution of an enchanted palace on that island, through the spilling of salt on the ground. In Da Vinci's picture of the Lord's Supper, Judas Iscariot is represented as overturning the salt

—an omen of the coming betrayal of Christ by that personage. In Russia, should a friend pass you the salt without smiling, a quarrel will follow. The Scotch put salt in a cow's first milk after calving. Even the Chinese throw salt into water from which a person has been rescued from drowning. All these practices point either to lustration or propitiation.

IV.

It has been suggested that the custom of the Sin-eater is in imitation of the Biblical scapegoat. 'And Aaron shall lay both his hands upon the head of the live goat, and confess over him all the iniquities of the children of Israel, and all their transgressions in all their sins, putting them upon the head of the goat, and shall send him away by the hand of a fit man into the wilderness. And the goat shall bear upon him all their iniquities unto a land not inhabited : and he shall let go the goat in the wilderness.'[1] This brings up the subject of charms and magic, and is illustrated in Wales, if not by the Sin-eater, by the cock and hen of St. Tegla's Well. This well is about half-way between Wrexham and Ruthin, in the parish of Llandegla, and has been considered efficacious in curing epilepsy. One of the common names of that complaint in Welsh is Clwyf y Tegla, (Tegla's disease). Relief is obtained by bathing in the well, and performing a superstitious ceremony in this manner : The patient repairs to the well after sunset, and washes himself in it ; then, having made an offering by throwing into the water fourpence, he walks round it three times, and thrice recites the Lord's Prayer. If of the male sex, he offers a cock ; if a woman, a hen. The bird is carried in a basket, first round the well,

[1] Levit. xvi., 21, 22.

then round the church, and the rite of repeating the
Pater Noster again performed. After all this, he
enters the church, creeps under the altar, and making
the Bible his pillow and the communion cloth his
coverlet, remains there until the break of day.
In the morning, having made a further offering of
sixpence, he leaves the cock (or hen, as the case
may be) and departs. 'Should the bird die, it is
supposed that the disease has been transferred to it,
and the man or woman consequently cured.'[1] The
custom is associated with the ancient Druids as well
as with the Jews, and its resemblance to the scapegoat is suggestive.

V.

The funeral procession, in rural districts where
hearses are unknown, wends its way graveward on
foot, with the corpse borne by the nearest relatives
of the deceased, a custom probably introduced in
Wales during their residence here by the Romans.
The coffin of Metellus, the conqueror of Macedon,
was borne by his four sons. The coffins of Roman
citizens held in high esteem by the Republic, were
borne by justices and senators, while those of the
enemies of the people were borne by slaves and
hired servants. As the Welsh procession winds its
way along the green lanes, psalms and hymns are
sung continually, except on coming to cross-roads.
Here the bier is set down, and all kneel and repeat
the Lord's Prayer. The origin of this custom, as
given by the Welsh, is to be found in the former
practice of burying criminals at cross-roads. It
was believed that the spirits of these criminals did
not go far away from the place where their bodies
lay, and the repeating of the Lord's Prayer was
supposed to destroy and do away with any evil

[1] Ab Ithel, 'Arch. Camb.' 1st Se., i., 184.

influence these spirits might have on the soul of the dear departed.[1]

The Welsh retain much of the superstitious feeling regarding the graves of criminals and suicides. There is indeed a strong prejudice against hanging, on account of the troublesome spirits thus let loose. The well-known leniency of a 'Cardigan jury' may be connected with this prejudice, though it is usually associated with a patriotic feeling. 'What! would you have hur hang hur own countryman?' is the famous response of a Cardigan juror, who was asked why he and his brethren acquitted a murderer. The tale may be only a legend; the fact it illustrates is patent. It is related that in a dispute between two Cardigan farmers, some fifty years ago, one of them killed the other. The jury, believing the killing was unintentional, acquitted the homicide; but 'whether the man was guilty or not, his neighbours and the people who lived in the district, and who knew the spot where the farmer was killed, threw a stone upon it whenever they passed, probably to show their abhorrence of the deed that had been perpetrated in that place. By this means a large heap of stones, which was allowed to remain for many years, arose.'[2] They were then removed to repair the turnpike. This custom is apparently Jewish. Hangings are almost unknown in Wales, whether from the extra morality of the people, or the prejudice above noted.

VI.

The legend of the Grassless Grave is a well-known Montgomeryshire tale, concerning a certain spot of earth in the graveyard of Montgomery Castle, upon which the verdure is less luxuriant than in other

[1] 'Cymru Fu,' 92. [2] 'Bye-gones,' March 22, 1876.

portions of the yard.   One dark November night,
many years ago, a man named John Newton, who
had been at Welshpool fair, set out for home.   Soon
after, he was brought back to Welshpool in the
custody of two men, who charged him with highway
robbery, a crime then punishable with death.   He
was tried, and executed, in spite of his protestations ;
and in his last speech, admitting he had committed
a former crime, but protesting he was innocent of
this, he said : 'I have offered a prayer to Heaven,
and believe it has been heard and accepted.   And
in meek dependence on a merciful God, whom I
have offended, but who, through the atonement of
His blessed Son, has, I trust, pardoned my offence,
I venture to assert that as I am innocent of the
crime for which I suffer, the grass, for one generation at least, will not cover my grave.'   For
thirty years thereafter, the grave was grassless ; a
bare spot in the shape of a coffin marked, amidst
the surrounding luxuriance, the place where lay the
penitent criminal, unjustly executed.   Then a
sacrilegious hand planted the spot with turf ; but it
withered as if blasted by lightning ; and the grave
is still grassless—certainly an unnecessary extension
of the time set by the defunct for its testimony to
his innocence.

VII.

A curious surviving custom at Welsh funerals is
the Offrwm, or parson's penny.   After having read
the burial service in the church, the parson stands
behind a table while a psalm is being sung, and to
him go the mourners, one and all, and deposit a
piece of money on the table.   The parson counts it,
states the amount, and pockets it.   If the mourner
depositing his offrwm be wealthy, he will give
perhaps a guinea ; if a farmer or tradesman, his

gift will be a crown; and if poor, he will lay down his sixpence. 'Each one that intended making an offering of silver, would go up to the altar in his turn, and after each one had contributed there would be a respite, after which those who gave copper as their offering went forward and did likewise; but no coppers were offered at any respectable funeral. These offerings often reached the sum of ten and even twenty pounds in the year.' Thus the Welsh work, 'Cymru Fu,' speaking as usual in the past tense; but the custom is a present-day one. The Welsh believe that this custom was originally intended to compensate the clergyman for praying for the soul of the departed. It has now ceased to mean anything more than a tribute of respect to the deceased, or a token of esteem towards the officiating clergyman.

In the parish of Defynog, Breconshire, there was a custom (up to 1843, when it seems to have ceased through the angry action of a lawless widower,) of giving to the parish clerk the best pair of shoes and stockings left behind by the defunct.[1]

A still more curious form of the offrwm, which also survives in many rural neighbourhoods, is called the Arian y Rhaw, or spade money. At the grave, the gravedigger rubs the soil off his spade, extends it for donations, and receives a piece of silver from each one in turn, which he also pockets. In Merionethshire the money is received at the grave in a bowl, instead of on the spade, and the gift is simply called the offrwm. 'I well recollect, when a lad,' says an entertaining correspondent,[2] 'at Llanrhaiadr-yn-Mochnant, seeing the clerk or sexton cleaning his spade with the palm of his hand, and blowing the remaining dust, so that the instrument

[1] 'Arch. Camb.,' 2nd Se., iv., 326. [2] 'Bye-gones,' Oct. 17, 1877.

of his calling should be clean and presentable, and then, with due and clerk-like gravity, presenting his polished spade, first to the "cyfneseifiaid" (next-of-kin), and then to the mourners one by one, giving all an opportunity of showing their respect to the dead, by giving the clerk the accustomed offrwm. At times the old clerk, "yr hen glochydd," when collecting the offrwm, rather than go around the grave to the people, to the no small annoyance of the friends, would reach his spade over the grave. At the particular time referred to, the clerk, having nearly had all the offrwm, saw that facetious wag and practical joker, Mr. B., extending his offering towards him from the opposite side of the grave. The clerk, as was his wont, extended the spade over the grave towards the offered gift. The opportunity for fun was not to be lost, and whilst placing his offrwm on the spade, Mr. B. pressed on one corner, and the spade turned in the hands of the unwitting clerk, emptying the whole offering into the grave, to the no small surprise of the clerk, who never forgot the lesson, and the great amusement of the standers-by.' It is noted in this connection that the sexton's spade 'was a terror to the superstitious, for if the gravedigger would but shake his spade at anyone, it was a matter of but short time ere the sexton would be called upon to dig the grave of that person who had come under the evil influence of the spade. . "Has the sexton shook his spade at you?" was a question often put to a person in bad health.'

VIII.

Until a recent date, burials without a coffin were common in some parts of Wales. Old people in Montgomeryshire not many years ago, could remember such burials, in what was called the cadach deupen, or cloth with two heads. Old Richard Griffith, of Trefeglwys, who died many years ago, recollected a burial in this fashion there, when the cloth gave way and was rent; whereupon the clergyman prohibited any further burials in that churchyard without a coffin. That was the last burial of the kind which took place in Montgomeryshire.[1]

In the middle ages there was a Welsh custom of burying the dead in the garment of a monk, as a protection against evil spirits. This was popular among the wealthy, and was a goodly source of priestly revenue.

IX.

Sul Coffa is an old Welsh custom of honouring the dead on the Sunday following the funeral, and for several succeeding Sundays, until the violence of grief has abated. In the Journal of Thomas Dinelly, Esquire, an Englishman who travelled through Wales and Ireland in the reign of Charles II.,[2] this passage occurs, after description of the wake, the keening, etc. : 'This done ye Irish bury their dead, and if it be in or neer ye burying place of that family, the servants and followers hugg kiss howle and weep over the skulls that are there digg'd up and once a week for a quarter of an year after come two or three and pay more noyse at the place.' The similarity in spirit between this and the Welsh Sul Coffa is as striking as the difference in practice. The Welsh walk quietly and gravely to the solemn mound beneath which rest the remains of the loved, and there kneeling in silence for five or ten minutes, pray or appear to pray.

The Sul Coffa of Ivan the Harper is a well-

---

[1] 'Bye-gones,' Nov. 22, 1876.
[2] Quoted in the Proceedings of the Kilkenny Arch. Soc., 1858.

known anecdote. Ivan the Harper was a noted character in his day, who desired that his coffa should be thus: 'I should like,' said he, on his death-bed, 'to have my coffa; but not in the old style. Instead of the old custom ask Williams of Merllyn and Richard the Harper to attend the church at Llanfwrog, and give these, my disciples, my two harps, and after the service is over, let them walk to my grave; let Williams sit at the head and Richard at the feet, of my grave, and let them play seven Welsh airs, beginning with Dafydd y Garreg Wen,' (David of the White Stone) 'and ending with, Toriad y Dydd,' (the Dawn.) 'The former is in a flat key, like death, and the latter is as sober as the day of judgment.' This request was religiously obeyed by the mourners on the ensuing Sul Coffa.

X.

Reference has been made, in the chapter on courtship and marriage, to the Welsh practice of planting graves with flowers. There are graves in Glamorganshire which have been kept blooming with flowers for nearly a century without interruption, through the loving care of descendants of the departed. By a most graceful custom which also prevailed until recently, each mourner at a funeral carried in his hand a sprig of rosemary, which he threw into the grave. The Pagan practice of throwing a sprig of cypress into the grave has been thought to symbolize the annihilation of the body, as these sprigs would not grow if set in the earth: whereas the rosemary was to signify the resurrection or up-springing of the body from the grave. The existing custom of throwing flowers and immortelles into the grave is derivable from the ancient practice. But the Welsh carry the association of graves and

floral life to the most lavish extreme, as has already
been pointed out. Shakspeare has alluded to this
in 'Cymbeline,' the scene of which tragedy is princi-
pally in Pembrokeshire, at and about Milford
Haven:

> *Arv.* With fairest flowers,
> Whilst summer lasts, and I live here, Fidele,
> I'll sweeten thy sad grave : Thou shalt not lack
> The flower, that's like thy face, pale primrose; nor
> The azur'd harebell, like thy veins ; no, nor
> The leaf of eglantine, whom not to slander,
> Outsweeten'd not thy breath.[1]

[1] 'Cymbeline,' Act iv., Sc. 2.

DAFYDD Y GARREG WEN.

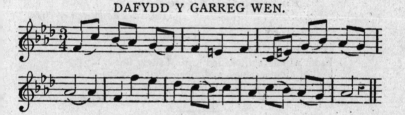

BOOK IV.

BELLS, WELLS, STONES, AND DRAGONS.

> Gorgons, and hydras, and chimeras dire.
> > MILTON : *Paradise Lost.*

> Then up there raise ane wee wee man
> > Franethe the moss-gray stane ;
> His face was wan like the collifloure,
> > For he nouthir had blude nor bane.'
> > > HOGG : *The Witch of Fife.*

> . . . where he stood,
> Of auncient time there was a springing well,
> From which fast trickled forth a silver flood,
> Full of great vertues, and for med'cine good : . . .
> For unto life the dead it could restore.
> > SPENSER : *Faery Queene.*

CHAPTER I.

Base of the Primeval Mythology—Bells and their Ghosts—The Bell that committed Murder and was damned for it—The Occult Powers of Bells—Their Work as Detectives, Doctors, etc.—Legend of the Bell of Rhayader—St. Illtyd's Wonderful Bell—The Golden Bell of Llandaff.

I.

THE human mind in its infancy turns instinctively to fetichism. The mind of primeval man resembled that of a child. Children have to learn by experience that the fire which burns them is not instigated by malice.[1] In his primitive condition, man per-

---

[1] A Mississippi negro-boy who was brought by a friend of mine from his southern home to a northern city, and who had never seen snow, found the ground one morning covered with what he supposed to be salt, and going out to get some, returned complaining that it 'bit his fingers.'

sonified everything in nature. Animate and inanimate objects were alike endowed with feelings,
passions, emotions, moral qualities. On this basis
rests the primeval mythology.

The numerous superstitions associated with bells,
wells and stones in Wales, excite constant inquiries
as regards their origin in fetichism, in paganism,
in solar worship, or in church observances. That
bells, especially, should suggest the supernatural to
the vulgar mind is not strange. The occult powers
of bells have place in the popular belief of many
lands. The Flemish child who wonders how the
voices got into the bells is paralleled by the Welsh
lad who hears the bells of Aberdovey talking in
metrical words to a musical chime. The ghosts of
bells are believed to haunt the earth in many parts
of Wales. Allusion has been made to those castle
bells which are heard ringing from the submerged
towers in Crumlyn lake. Like fancies are associated with many Welsh lakes. In Langorse Pool,
Breconshire, an ancient city is said to lie buried,
from whose cathedral bells on a calm day may be
heard a faint and muffled chime, pealing solemnly
far down in the sepial depths. A legend of Trefethin relates that in the church of St. Cadoc, at
that place, was a bell of wondrous powers, a gift
from Llewellyn ap Iorwerth, Lord of Caerleon. A
little child who had climbed to the belfry was struck
by the bell and killed, not through the wickedness
of the bell itself, but through a spell which had
been put upon the unfortunate instrument by an
evil spirit. But though innocent of murderous
intent, the wretched bell became forfeit to the
demons on account of its fatal deed. They seized
it and bore it down through the earth to the shadow-
realm of annwn. And ever since that day, when a

z

child is accidentally slain at Trefethin, the bell of St. Cadoc is heard tolling mournfully underneath the ground where it disappeared ages ago.

II.

There was anciently a belief that the sound of brass would break enchantment, as well as cause it ; and it is presumed that the original purpose of the common custom of tolling the bell for the dead was to drive away evil spirits. Originally, the bell was tolled not for the dead, but for the dying ; it was believed that evil spirits were hovering about the sick chamber, waiting to pounce on the soul as soon as it should get free from the body ; and the bell was tolled for the purpose of driving them away. Later, the bell was not tolled till death had occurred, and this form of the custom survives here, as in many lands. Before the Reformation there was kept in all Welsh churches a handbell, which was taken by the sexton to the house where a funeral was to be held, and rung at the head of the procession. When the voices of the singers were silent at the end of a psalm, the bell would take up the burden of complaint in measured and mournful tones, and ring till another psalm was begun. It was at this period deemed sacred. The custom survived long after the Reformation in many places, as at Caerleon, the little Monmouthshire village which was a bustling Roman city when London was a hamlet. The bell—called the bangu—was still preserved in the parish of Llanfair Duffryn Clwyd half-a-dozen years ago. I believe the custom of ringing a handbell before the corpse on its way through the streets is still observed at Oxford, when a university man is buried. The town marshal is the bellman for this office. The custom is associated with the same superstitious belief which is seen in the 'passing bell,' the notes of pure bronze freeing the soul from the power of evil spirits.

III.

The Welsh were formerly strong in the belief that bells could perform miracles, detect thieves, heal the sick, and the like. In many instances they were possessed of locomotive powers, and would transport themselves from place to place when they had occasion, according to their own sweet will, and without human intervention It is even recorded that certain handbells required to be tied with the double cord of an exorcism and a piece of twine, or they would get up and walk off in the night.

Bells which presaged storms, as well as other disasters, have been believed to exist in many parts of Wales. In Pembrokeshire the unexpected tolling of a church bell in the night is held to be the sure precursor of a calamity—a belief which may be paralleled in London, where there are still people who believe such tolling on the part of the great bell of St. Paul's portends disaster to the royal family. In the Cromwellian wars, the sacrilegious followers of the stern old castle-hater carried off a great bell from St. David's, Pembrokeshire. They managed to get it on shipboard, but in passing through Ramsey Sound the vessel was wrecked— a direct result, the superstitious said, of profanely treating the bell. Ever since that time, Pembroke people have been able to hear this sunken bell ring from its watery grave when a storm is rising.

IV.

The legend of the Bell of Rhayader perpetuates a class of story which reappears in other parts of

Great Britain. It was in the twelfth century that a certain contumacious knight was imprisoned in the castle of Rhayader. His wife, being devoted to him, and a good Catholic, besought the aid of the monks to get him out. They were equal to the occasion, at least in so far as to provide for her service a magical bell, which possessed the power of liberating from confinement any prisoner who should set it up on the wall and ring it. The wife succeeded in getting the bell secretly into her husband's possession, and he set it up on the wall and rang it. But although he had gathered his belongings together and was fully prepared to go, the doors of his prison refused to open. The castellan mocked at the magical bell, and kept the knight in durance vile. So therefore (for of course the story could not be allowed to end here) the castle was struck by lightning, and both it and the town were burned in one night—excepting only the wall upon which the magic bell was hanging. Nothing remains of the castle walls in this day.

V.

The bell of St. Illtyd was greatly venerated in the middle ages. A legend concerning this wonderful bell relates that a certain king had stolen it from the church, and borne it into England, tied about the neck of one of his horses. For this deed the king was destroyed, but repenting before his death, ordered the bell to be restored to its place in Wales. Without waiting to be driven, the horse with the bell about his neck set out for Wales, followed by a whole drove of horses, drawn by the melodious sound of the bell. Wonderful to tell, the horse was able to cross the river Severn and come into Wales, the great collection of horses following.

'Then hastening along the shore, and over the mountains, and through the woods, he came to the road which went towards Glamorgan, all the horses hearing, and following the sweet sound.' When they came to the banks of the river Taf, a clergy-man heard the sound of the bell, and went out to meet the horse, and they together carried the bell to the gate of St. Illtyd's church. There the horse bent down and loosed his precious burden from his neck, 'and it fell on a stone, from which fall a part of it was broken, which is to be seen until the present day, in memory of the eminent miracle.'[1]

Some thirty years ago a bell was discovered at Llantwit Major, in Glamorganshire, which was thought to be the identical bell of this saint. The village named was the scene of his exploits, many of which were miraculous to the point of Arabian Nights marvelousness. The discovered bell was inscribed 'Sancte Iltute, ora pro nobis,' and stood upon the gable of the quaint old town-hall. But though the bell was unmistakably ancient, it bore intrinsic evidence of having been cast long after the saint's death, when his name had become venerated. He was one of King Arthur's soldiers, who after-wards renounced the world, and founded several churches in Glamorganshire.

VI.

Among the many legends of Llandaff which still linger familiarly on the lips of the people is that of the bell of St. Oudoceus, second bishop of that see. In the ancient 'Book of Llandaff,' where are preserved the records of that cathedral from the earliest days of Christianity on this island, the legend is thus related : 'St. Oudoceus, being thirsty after under-

[1] 'Cambro-British Saints,' 492.

going labour, and more accustomed to drink water than any other liquor, came to a fountain in the vale of Llandaff, not far from the church, that he might drink, where he found women washing butter, after the manner of the country ; and sending to them his messengers and disciples, they requested that they would accommodate them with a vessel, that their pastor might drink therefrom ; who, ironically, as mischievous girls, said, "We have no cup besides that which we hold in our hands, namely, the butter." And the man of blessed memory taking it, formed one in the shape of a small bell, and he raised his hand so that he might drink therefrom, and he drank. And it remained in that form, that is, a golden one, so that it appeared to those who beheld it to consist altogether of the purest gold, which, by divine power, is from that day reverently preserved in the church of Llandaff in memory of the holy man, and it is said that by touching it health is given to the diseased.'[1]

[1] 'Liber Landavensis,' 378.

CLYCHAU ABERDYFI.

(The Bells of Aberdovey.)

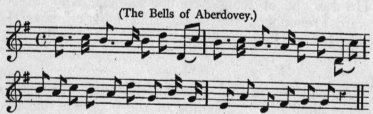

CHAPTER II.

Mystic Wells—Their Good and Bad Dispositions—St. Winifred's Well
—The Legend of St. Winifred—Miracles—St. Tecla's Well—St.
Dwynwen's—Curing Love-sickness—St. Cynfran's—St. Cynhafal's
—Throwing Pins in Wells—Warts—Barry Island and its Legends—
Ffynon Gwynwy—Propitiatory Gifts to Wells—The Dreadful
Cursing Well of St. Elian's—Wells Flowing with Milk—St. Illtyd's—
Taff's Well—Sanford's Well—Origins of Superstitions of this Class.

I.

THE waters of mystery which flow at Lourdes, in
France, are paralleled in numberless Welsh parishes.
In every corner of Cambria may be found wells
which possess definite attributes, malicious or beneficent, which they are popularly supposed to actively
exert toward mankind. In almost every instance,
the name of the tutelary saint to whom the well is
consecrated is known to the peasantry, and generally
they can tell you something about him, or her.
Unnumbered centuries have elapsed since the saint
lived; nay, generation upon generation has perished
since any complete knowledge of his life or character
existed, save in mouldering manuscripts left by
monks, themselves long turned to dust; yet the
tradition of the saint as regards the well is there, a
living thing beside its waters. However lightly
some forms of superstition may at times be treated
by the vulgar, they are seldom capable of irreverent
remark concerning the well. In many cases this
respect amounts to awe.

These wells are of varying power and disposition.
Some are healing wells; others are cursing wells;

still others combine the power alike to curse and to cure. Some are sovereign in their influence over all the diseases from which men suffer, mental and moral as well as physical; others can cure but one disease, or one specific class of diseases; and others remedy all the misfortunes of the race, make the poor rich, the unhappy happy, and the unlucky lucky. That these various reputations arose in some wells from medicinal qualities found by experience to dwell in the waters, is clear at a glance; but in many cases the character of the patron saint gives character to the well. In parishes dedicated to the Virgin Mary there will almost inevitably be found a Ffynon Mair, (Well of Mary,) the waters of which are supposed to be purer than the waters of other wells. Sometimes the people will take the trouble to go a long distance for water from the Ffynon Mair, though a good well may be nearer, in whose water chemical analysis can find no difference. Formerly, and indeed until within a few years past, no water would do for baptizing but that fetched from the Ffynon Mair, though it were a mile or more from the church. That the water flowed southward was in some cases held to be a secret of its virtue. In other instances, wells which opened and flowed eastward were thought to afford the purest water.

II.

Most renowned and most frequented of Welsh wells is St. Winifred's, at Holywell. By the testimony of tradition it has been flowing for eleven hundred and eighty years, or since the year 700, and during all this time has been constantly visited by throngs of invalids; and that it will continue to be so frequented for a thousand years to come is not doubted, apparently, by the members of the Holy-

well Local Board, who have just taken a lease of
the well from the Duke of Westminster for 999
years more, at an annual rental of £1. The town
of Holywell probably owes not only name but existence to this well. Its miraculous powers are extensively believed in by the Welsh, and by people
from all parts of Great Britain and the United
States; but Drayton's assertion that no dog could
be drowned in its waters, on account of their beneficent disposition, is not an article of the existing
faith. The most prodigious fact in connection with
this wonderful fountain, when its legendary origin is
contemplated, is its size, its abounding life, the great
volume of its waters. • A well which discharges
twenty-one tons of water per minute, which feeds
an artificial lake and runs a mill, and has cured unnumbered thousands of human beings of their ills
for hundreds of years, is surely one of the wonders
of the world, to which even mystic legend can only
add one marvel more.

The legend of St. Winifred, or Gwenfrewi, as
she is called in Welsh, was related by the British
monk Elerius in the year 660, or by Robert of
Salop in 1190, and is in the Cotton MSS. in the
British Museum. It is there written in characters considered to be of the middle of the eleventh century.
Winifred was the daughter of a valiant soldier in
North Wales; from her youth she loved a heavenly
spouse, and refused transitory men. One day Caradoc, a descendant of royal stock, came to her house
fatigued from hunting wild beasts, and asked Winifred for drink. But seeing the beauty of the nymph
he forgot his thirst in his admiration, and at once
besought her to treat him with the familiarity of a
sweetheart. Winifred refused, asserting that she
was engaged to be married to another. Caradoc

became furious at this, and said, 'Leave off this foolish, frivolous, and trifling mode of speaking, and consent to my wish.' Then he asked her to be his wife. Finding he would not be denied, Winifred had recourse to a stratagem to escape from him: she pretended to comply, but asked leave to first make a becoming toilet. Caradoc agreed, on condition that she should make it quickly. The girl went through her chamber with swift feet into the valley, and was escaping, when Caradoc perceived the trick, and mounting his horse spurred after her. He overtook her at the very door of the monastery to which she was fleeing; before she could place her foot within the threshold he struck off her head at one blow. St. Beino coming quickly to the door saw bloody Caradoc standing with his stained sword in his hand, and immediately cursed him as he stood, so that the bloody man melted in his sight like wax before a fire. Beino then took the virgin's head (which had been thrown inside the door by the blow which severed it) and fitted it on the neck of the corpse. Winifred thereupon revived, with no further harm than a small line on her neck. But the floor upon which her bloody head had fallen, cracked open, and a fountain sprang up like a torrent at the spot. 'And the stones appear bloody at present as they did at first, and the moss smells as frankincense, and it cures divers diseases.'[1] Thus far the monastic legend. Some say that Caradoc's descendants were doomed to bark like dogs.

Among the miracles related of Winifred's well by her monkish biographer is one characterized as 'stupendous,' concerning three bright stones which were seen in the middle of the ebullition of the fountain, ascending and descending, 'up and down

[1] 'Cambro-British Saints,' 519.

by turns, after the manner of stones projected by a shooter.' They so continued to dance for many years, but one day an unlucky woman was seized with a desire to play with the stones. So she took hold of one; whereat they all vanished, and the woman died. This miracle was supplemented by that of a man who was rebuked for theft at the fountain; and on his denying his guilt, the goat which he had stolen and eaten became his accuser by uttering an audible bleating from his belly. But the miracles of Winifred's well are for the most part records of wonderful cures from disease and deformity. Withered and useless limbs were made whole and useful; the dumb bathed in the water, came out, and asked for their clothes; the blind washed and received their sight; lunatics 'troubled by unclean spirits' were brought to the well in chains, 'tearing with their teeth and speaking vain things,' but returned homeward in full possession of their reason. Fevers, paralysis, epilepsy, stone, gout, cancers, piles—these are but a few of the diseases cured by the marvellous well, on the testimony of the ancient chronicler of the Cotton MSS. 'Nor is it to be hidden in the silence of Lethean oblivion that after the expulsion of the Franks from all North Wales' the fountain flowed with a milky liquor for the space of three days. A priest bottled some of it, and it 'was carried about and drunk in all directions,' curing diseases in the same manner as the well itself.

III.

Only second in fame to Winifred's, among the Welsh themselves, is St. Tecla's well, or Ffynon Tegla, in Denbighshire. It springs out of a bog called Gwern Degla, about two hundred yards from the parish church of Llandegla. Some account of the peculiar superstitious ceremony connected with this well has already been given, in the chapter treating of the sin-eater. It is there suggested that the cock to which the fits are transferred by the patient at the well is a substitute for the scapegoat of the Jews. The parish clerk of Llandegla in 1855 said that an old man of his acquaintance 'remembered quite well seeing the birds staggering about from the effects of the fits' which had been transferred to them.

IV.

Of great celebrity in other days was St. Dwynwen's well, in the parish of Llandwyn, Anglesea. This saint being patron saint of lovers, her well possessed the property of curing love-sickness. It was visited by great numbers, of both sexes, in the fourteenth century, when the popular faith in its waters seems to have been at its strongest. It is still frequented by young women of that part of the country when suffering from the woes inflicted by Dan Cupid. That the well itself has been for many years covered over with sand does not prevent the faithful from displaying their devotion; they seek their cure from 'the water next to the well.' Ffynon Dwynwen, or Fountain of Venus, was also a name given to the sea, according to the Iolo MSS.; and in the legend of Seithenhin the Drunkard, in the 'Black Book of Carmarthen,' this stanza occurs:

> Accursed be the damsel,
> Who, after the wailing,
> Let loose the Fountain of Venus, the raging deep.[1]

---

[1] 'Black Book of Carmarthen,' xxxviii. (An ancient MS. in the Hengwrt collection, which belonged of old to the priory of Black Canons at Carmarthen, and at the dissolution of the religious houses in Wales, when their libraries were dispersed, was given by the treasurer of St. David's Church to Sir John Price, one of Henry VIII.'s commissioners.)

The story of Aphrodite, born from the foam of the sea, need only be alluded to here.

V.

Several wells appear to have been devoted to the cure of the lower animals' diseases. Such was the well of Cynfran, where this ejaculation was made use of: ' Rhad Duw a Chynfran lwydd ar y da!' —(the grace of God and the blessed Cynfran on the cattle.) This Cynfran was one of the many sons of the patriarch Brychan, and his well is near Abergeleu. Pennant speaks also of a well near Abergeleu, which he calls St. George's well, and says that there the British Mars had his offering of horses; 'for the rich were wont to offer one, to secure his blessing on all the rest. He was the tutelar saint of those animals.'

VI.

St. Cynhafal's well, on a hillside in Llangynhafal parish, Denbighshire, is one of those curing wells in which pins are thrown. Its specialty is warts. To exorcise your wart you stick a pin in it and then throw the pin into this well; the wart soon vanishes. The wart is a form of human trouble which appears to have been at all times and in all countries a special subject of charms, both in connection with wells and with pins. Where a well of the requisite virtue is not conveniently near, the favourite form of charm for wart-curing is in connection with the wasting away of some selected object. Having first been pricked into the wart, the pin is then thrust into the selected object—in Gloucestershire it is a snail—and then the object is buried or impaled on a blackthorn in a hedge, and as it perishes the wart will disappear. The scapegoat principle of the sin-eater also appears in connection with charming away warts, as where a 'vagrom man' counts your warts, marks their number in his hat, and goes away, taking the warts with him into the next county—for a trifling consideration.[1]

VII.

On Barry Island, near Cardiff, is the famous well of St. Barruc, or Barri, which was still frequented by the credulous up to May, 1879, at which time the island was closed against visitors by its owner, Lord Windsor, and converted into a rabbit warren. Tradition directs that on Holy Thursday he who is troubled with any disease of the eyes shall go to this well, and having thoroughly washed his eyes in its water, shall drop a pin in it. The innkeeper there formerly found great numbers of pins—a pint, in one instance—when cleaning out the well. It had long been utterly neglected by the sole resident of the island, whose house was a long distance from the well, at a point nearer the main land; but pins were still discovered there from time to time. There was in old days a chapel on this island; no vestige of it remains. Tradition says that St. Barruc was buried there, and the now barren and deserted isle appears to have been anciently a popular place among the saints. St. Cadoc had one of his residences there.[2] He was one day sitting on a hill-top in that island when he saw the two saints Barruc and Gwalches drawing near in a boat, and as he looked the boat was overturned by the wind. Both

---

[1] A popular belief among boys in some parts of the United States that warts can be rubbed off upon a toad impaled with a sharp stick; as the toad dies the warts will go. *Per contra*, this cruel faith is offset by a theory that toads if ill-treated can spit upon their aggressor hands and thus cause warts.

[2] 'Cambro-British Saints,' 336.

saints were drowned, and Cadoc's manual book, which they had in the boat with them, was lost in the sea. But when Cadoc proceeded to order his dinner, a salmon was brought to him which being cut open was found to have the missing manual book in its belly in an unimpaired condition. Concerning another saint whose name was Barri, a wonderful story is told that one day being on a visit to St. David he borrowed the latter's horse and rode across the sea from Pembrokeshire to the Irish coast. Many have supposed this Barri to be the same person as Barruc, but they were two men.

This romantic island was anciently celebrated for certain ghastly noises which were heard in it— sounds resembling the clanking of chains, hammering of iron, and blowing of bellows—and which were supposed to be made by the fiends whom Merlin had set to work to frame the wall of brass to surround Carmarthen. So the noises and eruptions of Etna and Stromboli were in ancient times ascribed to Typhon or Vulcan. But in the case of Barry I have been unable, by any assistance from imagination, to detect these mystic sounds in our day. Camden, in his 'Britannica,' makes a like remark, but says the tradition was universally prevalent. The judicious Malkin, however, thinks it requires but a moderate stretch of fancy to create this cyclopean imagery, when the sea at high tides is often in possession of cavities under the very feet of the stranger, and its voice is at once modified and magnified by confinement and repercussion.[1]

VIII.

Another well whose specialty is warts is a small spring called Ffynon Gwynwy, near Llangelynin

[1] Malkin's 'South Wales,' 132.

church, Carnarvonshire. The pins used here must be crooked in order to be efficacious. It is said that fifty years ago the bottom of this little well was covered with pins ; and that everybody was careful not to touch them, fearing that the warts deposited with the pins would grow upon their own hands if they did so.[1] At present the well is overgrown with weeds, like that on Barry Island.

IX.

The use of pins for purposes of enchantment is one of the most curious features of popular super-stition. Trivial as it appears to superficial observa-tion, it can be associated with a vast number of mystic rites and ceremonials, and with times the most ancient. There is no doubt that before the invention of pins in this country small pieces of money were thrown into the well instead ; indeed it was asserted by a writer in the 'Archæologia Cambrensis' in 1856 that money was still thrown into St. Tecla's well, by persons desirous of re-covering from fits. That the same practice pre-vailed among the Romans is shown by Pliny, who speaks of the sacred spring of the Clitumnus, so pure and clear that you may count the pieces of money that have been thrown into it, and the shining pebbles at the bottom. And in connection with the Welsh well of St. Elian there was for-merly a box into which the sick dropped money as they nowadays drop a pin into that well. This box was called cyff-elian, and was in the form of a trunk studded with nails, with an aperture in the top through which the money was dropped. It is said to have got so full of coins that the parishioners opened it, and with the contents purchased three

[1] 'Arch. Camb.,' 3rd Se., xiii., 61.

farms. The presentation of pins to the well, though now a meaningless rite on the part of those who practice it, was originally intended as a propitiatory offering to the evil spirit of the well. In some instances the heathen faith is virtually restored, and the well endowed with supernatural powers irrespective of the dedication of its waters to a Christian saint. Indeed in the majority of cases where these wells are now resorted to by the peasantry for any other than curative purposes, the fetichistic impulse is much more conspicuous than any influence associated with religious teaching.

X.

St. Elian's is accounted the most dreadful well in Wales. It is in the parish of Llanelian, Denbighshire. It is at the head of the cursing wells, of which there are but few in the Principality, and holds still a strong influence over the ignorant mind. The popular belief is that you can 'put' your enemy 'into' this well, i.e., render him subject to its evil influence, so that he will pine away and perhaps die unless the curse be removed. The degree and nature of the curse can be modified as the 'offerer' desires, so that the obnoxious person will suffer aches and pains in his body, or troubles in his pocket—the slings and arrows of outrageous fortune. The minister of the well appears to be some heartless wretch residing in the neighbourhood, whose services are enlisted for a small fee. The name of the person to be 'put into' the well is registered in a book kept by the wretch aforesaid, and a pin is cast into the well in his name, together with a pebble inscribed with its initials. The person so cursed soon hears of it, and the fact preys on his mind; he imagines for himself every conceivable ill,

and if gifted with a lively faith soon finds himself reduced to a condition where he cannot rest till he has
secured the removal of the curse. This is effected
by a reversal of the above ceremonies—erasing the
name, taking out the pebble, and otherwise ap-
peasing the spirit of the well. It is asserted that
death has in many instances resulted from the curse
of this wickedly malicious well.[1]

XI.

Occasionally the cursing powers of a well were
synonymous with curing powers. Thus a well
much resorted to near Penrhos, was able to curse a
cancer, i.e., cure it. The sufferer washed in the water,
uttering curses upon the disease, and also dropping
pins around the well. This well has been drained
by the unsympathizing farmer on whose land it was,
on account of the serious damage done to his crops
by trespassers.

XII.

Wells from which milk has flowed have been
known in several places. That Winifred's well
indulged in this eccentricity on one occasion has
been noted. The well of St. Illtyd is celebrated
for the like performance. This well is in Glamorganshire, in the land called Gower, near Swansea. It was about the nativity of John the Baptist,
on the fifth day of the week, in a year not specified, but certainly very remote, that for three hours
there flowed from this well a copious stream
of milk instead of water. That it was really milk
we are not left in any possible doubt, for 'many
who were present testified that while they were
looking at the milky stream carefully and with
astonishment, they also saw among the gravel

[1] 'Camb. Pop. Ant.,' 247. See also 'Arch. Camb.,' 1st Se., i. 46.

curds lying about in every direction, and all around
the edge of the well a certain fatty substance floating
about, such as is collected from milk, so that butter
can be made from it.'[1]

The origin of this well is a pleasing miracle, and
recalls the story of Canute; but while Canute's
effort to command the sea was a failure in the
eleventh century, that of St. Illtyd five hundred
years earlier was a brilliant success. It appears
that the saint was very pleasantly established on
an estate consisting of a field surrounded on all
sides by plains, with an intermediate grove, but was
much afflicted by the frequent overflowings of the
sea upon his land. In vain he built and rebuilt a
very large embankment of mud mixed with stones,
the rushing waves burst through again and again.
At last the saint's patience was worn out, and he
said, ' I will not live here any longer ; I much wished
it, but troubled with this marine molestation, it is
not in my power. It destroys my buildings, it flows
to the oratory which we built with great labour.'
However, the place was so convenient he was loth
to leave it, and he prayed for assistance. On the
night before his intended departure an angel came
to him and bade him remain, and gave him instructions for driving back the sea. Early in the morning
Illtyd went to the fluctuating sea and drove it back ;
it receded before him ' as if it were a sensible animal,'
and left the shore dry. Then Illtyd struck the
shore with his staff, 'and thereupon flowed a very
clear fountain, which is also beneficial for curing
diseases, and which continues to flow without a
falling off ; and what is more wonderful, although it
is near the sea, the water emitted is pure.'[2]

[1] ' Arch. Camb.,' 1st Se., iii., 264.
[2] ' Cambro-British Saints,' 478.

XIII.

Some of the Welsh mystic wells are so situated that they are at times overflowed by the waters of the sea, or of a river. Taff's well, in Glamorganshire, a pleasant walk from Cardiff, is situated practically in the bed of the river Taff. One must wade through running water to reach it, except in the summer season, when the water in the river is very low. A rude hut of sheet iron has been built over it. This well is still noted for its merits in healing rheumatism and kindred ailments. The usual stories are told of miraculous cures. A primitive custom of the place is that when men are bathing at this well they shall hang a pair of trousers outside the hut; women, in their turn, must hang out a petticoat or bonnet.

At Newton Nottage, Glamorganshire, a holy well called Sanford's is so situated that the water is regulated in the well by the ocean tides. From time immemorial wondrous tales have been told of this well, how it ebbs and flows daily in direct contrariety to the tidal ebb and flow. The bottom of the well is below high-water mark on the beach, where it has an outlet into the sea. At very low tides in the summer, when the supply of water in the well is scanty, it becomes dry for an hour or two after low water. When the ocean tide rises, the sea-water banks up and drives back the fresh water, and the well fills again and its water rises. The villagers are accustomed to let the well-water rise through what they call the 'nostrils of the well,' and become settled a little before they draw it. Of course this phenomenon has been regarded as something supernatural by the ignorant for ages, and upon the actual visible phenomena have been built

a number of magical details of a superstitious character.

XIV.

The wide prevalence of some form of water-
worship among Aryan peoples is a fact of great
significance. Superstitions in connection with British
wells are generally traceable to a Druidic origin.
The worship of natural objects in which the British
Druids indulged, particularly as regards rivers
and fountains, probably had a connection with
traditions of the flood. When the early Christian
preachers and teachers encountered such superstitions among the people, they carefully avoided
giving unnecessary offence by scoffing at them; on
the contrary they preferred to adopt them, and to
hallow them by giving them Christian meanings.
They utilized the old Druidic circles as places of
worship, chose young priests from among the educated Druids, and consecrated to their own saints
the mystic wells and fountains. In this manner
were continued practices the most ancient. As
time passed on, other wells were similarly sanctified,
as the new religion spread and parish churches were
built. Disease and wickedness being intimately
associated in the popular mind—epileptics and like
sufferers being held to be possessed of devils, and
even such vulgar ills as warts and wens being
considered direct results of some evil deed, suffered
or performed—so the waters of Christian baptism
which cleansed from sin, cleansed also from disease.
Ultimately the virtue of the waters came to be
among the vulgar a thing apart from the rite of
baptism; the good was looked upon as dwelling in
the waters themselves, and the Christian rite as not
necessarily an element in the work of regeneration.
The reader who will recall what has been said in

the chapter on changelings, in the first part of this volume, will perceive a survival of the ancient creed herein, in the notion that baptism is a preventive of fairy babe-thievery. Remembering that the changeling notion is in reality nothing but a fanciful way of accounting for the emaciation, ugliness, idiocy, bad temper—in a word, the illness—of the child, it will be seen that the rite of baptism, by curing the first manifestations of evil in the child's system, was the orthodox means of preventing the fairies from working their bad will on the poor innocent.

CHAPTER III.

Personal Attributes of Legendary Welsh Stones—Stone Worship—
Canna's Stone Chair—Miraculous Removals of Stones—The Walk-
ing Stone of Eitheinn—The Thigh Stone—The Talking Stone in
Pembrokeshire—The Expanding Stone—Magic Stones in the
'Mabinogion'—The Stone of Invisibility—The Stone of Remem-
brance—Stone Thief-catchers—Stones of Healing—Stones at Cross
Roads—Memorials of King Arthur—Round Tables, Carns, Pots,
etc.—Arthur's Quoits—The Gigantic Rock-tossers of Old—Mol
Walbec and the Pebble in her Shoe—The Giant of Trichrug—
Giants and the Mythology of the Heavens—The Legend of Rhitta
Gawr.

I.

In the traditions concerning Welsh stones, abundant
personal attributes are accorded them, such as in
nature belong only to animals. They were endowed
with volition and with voice; they could travel from
place to place without mortal aid; they would move
uneasily when disturbed by human contact; they
expanded and contracted at will; they clung to
people who touched them with profane or guilty
purpose; they possessed divers qualities which made
them valuable to their possessors, such as the power
of rendering them invisible, or of filling their pockets
with gold. In pursuing the various accounts of these
stones in Welsh folk-lore we find ourselves now in
fairy-land, now in the domains of mother church,
now listening to legends of enchantment, now to
tales of saintly virtue, now giving ear to a magician,
now to a monk. Stone-worship, of which the existing superstitions are remains, was so prevalent under
the Saxon monarchy, that it was forbidden by law in
the reign of Edgar the Peaceable, (ninth century,)

and when Canute came, in the following century, he also found it advisable to issue such a law. That this pagan worship was practised from a time of which there is now no record, is not questioned; and the perpetuation of certain features of this worship by the early Christians was in spite of the laws promulgated for its suppression by a Christian king. In this manner the monks were enabled to draw to themselves the peasantry in whose breasts the ancient superstition was strong, and who willingly substituted the new story for the old, so long as the underlying belief was not rudely uprooted.

II.

Among the existing stones in Wales with which the ancient ideas of occult power are connected, one in Carmarthenshire is probably unique of its kind. It is called Canna's Stone, and lies in a field adjoining the old church of Llangan, now remote from the population whose ancestors worshipped in it. The church was founded by an Armorican lady of rank named Canna, who was sainted. The stone in question forms a sort of chair, and was used in connection with a magic well called Ffynon Canna, which is now, like the church, deserted and wretched. Patients suffering from ague, in order to profit by its healing power, must sit in the chair of Canna's stone, after drinking of the water. If they could manage to sleep while in the chair, the effect of the water was supposed to be made sure. The process was continued for some days, sometimes for two or three weeks.

In the middle of this parish there is a field called Parc y Fonwent, or the churchyard-field, where, according to local tradition, the church was to have been originally built; but the stones brought to the spot during the day were at night removed by invisible hands to the site of the present church. Watchers in the dark heard the goblins engaged in this work, and pronouncing in clear and correct Welsh these words, 'Llangan, dyma'r fan,' which mean, 'Llangan, here is the spot.'

Similar miraculous removals of stones are reported and believed in other parts of Wales. Sometimes visible goblins achieve the work; sometimes the stones themselves possess the power of locomotion. The old British historian Nennius[1] speaks of a stone, one of the wonders of the Isle of Anglesea, which walks during the night in the valley of Eitheinn. Being once thrown into the whirlpool Cerevus, which is in the middle of the sea called Menai, it was on the morrow found on the side of the aforesaid valley. Also in Builth is a heap of stones, upon which is one stone bearing the impress of a dog's foot. This was the famous dog of King Arthur, named Cabal, which left its footprint on this stone when it hunted the swine Troynt. Arthur himself gathered this heap of stones, with the magic stone upon it, and called it Carn Cabal; and people who take away this stone in their hands for the space of a day and a night cannot retain it, for it returns itself to the heap. The Anglesea stone is also mentioned by Giraldus, through whom it achieved celebrity under the name of Maen Morddwyd, or the Thigh Stone —'a stone resembling a human thigh, which possesses this innate virtue, that whatever distance it may be carried it returns of its own accord the following night. Hugh, Earl of Chester, in the reign of King Henry I., having by force occupied this island and the adjacent country, heard of the miraculous power of this stone, and for the purpose of

[1] Harleian MSS., 3859.

trial ordered it to be fastened with strong iron chains to one of a larger size and to be thrown into the sea; on the following morning, however, according to custom, it was found in its original position, on which account the Earl issued a public edict that no one from that time should presume to move the stone from its place. A countryman also, to try the powers of this stone, fastened it to his thigh, which immediately became putrid, and the stone returned to its original situation.'[1] This stone ultimately lost its virtues, however, for it was stolen in the last century and never came back.

III.

The Talking Stone Llechlafar, or stone of loquacity, served as a bridge over the river Alyn, bounding the churchyard of St. David's in Pembrokeshire, on the northern side. It was a marble slab worn smooth by the tread of many feet, and was ten feet long, six feet broad, and one foot thick. Ancient tradition relates that one day 'when a corpse was being carried over it for interment the stone broke forth into speech, and by the effort cracked in the middle, which fissure is still visible; and on account of this barbarous and ancient superstition the corpses are no longer brought over it.'[2]

In this same parish of St. David's, there was a flight of steps leading down to the sea, among which were a certain few which uttered a miraculous sound, like the ringing of a bell. The story goes that in ancient times a band of pirates landed there and robbed the chapel. The bell they took away to sea with them, but as it was heavy they rested it several times on their way, and ever since that day

---

[1] Sir R. C. Hoare's Giraldus, ' Itin. Camb.,' ii., 104.
[2] Ibid., ii., 8.

the stones it rested upon have uttered these mysterious sounds when struck.

Also in this parish is the renowned Expanding
Stone, an excavation in the rock of St. Gowan's
chapel, which has the magic property of adapting
itself to the size of the person who gets into it,
growing smaller for a small man and larger for a
large one. Among its many virtues was that if
a person got into it and made a wish, and did not
change his mind while turning about, the wish
would come true. The original fable relates that
this hollow stone was once solid; that a saint
closely pursued by Pagan persecutors sought shelter
of the rock, which thereupon opened and received
him, concealing him till the danger was over and
then obligingly letting him out.

This stone may probably be considered as the
monkish parallel for the magic stones which confer
on their possessor invisibility, as we find them in the
romances of enchantment. In the 'Mabinogion'
such stones are frequently mentioned, usually in the
favourite form of a gem set within a ring. 'Take
this ring,' says the damsel with yellow curling hair,[1]
'and put it on thy finger, with the stone inside thy
hand; and close thy hand upon the stone. And as
long as thou concealest it, it will conceal thee.' But
when it is found, as we find in following these clues
further, that this Stone of Invisibility was one of
the Thirteen Rarities of Kingly Regalia of the
Island of Britain; that it was formerly kept at
Caerleon, in Monmouthshire, the city whence St.
David journeyed into Pembrokeshire; and that it
is mentioned in the Triads thus: 'The Stone of the
Ring of Luned, which liberated Owen the son of
Urien from between the portcullis and the wall;

[1] Lady Charlotte Guest's 'Mabinogion,' 13.

whoever concealed that stone the stone or bezel
would conceal him,' the strong probability appears
that we are dealing with one and the same myth
in the tale of magic and in the monkish legend.
Traced back to a period more remote than that
with which these Welsh stories ostensibly deal, we
should find their prototype in the ring of Gyges.

The Stone of Remembrance is another stone mentioned in the 'Mabinogion,' also a jewel, endowed
with valuable properties which it imparts not merely
to its wearer, but to any one who looks upon it.
'Rhonabwy,' says Iddawc to the enchanted dreamer
on the yellow calf-skin, 'dost thou see the ring with
a stone set in it, that is upon the Emperor's hand?'
'I see it,' he answered. 'It is one of the properties
of that stone to enable thee to remember that thou
seest here to-night, and hadst thou not seen the
stone, thou wouldst never have been able to remember aught thereof.'[1] Still another stone of rare
good qualities is that which Peredur gave to Etlym,
in reward for his attendance,[2] the stone which was
on the tail of a serpent, and whose virtues were such
that whosoever should hold it in one hand, in the
other he would have as much gold as he might
desire. Peredur having vanquished the serpent and
possessed himself of the stone, immediately gave it
away, in that spirit of lavish free-handedness which
so commonly characterizes the heroes of chivalric
British romance.

IV.

In the church of St. David's of Llanfaes, according to Giraldus, was preserved among the relics
a stone which caught a thieving boy in the act of
robbing a pigeon's nest, and held him fast for three
days and nights. Only by assiduous and long-con-

---

[1] Lady Charlotte Guest's 'Mabinogion,' 303.　　　[2] Ibid., 111.

tinued prayer were the unhappy boy's parents able
to get him loose from the terrible stone, and the
marks of his five fingers remained ever after impressed upon it, so that all might see them. There
was a stone of similar proclivities in the valley of
Mowddwy, which did good service for the church.
A certain St. Tydecho, a relation of King Arthur,
who slept on a blue rock in this valley, was persecuted by Maelgwn Gwynedd. One day this wicked
knight came with a pack of white dogs to hunt in
that neighbourhood, and sat down upon the saint's
blue stone. When he endeavoured to get up he
found himself fastened to his seat so that he could
not stir, in a manner absurdly suggestive of French
farces ; and he was obliged to make up matters with
the saint. He ceased to persecute the good man,
and to make amends for the past gave him the
privilege of sanctuary for a hundred ages.[1]

V.

As for Stones of Healing, with qualities resembling
those abiding in certain wells, they appear in many
shapes. Now it is a maenhir, against which the
afflicted peasant must rub himself ; now it is a pebble
which he must carry in his pocket. The inevitable
wart reappears in this connection ; the stone which
cures the wart is found by the roadside, wrapped in
a bit of paper, and dropped on a cross-road ; to him
who picks it up the wart is transferred. Children in
Pembrokeshire will not at the present day pick up a
small parcel on a cross-road, suspecting the presence
of the wart-bearing stone. In Carmarthen ,are still
to be found traces of a belief in the Alluring Stone,
whose virtue is that it will cure hydrophobia. It is

---

[1] 'Celtic Remains,' 420. (Printed for the Cambrian Arch. Soc.,
London, 1878.)

represented as a soft white stone, about the size of a man's head, originally found on a farm called Dysgwylfa, about twelve miles from Carmarthen town. Grains were scraped from the stone with a knife, and administered to the person who had been bitten by a rabid dog; and a peculiarity of the stone was that though generation after generation had scraped it, nevertheless it did not diminish in size. A woman who ate of this miraculous stone, after having been bitten by a suspicious cur, testified that it caused 'a boiling in her blood.' The stone was said to have fallen from the sky in the first instance.

VI.

Stones standing at cross-roads are seldom without some superstitious legend. A peasant pointed out to me, on a mountain-top near Crumlyn, Monmouthshire, a cross-roads stone, beneath which, he asserted, a witch sleeps by day, coming forth at night. 'Least they was say so,' he explained, with a nervous look about him, 'but there you! *I* was never see anything, an' I was pass by there many nights— yes, indeed, often.' The man's eagerness to testify against the truth of the tradition was one of the most impressive illustrations possible of lingering superstitious awe in this connection.

A famous Welsh witch, who used to sleep under a stone at Llanberis, in North Wales, was called Canrig Bwt, and her favourite dish at dinner was children's brains. A certain criminal who had received a death-sentence was given the alternative of attacking this frightful creature, his life to be spared should he succeed in destroying her. Arming himself with a sharp sword, the doomed man got upon the stone and called on Canrig to come out. 'Wait till I have finished eating the brains in this sweet little skull,' was her horrible answer. However, forth she came presently, when the valiant man cut off her head at a blow. To this day they scare children thereabout with the name of Canrig Bwt.

VII.

In every part of Wales one encounters the ancient memorials of King Arthur—sometimes to be dimly connected with the historical character, but more often with the mythical figure—each with its legend, or its bundle of legends, poetic, patriotic, or superstitious. Arthur's Round Table at Caerleon, Monmouthshire, is as well known to every boy in the neighbourhood as any inn or shop of the village. It is a grass-grown Roman amphitheatre, whence alabaster statues of Adrian's day have been disinterred. There is also an Arthur's Round Table in Denbighshire, a flat-topped hill thus called, and in Anglesea another, near the village of Llanfihangel. Arthur's Seat, Arthur's Bed, Arthur's Castle, Arthur's Stone, Arthur's Hill, Arthur's Quoit, Arthur's Board, Arthur's Carn, Arthur's Pot—these are but a few of the well-known cromlechs, rocking-stones, or natural objects to be found in various neighbourhoods. They are often in duplicates, under these names, but they never bear such titles by other authority than traditions reaching back into the dark ages. Some of the stories and superstitions which attach to them are striking, and of the most fascinating interest to the student of folk-lore; others are merely grotesque, as in the case of Arthur's Pot. This is under a cromlech at Dolwillim, on the banks of the Tawe, and in the stream itself when the water is high; it is a circular hole of considerable depth, accurately bored in the stone by the action of the water. This hole is called Arthur's

Pot, and according to local belief was made by
Merlin for the hero king to cook his dinner in.
Arthur's Quoits are found in many parts of the
country. A large rock in the bed of the Sawdde
river, on the Llangadock side of Mynydd Du, (the
Black Mountain,) is one of these quoits. The story
is that the king one day flung it from the summit of
Pen Arthur, a mile away. There is another large
rock beside it, which was similarly flung down by a
lady of Arthur's acquaintance, whose gigantic proportions may be guessed from the fact that this
boulder was a pebble in her shoe, which annoyed
her.

VIII.

Upon this hint there opens out before the inquirer
a wealth of incident and illustration, in connection
with gigantic Britons of old time who hurled huge
rocks about as pebbles. There is the story of the
giant Idris, who dwelt upon Cader Idris, and who
found no less a number than three troublesome
pebbles in his shoe as he was out walking one day,
and who tossed them down where they lie on the
road from Dolgelley to Machynlleth, three bulky
crags. There are several legends about Mol
Walbec's pebbles in Breconshire. This lusty dame
has a full score of shadowy castles on sundry heights
in that part of Wales; and she is said to have built
the castle of Hay in one night. In performing this
work she carried the stones in her apron; one of
these—a pebble about a foot thick and nine feet
long—fell into her shoe. At first she did not notice
it, but by-and-by it began to annoy her, and she
plucked it out and threw it into Llowes churchyard,
three miles away, where it now lies. In many parts of
Wales where lie rude heaps of stones, the peasantry
say they were carried there by a witch in her apron.

The gigantic creatures whose dimensions are indicated by these stones reappear continually in Welsh folk-lore. Arthur is merely the greatest among them; all were of prodigious proportions. Hu Gadarn, Cadwaladr, Rhitta Gawr, Brutus, Idris, are all members of the shadowy race whose 'quoits' and 'pebbles' are scattered about Wales. The remains at Stonehenge have been from time immemorial called by the Cymry the Côr Gawr, Circle or Dance of Giants. How the Carmarthen enchanter, Merlin, transported these stones hither from Killara mountain in Ireland by his magic art, everybody knows. It is only necessary that a stone should be of a size to make the idea of removing it an apparently hopeless one—that Merlin or some other magician brought it there by enchantment, or that Arthur or some other giant tossed it there with his mighty arm, is a matter of course.[1] The giant of Trichrug, (a fairy haunt in Cardiganshire,) appears to have been the champion pebble-tosser of Wales, if local legend may be trusted. Having invited the neighbouring giants to try their strength with him in throwing stones, he won the victory by tossing a huge rock across the sea into Ireland. His grave is traditionally reported to be on that mountain, and to possess the same properties as the Expanding Stone, for it fits any person who lies down in it, be he tall or short. It has the further virtue of imparting extraordinary strength to any one lying in it; but if he gets into it with arms upon his person they will be taken from him and he will never see them more.

[1] It is noteworthy that most of the great stones of these legends appear to have really been transported to the place where they are now found, being often of a different rock than that of the immediate locality. To what extent the legends express the first vague inductions of early geological observers, is a question not without interest.

2 B

IX.

The gigantic stone-tossers of Wales associate themselves without effort with the mythology of the heavens. One of their chiefest, Idris, was indeed noted as an astrologer, and is celebrated as such in the Triads:

> Idris Gawr, or the Giant Idris;
> Gwydion, or the Diviner by Trees;
> Gwyn, the Son of Nudd, the Generous;
> So great was their knowledge of the stars, that they could foretell whatever might be desired to be known until the day of doom.

And among Welsh legends none is more familiar than that of Rhitta Gawr, wherein the stars are familiarly spoken of as cows and sheep, and the firmament as their pasture.

CHAPTER IV.

Early Inscribed Stones—The Stone Pillar of Banwan Bryddin, near Neath—Catastrophe accompanying its Removal—The Sagranus Stone and the White Lady—The Dancing Stones of Stackpool—Human Beings changed to Stones—St. Ceyna and the Serpents—The Devil's Stone at Llanarth—Rocking Stones and their accompanying Superstitions—The Suspended Altar of Loin-Garth—Cromlechs and their Fairy Legends—The Fairies' Castle at St. Nicholas, Glamorganshire—The Stone of the Wolf Bitch—The Welsh Melusina—Parc y Bigwrn Cromlech—Connection of these Stones with Ancient Druidism.

I.

PALEOGRAPHIC students are more or less familiar with about seventy early inscribed stones in Wales. The value of these monuments, as corroborative evidence of historical facts, in connection with waning popular traditions, is well understood. Superstitious prejudice is particularly active in connection with stones of this kind. The peasantry view them askance, and will destroy them if not restrained, as they usually are, by fear of evil results to themselves. Antiquaries have often reason to thank superstition for the existence in our day of these ancient monuments. But there is a sort of progressive movement towards enlightenment which carries the Welsh farmer from the fearsome to the destructive stage, in this connection. That dangerous thing, a little knowledge, sometimes leads its imbiber beyond the reach of all fear of the guardian fairy or demon of the stone, yet leaves him still so superstitious regarding it that he believes its influence to be baleful, and its destruction a sort of duty. It was the common opinion of the peasantry of the parish in

which it stood, that whoever happened to read the
inscription on the Maen Llythyrog, an early inscribed
stone on the top of a mountain near Margam Abbey,
in Glamorganshire, would die soon after. In many
instances the stones are believed to be transformed
human beings, doomed to this guise for some sin,
usually an act of sacrilege. Beliefs of this character
would naturally be potent in influencing popular
feeling against the stones. But on the other hand,
however desirable might be their extinction, there
would be perils involved, which one would rather his
neighbour than himself should encounter. Various
awful consequences, but especially the most terrific
storms and disturbances of the earth, followed any
meddling with them.

At Banwan Bryddin, a few miles from Neath, a
stone pillar inscribed 'MARCI CARITINI FILII BERICII,'
long stood on a tumulus which by the peasants was
considered a fairy ring. The late Lady Mackworth
caused this stone to be removed to a grotto she was
constructing on her grounds, and which she was
ornamenting with all the curious stones she could
collect. An old man who was an under-gardener
on her estate, and who abounded with tales of
goblins, declaring he had often had intercourse with
these strange people, told the Rev. Mr. Williams of
Tir-y-Cwm, that he had always known this act of
sacrilege would not go unpunished by the guardians
of the stone. He had more than once seen these
sprites dancing of an evening in the rings of Banwan
Bryddin, where the 'wonder stone' stood, but never
since the day the stone was removed had any mortal
seen them. Upon the stone, he said, were written
mysterious words in the fairy language, which no
one had ever been able to comprehend, not even
Lady Mackworth herself. When her ladyship re-

moved the stone to Gnoll Gardens the fairies were very much annoyed; and the grotto, which cost Lady Mackworth thousands of pounds to build, was no sooner finished than one night, Duw'n catwo ni! there was such thunder and lightning as never was heard or seen in Glamorganshire before; and next morning the grotto was gone! The hill had fallen over it and hidden it for ever. 'Iss indeed,' said the old man, 'and woe will fall on the Cymro or the Saeson that will dare to clear the earth away. I myself, and others who was there, was hear the fairies laughing loud that night, after the storm has cleared away.'

II.

The Sagranus Stone at St. Dogmell's, Pembrokeshire, was formerly used as a bridge over a brook not far from where it at present stands—luckily with its inscribed face downwards, so that the sculpture remained unharmed while generations were tramping over it. During its use as a bridge it bore the reputation of being haunted by a white lady, who was constantly seen gliding over it at the witching hour of midnight. No man or woman could be induced to touch the strange stone after dark, and its supernatural reputation no doubt helped materially in its preservation unharmed till the present time. It is considered on paleographic grounds to be of the fourth century.

In Pembrokeshire also are found the famous Dancing Stones of Stackpool. These are three upright stones standing about a mile from each other, the first at Stackpool Warren, the second further to the west, on a stone tumulus in a field known as Horestone Park, and the third still further westward. One of many traditions concerning them is to the effect that on a certain day they meet

and come down to Sais's Ford to dance, and after
their revel is over return home and resume their
places.

III.

There is a curious legend regarding three stones
which once stood on the top of Moelfre Hill, in Carnarvonshire, but which were long ago rolled to the
bottom of the hill by 'some idle-headed youths'
who dug them up. They were each about four feet
high, standing as the corners of a triangle; one was
red as blood, another white, and the third a pale
blue. The tradition says that three women, about
the time when Christianity first began to be known
in Britain, went up Moelfre Hill on a Sabbath morning to winnow their corn. They had spread their
winnowing sheet upon the ground and begun their
work, when some of their neighbours came to them
and reprehended them for working on the Lord's
day. But the women, having a greater eye to their
worldly profit than to the observance of the fourth
commandment, made light of their neighbours'
words, and went on working. Thereupon they were
instantly transformed into three pillars of stone, each
stone of the same colour as the dress of the woman
in whose place it stood, one red, one white, and the
third bluish.

Legends of the turning to stone of human beings
occur in connection with many of the meini hirion
(long stones). Near Llandyfrydog, Anglesea, there
is a maenhir of peculiar shape. From one point of
view it looks not unlike the figure of a humpbacked
man, and it is called 'Carreg y Lleidr,' or the
Robber's Stone. The tradition connected with it is
that a man who had stolen the church Bible, and
was carrying it away on his shoulder, was turned
into this stone, and must stand here till the last
trump sets him free.

At Rolldritch (Rhwyldrech ?) there is or was a circle of stones, concerning which tradition held that they were the human victims of a witch who, for some offence, transformed them to this shape. In connection with this circle is preserved another form of superstitious belief very often encountered, namely, that the number of stones in the circle cannot be correctly counted by a mortal.[1]

It is noteworthy that the only creature which shares with man the grim fate of being turned to stone, in Welsh legends, is the serpent. The monkish account of St. Ceyna, one of the daughters of Prince Brychan, of Breconshire, relates that having consecrated her virginity to the Lord by a perpetual vow, she resolved to seek some desert place where she could give herself wholly up to meditation. So she journeyed beyond the river Severn, 'and there meeting a woody place, she made her request to the prince of that country that she might be permitted to serve God in that solitude. His answer was that he was very willing to grant her request, but that the place did so swarm with serpents that neither man nor beast could inhabit it. But she replied that her firm trust was in the name and assistance of Almighty God to drive all that poisonous brood out of that region. Hereupon the place was granted to the holy virgin, who, prostrating herself before God, obtained of him to change the serpents and vipers into stones. And to this day the stones in that region do resemble the windings of serpents, through all the fields and villages, as if they had been framed by the hand of the sculptor.' The scene of this legend is mentioned by Camden as being at a place near Bristol, called Keynsham, 'where abundance of that fossil called by the naturalists Cornu Ammonis is dug up.'

[1] Roberts, 'Camb. Pop. Ant.,' 220.

IV.

Our old friend the devil is once more to the fore when we encounter the inscribed stone of the twelfth century, which stands in the churchyard of Llanarth, near Aberaeron, in Cardiganshire. A cross covers this stone, with four circular holes at the junction of the arms. The current tradition of the place regarding it is that one stormy night, there was such a tremendous noise heard in the belfry that the whole village was thrown into consternation. It was finally concluded that nobody but the diawl could be the cause of this, and therefore the people fetched his reverence from the vicarage to go and request the intruder to depart. The vicar went up into the belfry, with bell, book, and candle, along the narrow winding stone staircase, and, as was anticipated, there among the bells he saw the devil in person. The good man began the usual 'Conjurate in nomine,' etc., when the fiend sprang up and mounted upon the leads of the tower. The vicar was not to be balked, however, and boldly followed up the remainder of the staircase and got also out upon the leads. The devil finding himself hard pressed, had nothing for it but to jump over the battlements of the tower. He came down plump among the gravestones below, and falling upon one, made with his hands and knees the four holes now visible on the stone in question, which among the country people still bears the name of the Devil's Stone.

V.

The logan stones in various parts of Wales, which vibrate mysteriously under the touch of a child's finger, and rock violently at a push from a man's stronger hand, are also considered by the

superstitious a favourite resort of the fairies and the
diawl. The holy aerolite to which unnumbered
multitudes bow down at Mecca is indeed no stranger
thing than the rocking-stone on Pontypridd's sky-
perched common. Among the marvellous stones
in Nennius is one concerning a certain altar in Loin-
garth, in Gower, 'suspended by the power of God,'
which he says a legend tells us was brought thither
in a ship along with the dead body of some holy
man who desired to be buried near St. Illtyd's
grave, and to remain unknown by name, lest he
should become an object of too reverent regard; for
Illtyd dwelt in a cave there, the mouth of which
faced the sea in those days; and having received
this charge, he buried the corpse, and built a church
over it, enclosing the wonderful altar, which testified
by more than one astounding miracle the Divine
power which sustained it. This is thought to be a
myth relating to some Welsh rocking-stone no longer
known. The temptation to throw down stones of
this character has often been too much for the
destruction-loving vulgarian, both in Wales and in
other parts of the British islands; but the offenders
have seldom been the local peasantry, who believe
that the guardians of the stone—the fairies or the
diawl, as the case may be—will heavily avenge
its overthrow on the overthrowers.

VI.

Venerable in their hoary antiquity stand those
monuments of a long-vanished humanity, the cromlechs which are so numerous in Wales, sharing with
the logan and the inscribed stone the peasant's superstitious interest. Even more than the others, these
solemn rocks are surrounded with legends of enchantment. They figure in many fairy-tales like that of

the shepherd of Frennifawr, who stood watching their mad revelry about the old cromlech, where they were dancing, making music on the harp, and chasing their companions in hilarious sort. That the fairies protect the cromlechs with special care, as they also do the logans and others, is a belief the Welsh peasant shares with the superstitious in many lands. There is a remarkable cromlech near the hamlet of St. Nicholas, Glamorganshire, on the

THE FAIRY FROLIC AT THE CROMLECH.

estate of the family whose house has the honour of being haunted by the ghost of an admiral. This cromlech is called, by children in that neighbourhood, 'Castle Correg.' A Cardiff gentleman who asked some children who were playing round the cromlech, what they termed it, was struck by the name, which recalled to him the Breton fairies thus designated.[1] The korreds and korregs of Brittany

[1] Mr. J. W. Lukis, in an address before the Cardiff Nat. Soc. in July, 1874.

closely resemble the Welsh fairies in numberless details. The korreds are supposed to live in the cromlechs, of which they are believed to have been the builders. They dance around them at night, and woe betide the unhappy peasant who joins them in their roundels.[1] Like beliefs attach to cromlechs in the Haute Auvergne, and other parts of France. A cromlech at Pirols, said to have been built by a fée, is composed of seven massive stones, the largest being twelve feet long by eight and a half feet wide. The fée carried these stones hither from a great distance, and set them up; and the largest and heaviest one she carried on the top of her spindle, and so little was she incommoded by it that she continued to spin all the way.[2]

VII.

Among the Welsh peasantry the cromlechs are called by a variety of names, one interesting group giving in Cardiganshire 'the Stone of the Bitch,' in Glamorganshire 'the Stone of the Greyhound Bitch,' in Carmarthenshire and in Monmouthshire 'the Kennel of the Greyhound Bitch,' and in some other parts of Wales 'the Stone of the Wolf Bitch.' These names refer to no fact of modern experience; they are legendary. The Cambrian form of the story of Melusina is before us here, with differing details. The wolf-bitch of the Welsh legend was a princess who for her sins was transformed to that shape, and thus long remained. Her name was Gast Rhymhi, and she had two cubs while a wolf-bitch, with which she dwelt in a cave. After long suffering in this wretched guise, she and her cubs were restored to their human form 'for Arthur,' who

[1] Keightley, 'Fairy Mythology,' 432.
[2] Cambry, 'Monuments Celtiques,' 232.

sought her out. The unfortunate Melusina, it will
be remembered, was never entirely robbed of her
human form.

'Ange par la figure, et serpent par le reste,'

she was condemned by the lovely fay Pressina to
become a serpent from the waist downwards, on
every Saturday, till she should meet a man who
would marry her under certain specified conditions.
The monkish touch is on the Welsh legend, in the
medieval form in which we have it in the Mabinogi
of 'Kilhwch and Olwen.' The princess is transformed into a wolf-bitch 'for her sins,' and when
restored, although it is for Arthur, 'God did change'
her to a woman again.[1]

VIII.

In a field called Parc-y-Bigwrn, near Llanboidy,
Carmarthenshire, are the remains of a cromlech
destroyed many years ago, concerning which an old
man named John Jones related a superstitious tale.
It was to the effect that there were ten men engaged
in the work of throwing it down, and that when
they were touching the stone they became filled
with awe; and moreover, as the stone was being
drawn away by six horses the road was suddenly
rent asunder in a supernatural manner. This is a
frequent phenomenon supposed by the Welsh peasantry to accompany the attempt to move a cromlech. Another common catastrophe is the breaking
down of the waggon—not from the weight of the
stone, but through the displeasure of its goblin
guardians. Sometimes this awful labour is accompanied by fierce storms of hail and wind, or violent
thunder and lightning; sometimes by mysterious

[1] 'Mabinogion,' 259.

noises, or swarms of bees which are supposed to be fairies in disguise.

IX.

A very great number of fanciful legends might be related in connection with stones of striking shape, or upon which there are peculiar marks and figures; but enough of this store of folk-lore has been given to serve present ends. If more were detailed, there would in all cases be found a family resemblance to the legends which have been presented, and which lead us now into the enchanted country where Arthur reigns, now wandering among the monkish records of church and abbey, now to the company of the dwarfs and giants of fairyland. That the British Druids regarded many of these stones with idolatrous reverence, is most probable. Some of them, as the cromlechs and logans, they no doubt employed in their mystic rites, as being symbols of the dimly descried Power they worshipped. Of their extreme antiquity there is no question. The rocking-stones may be considered natural objects, though they were perhaps assisted to their remarkable poise by human hands. The cromlechs were originally sepulchral chambers, unquestionably, but they are so old that neither history nor tradition gives any aid in assigning the date of their erection. Opinions that they were once pulpits of sun-worship, or Druidic altars of sacrifice, are not unwarranted, perhaps, though necessarily conjectural. The evidence that the inscribed stones are simply funeral monuments, is extensive and conclusive. Originally erected in honour of some great chief or warrior, they were venerated by the people, and became shrines about which the latter gathered in a spirit of devotion. With the lapse of ages, the warrior was forgotten; even the language in which he was commemorated decayed, and the marks on the stones became to the peasantry meaningless hieroglyphics, to which was given a mysterious and awful significance ; and so for unnumbered centuries the tombstone remained an object of superstitious fear and veneration.

CHAPTER V.

I.

In the prominent part played by storm—torrents of rain, blinding lightning, deafening thunder — in legends of disturbed cromlechs, and other awful stones, is involved the ancient belief that these elements were themselves baleful spirits, which could be evoked by certain acts. They were in the service of fiends and fairies, and came at their bidding to avenge the intrusion of venturesome mortals, daring to meddle with sacred things. This fascinating superstition is preserved in numberless Welsh legends relating to hidden treasures, buried under cromlechs or rocky mounds, or in caverns. In the 'Mabinogion' it appears in the enchanted barrier to the Castle of the Lady of the Fountain. Under a certain tall tree in the midst of a wide valley there was a fountain, 'and by the side of the fountain a marble slab, and on the marble slab a silver bowl, attached by a chain of silver, so that it may not be carried away. Take the bowl and throw a bowlful of water on the slab,' says the black giant of the wood to Sir Kai, 'and thou wilt hear a mighty peal of thunder, so that thou wilt think that heaven and earth are trembling with its fury. With the thunder there will come a shower so severe that it will be scarce possible for thee to endure it and live. And the shower will be of hailstones; and after the shower the weather will become fair, but every leaf that was upon the tree will have been carried away by the shower.'[1] Of course the knight dares this awful obstacle, throws the bowlful of water upon the slab, receives the terrible storm upon his shield, and fights the knight who owned the fountain, on his coming forth. Sir Kai is worsted, and returns home to Arthur's court; whereupon Sir Owain takes up the contest. He sallies forth, evokes the storm, encounters the black knight, slays him, and becomes master of all that was his—his castle, his lands, his wife, and all his treasures.

The peasant of to-day who sets out in quest of hidden treasures evokes the avenging storm in like manner. Sometimes the treasure is in the ground, under a cromlech or a carn; he digs, and the thunder shakes the air, the lightnings flash, torrents descend, and he is frustrated in his search. Again, the treasure is in a cavern, guarded by a dragon, which belches forth fire upon him and scorches his eye-balls. Welsh folk-lore is full of legends of this character; and the curious way in which science and religion sometimes get mixed up with these superstitions is most suggestive—as in the cases of the falling of Coychurch tower, and the Red Lady of Paviland. The latter is the name given a skeleton found by Dr. Buckland in his exploration of the Paviland caves, the bones of which were stained

[1] 'Mabinogion,' 8.

by red oxide of iron. The vulgar belief is that the Red Lady was entombed in the cave by a storm while seeking treasure there—a legend the truth of which no one can dispute with authority, since the bones are certainly of a period contemporary with the Roman rule in this island. Coins of Constantine were found in the same earth, cemented with fragments of charcoal and bone ornaments. In the case of Coychurch tower, it undoubtedly fell because it was undermined by a contractor who had the job of removing certain defunct forefathers from their graves near its base. Some eighteen hundred skulls were taken from the ground and carted off to a hole on the east side of the church. But the country folk pooh-pooh the idea that the tower fell for any reason other than sheer indignation and horror at the disturbance of this hallowed ground by utilitarian pickaxe and spade. They call your attention to the fact that not only did the venerable tower come crashing down, after having stood for centuries erect, but that in falling it struck to the earth St. Crallo's cross—an upright stone in the churchyard as venerable as itself—breaking it all to pieces.

II.

A hollow in the road near Caerau, in Cardiganshire, 'rings when any wheeled vehicle goes over it.' Early in this century, two men having been led to believe that there were treasures hidden there (for a fairy in the semblance of a gipsy had appeared and thrown out hints on the fascinating subject from time to time), made up their minds to dig for it. They dug accordingly until they came, by their solemn statement, to the oaken frame of a subterranean doorway; and feeling sure now, that they had serious work before them, prepared for

the same by going to dinner. They had no sooner
gone than a terrible storm arose; the rain fell in
torrents, the thunder pealed and the lightning
flashed. When they went back to their work, the
hole they had digged was closed up; and nothing
would convince them that this was done by any
other than a supernatural agency. Moreover, but
a little above the place where they were, there
had been no rain at all.[1]

III.

There is a current belief among the peasants
about Moel Arthur—a mountain overlooking the
Vale of Clwyd—that treasure, concealed in an iron
chest with a ring-handle to it, lies buried there.
The place of concealment is often illuminated at
night by a supernatural light. Several people thereabouts are known to have seen the light, and there
are even men who will tell you that bold adventurers
have so far succeeded as to grasp the handle of the
iron chest, when an outburst of wild tempest wrested
it from their hold and struck them senseless. Local
tradition points out the place as the residence of an
ancient prince, and as a spot charmed against the
spade of the antiquary. 'Whoever digs there,' said
an old woman in Welsh to some men going home
from their work on this spot, after a drenching wet
day, 'is always driven away by thunder and lightning and storm; you have been served like everybody else who has made the attempt.'

IV.

So prevalent are superstitions of this class even
in the present day that cases get into the newspapers now and then. The 'Herald Cymraeg' of

[1] 'Arch. Camb.' 3rd Se., ix., 306.

September 25, 1874, gave an account of some ex-
cavations made at Pant-y-Saer cromlech, Anglesea,
by the instigation of John Jones of Llandudno, 'a
brother of Isaac Jones, the present tenant of Pant-y-
Saer,' at the time on a visit to the latter. The
immediately exciting cause of the digging was a
dream in which the dreamer was told that there
was a pot of treasure buried within the cromlech's
precincts. The result was the revelation of a large
number of human bones, among them five lower
jaws with the teeth sound; but no crochan aur
(pitcher of gold) turned up, and the digging was
abandoned in disgust. Is it credible that between
this account and the following yawns the gulf of
seven hundred years? Thus Giraldus: In the province of Kemeys, one of the seven cantrefs of
Pembrokeshire, 'during the reign of King Henry I.,
a rich man who had a residence on the northern
side of the Preseleu mountains was warned for three
successive nights by dreams that if he put his hand
under a stone which hung over the spring of a
neighbouring well called the Fountain of St. Ber-
nacus, he should find there a golden chain; obeying
the admonition, on the third day he received from a
viper a deadly wound in his finger; but as it appears
that many treasures have been discovered through
dreams, it seems to me probable that some ought
and some ought not to be believed.'[1]

v.

In a certain cavern in Glamorganshire, called the
Ogof Cigfrain, or Cavern of the Ravens, is said to
be a chest of gold, watched over by two birds of
gloomy plumage, in a darkness so profound that
nothing can be seen but the fire of their sleepless

[1] Sir R. C. Hoare's Giraldus, 'Itin. Camb.' ii., 37.

eyes. To go there with the purpose of disturbing
them is to bring on a heaving and rolling of the
ground, accompanied by thunder and lightning. A
swaggering drover from Brecknockshire, though
warned by a 'dark woman' that he had better not
try it, sneered that 'a couple of ravens were a fine
matter to be afraid of indeed!' and ventured into
the cavern, with a long rope about his waist, and a
lantern in his hand. Some men who accompanied
him (seeing that he was bent on this rash and dangerous emprise,) held the coil of rope, and paid it
out as he went further and further in. The result
was prompt and simple : the sky cracked with loud
bursts of thunder and flashes of lightning, and the
drover roared with affright and rushed out of the
dark cavern with his hair on end. No coaxing
ever prevailed on him to reveal the terrible sights
he had seen ; when questioned he would only
repeat in Welsh the advice of 'Punch' to those
about to marry, viz., 'Peidiwch!'

VI.

In the legend of Castell Coch, instead of a raven
it is a pair of huge eagles which watch the treasure.
Castell Coch is an easy and pleasant two hours' walk
from Cardiff Castle, with which it is vulgarly believed
to be connected by a subterranean passage. A short
time ago—well, to be precise, a hundred years ago,
but that is no time at all in the history of Castell
Coch, which was a crumbling ruin then as it is now [1]
—in or about the year 1780, a reduced lady was
allowed to fit up three or four rooms in the ruin as
a residence, and to live there with two old servants
of her house. One night this lady was awakened

---

[1] It is at present being entirely restored and made habitable by its
owner, Lord Bute.

from her sleep to receive the visit of a venerable ghost in a full dress-suit of an earlier century, who distressed her by his troubled countenance and vexed her by his eccentric behaviour, for when she spoke to him from the depths of her nightcap he at once got through the wall. He came on subsequent nights so often, and frightened the servants so much by the noise he made—in getting through the wall, of course—that the lady gave up her strange abode, and was glad to pay house rent ever after in other parts. This old ghost was in the flesh proprietor of the castle, it appears, and during the civil wars buried an iron chest full of gold in the subterranean passage—which is still there, guarded by two large eagles. A party of gentlemen who somewhere about 1800 attempted to explore the passage saw the eagles, and were attacked by the birds of freedom so fiercely that they retreated in disorder. Subsequently they returned with pistols and shot the eagles, which resented this trifling impertinence by tearing the treasure-seekers in a shocking manner. After having recovered from their wounds, the determined Welshmen renewed the attack — this time with silver bullets, which they had got blessed by a good-natured priest. The bullets rattled harmlessly on the feathers of the terrible birds; the ground shook under foot; rain descended in torrents; with their great wings the eagles beat out the gold-hunters' torches, and they barely escaped with their lives.

VII.

The shadowy Horror which keeps vigil over these hidden treasures is now a dragon, again a raven or an eagle, again a worm. In the account of the treasure-seeker of Nantyglyn, it is a winged creature of unknown nature, a 'mysterious incubus,' which

broods over the chest in the cave. The terrible
Crocodile of the Lake, which was drawn from its
watery hiding-place by the Ychain Banog, or Prominent Oxen of Hu Gadarn, is also sometimes called
a dragon (draig) in those local accounts which survive in the folk-lore of several different districts.
It infested the region round about the lake where
it lay concealed, and the mighty oxen so strained
themselves in the labour of drawing it forth that
one of them died and the other rent the mountain
in twain with his bellowing. Various legends of
Sleeping Warriors appear in Welsh folk-lore, in
which the dragon is displaced by a shadowy army
of slumbering heroes, lying about in a circle, with
their swords and shields by their sides, guarding
great heaps of gold and silver. Now they are Owen
Lawgoch and his men, who lie in their enchanted
sleep in a cavern on the northern side of Mynydd
Mawr, in Carmarthenshire; again they are Arthur
and his warriors, asleep in a secret ogof under
Craig-y-Ddinas, waiting for a day when the Briton
and the Saxon shall go to war, when the noise of
the struggle will awaken them, and they will re-
conquer the island, reduce London to dust, and
re-establish their king at Caerleon, in Monmouthshire.

Dragon or demon, raven or serpent, eagle or
sleeping warriors, the guardian of the underground
vaults in Wales where treasures lie is a personification of the baleful influences which reside in caverns,
graves, and subterraneous regions generally. It is
something more than this, when traced back to its
source in the primeval mythology; the dragon
which watched the golden apples of Hesperides, and
the Payshtha-more, or great worm, which in Ireland
guards the riches of O'Rourke, is the same mala-

rious creature which St. Samson drove out of Wales.
According to the monkish legend, this pestiferous
beast was of vast size, and by its deadly breath had
destroyed two districts. It lay hid in a cave, near
the river. Thither went St. Samson, accompanied
only by a boy, and tied a linen girdle about the creature's neck, and drew it out and threw it headlong
from a certain high eminence into the sea.[1] This
dreadful dragon became mild and gentle when addressed by the saint; did not lift up its terrible
wings, nor gnash its teeth, nor put out its tongue to
emit its fiery breath, but suffered itself to be led to
the sea and hurled therein.[2] In the 'Mabinogion,'
the dragon which fights in Lludd's dominion is mentioned as a plague, whose shriek sounded on every
May eve over every hearth in Britain; and it 'went
through people's hearts, and so scared them, that the
men lost their hue and their strength, and the women
their children, and the young men and maidens lost
their senses.'[3] 'Whence came the *red* dragon of
Cadwaladr?' asks the learned Thomas Stephens.[4]
'Why was the Welsh dragon in the fables of Merddin,
Nennius, and Geoffrey, described as *red*, while the
Saxon dragon was *white?*' The question may remain long unanswered, for the reason that there is
no answer outside the domain of fancy, and therefore no reason which could in our day be accepted
as reasonable.[5] The Welsh word 'dragon' means
equally a dragon and a leader in war. Red was the
most honourable colour of military garments among

---

[1] 'Liber Landavensis,' 301.   [2] Ibid., 347.
[3] 'Mabinogion,' 461.   [4] 'Literature of the Kymry,' 25.
[5] Mr. Conway, in his erudite chapter on the Basilisk, appears to
think that the red colour of the Welsh dragon, in the legend of Merlin
and Vortigern, determines its moral character; that it illustrates the
evil principle in the struggle between right and wrong, or light and
darkness, as black does in the Persian legends of fighting serpents.—
'Demonology and Devil-Lore,' p. 369. (London, Chatto and Windus,
1879.)

the British in Arthur's day; and Arthur wore a
dragon on his helmet, according to tradition.

> His haughty helmet, horrid all with gold,
>   Both glorious brightness and great terror bred,
> For all the crest a dragon did enfold
>   With greedy paws. [1]

But the original dragon was an embodiment of
mythological ideas as old as mankind, and older
than any written record. The mysterious beast of
the boy Taliesin's song, in the marvellous legend of
Gwion Bach, is a dragon worthy to be classed with
the gigantic conceptions of the primeval imagination,
which sought by these prodigious figures to explain
all the phenomena of nature. 'A noxious creature
from the rampart of Satanas,' sings Taliesin; with
jaws as wide as mountains; in the hair of its two
paws there is the load of nine hundred waggons, and
in the nape of its neck three springs arise, through
which sea-roughs swim.' [2]

VIII.

For the prototype of the dragon-haunted caves
and treasure-hills of Wales, we must look to the
lightning caverns of old Aryan fable, into which no
man might gaze and live, and which were in fact
the attempted explanation of thunderstorms, when
the clouds appeared torn asunder by the lightning.

Scholars have noted the impressive fact that the
ancient Aryan people had the same name for cloud
and mountain; in the Old Norse, 'klakkr' means
both cloud and rock, and indeed the English word
cloud has been identified with the Anglo-Saxon
'clûd,' rock.[3] Equally significant here is the fact that
in the Welsh language 'draig' means both lightning
and dragon.

---

[1] Spenser, 'Faerie Queene.'   [2] 'Mabinogion,' 484.
[3] Max Müller, 'Rig-Veda,' i. 44. And see Mr. Baring-Gould's
'Curious Myths of the Middle Ages,' etc.

Primeval man, ignorant that the cloud was in any way different in structure from the solid mountains whose peaks it emulated in appearance, started back aghast and trembling when with crashing thunders the celestial rocks opened, displaying for an instant the glowing cavern whose splendour haunted his dreams. From this phenomenon, whose goblins modern science has tamed and taught to run errands along a wire, came a host of glittering legends, the shining hammer of Thor, the lightning spear of Odin, the enchanted arrow of Prince Ahmed, and the forked trident of Poseidon, as well as the fire-darting dragons of our modern folk-lore.

INDEX

A.

B.

2 D 2